Western Spectacle of Governance and the Emergence of Humanitarian World Politics

Western Spectacle
of Governance and the
Emergence of Humanitarian
World Politics

Mika Aaltola

WESTERN SPECTACLE OF GOVERNANCE AND THE EMERGENCE
OF HUMANITARIAN WORLD POLITICS

Copyright © Mika Aaltola, 2009.

First published in 2009 by PALGRAVE MACMILLAN® in the United States -
a division of St. Martin's Press LLC, 175 Fifth Avenue, New York, NY 10010.

Where this book is distributed in the UK, Europe and the rest of the world,
this is by Palgrave Macmillan, a division of Macmillan Publishers Limited,
registered in England, company number 785998, of Houndmills,
Basingstoke, Hampshire RG21 6XS.

Palgrave Macmillan is the global academic imprint of the above companies
and has companies and representatives throughout the world.

Palgrave® and Macmillan® are registered trademarks in the United States,
the United Kingdom, Europe and other countries.

ISBN-13: 978–0–230–61634–9
ISBN-10: 0–230–61634–8

Library of Congress Cataloging-in-Publication Data is available from the
Library of Congress.

A catalogue record of the book is available from the British Library.

Design by Integra Software Services

First edition: June 2009

10 9 8 7 6 5 4 3 2 1

Printed in the United States of America.

Contents

List of Figures

1

Introduction

Humanitarianism has arguably become the key frame through which the multifarious actors of the world evaluate each other's legitimacy and determine their roles in the current world. The emerging "humanitarian paradigm" has become an essential expression of what is meant by "international community" and the contemporary world order behind it. This book examines the patterns of co-option and collaboration between the ethical and political traditions of humanitarianism in various world political spectacles: September 11, 2001 (9/11), the wars in Iraq and Afghanistan, Darfur, SARS and avian flu, and the U.S. transformational HIV/AIDS diplomacy.

This work is about bodily pain. It concerns itself mainly with the different sentiments of compassion that arise from the suffering of individuals, but it also looks at bodies of different quality. While composing the theme, I remember serendipitously crossing paths with Elaine Scarry's 1983 book, *Bodies in Pain*. In it, I saw many bridgeheads to the politics of pain and to political pain.

As one can imagine, Scarry's topic was full of morbidity: The words and visuals in it contain contorted and convulsing human bodies, vivid images of agony, and an account of the unmaking of the body through torture and war. The schema contained in the book was about the unmaking of an individual's world, which comes with twisted bent-over human bodies.

While giving a lecture about the book in a course about the politics of pandemic diseases, I drew a connection between it and Susan Sontag's classic about bodily decomposition, *Illness as a Metaphor*. Sontag, in her flawed yet pioneering work, ponders over the cultural history of the condition of being sick in Western societies. Distinct diseases have a highly readable social meaning, with long and mutating historical roots. The most horrid and culturally memorable of these diseases involve the regressive bodily processes of decomposition. They are readable not only in a cognitive way, but also in a more emotional way of terror and horror.

These interpretations of "dis-eased" bodies and their supposed external markings permeate cultures and communities. They render bodies as categorized, profiled, and, subsequently, differentially treated. It is clear that the embodied language of pain and disease has deep political significance. This language deals with securing communities at a level that is rarely quite cognitive. More often, it is emotional and, at the more social level, sentimental.

I vividly remember my first conscious rendezvous with what Sontag calls "the citizens of the kingdom of the sick": I was in India as a trainer in an HIV/AIDS awareness program. Before our first visit to a hospital that had many HIV patients as well as many terminally ill people with AIDS, I felt anxiety. My intellectual safeguards and educational need to teach health-related responsibility faded in the face of the more primal fear of seeing the skins, bodies, and faces of death. The grammar of this fear and horror is quasi-cognitive. It is revelatory language, meaningful only as a part of a particular community's cultural history as the case of HIV/AIDS clearly demonstrates. The history itself is not enough to adequately appreciate the differential impacts of the language of bodily decomposition. Insight into communal power relations provides much meaning into our feverish chills in the face of dis-ease. This is especially true when we move from the suffering of individuals to other political bodies, such as communities (e.g., crime-infested neighborhoods), regions (e.g., Africa as a diseased continent), and empires (e.g., Soviet malaise).

Thus, in an important way, this revelatory language is meaningful only as a constitutive part of a particular power hierarchy. Any changes in the power hierarchy are felt and sensed. Any regressive process is a source of alarm, securing, and fear. Any such shifts in the power hierarchy are sources of worry because the hierarchy is dynamic and labile. Any change is inherently contagious. Humanitarianism as compassion for the distant other can be thought of in such a context.

My aim is to locate humanitarian compassion among the political emotions that are felt in integrated power hierarchies worldwide. Compassion tied with the "nearest is dearest" theme is closely connected with compassion "for the distant other." The political sentiment of hatred is common construction material for both types of political compassion, as is the sentiment of injustice. Evidently, the list of the ways of feeling world politics is long. In a way, communities and world orders are our second and third bodies. We feel "bodily" processes in them because the mere thought of their extreme forms sends shivers down our spines. In lived "world politics," these shivers, chills, and fevers are easily caught. Humanitarianism is among them. It both excites and stimulates and causes worry and horror.

Both the aforementioned books, *Illness as a Metaphor* and *Bodies in Pain*, provide the groundwork for my guiding idea in this work. Bodily processes matter and are iconically readable. They are personally emotional in a way that is conditioned and constructed by the prevailing imagination of the local and global power hierarchy. However, the key question that we need to ponder over is, "What bodies are we talking about?" Thinking about this question opens another bridgehead into this book. The starting point is that our skins are overlapping and multiple. I will make the case that we live in and are constituted by a diversity of bodies. The sensations, sentiments, and emotions attached with these different bodies vary. The suffering, agony, twisting, and convulsions of our individual bodies are felt by others. In the same way, the pain of larger social bodies is inherently connected with those of our own. We feel through and with the other bodies. One may argue that world politics, and especially sentiments for the distant others, provides the largest possible context for such felt and lived bodies.

The longing for the distant other has provided much of the fuel for charitable, compassionate, and colonial impulses. From orientalism to modern-day humanitarianism, the relationship between the top and the bottom of the world hierarchy has resulted in a lot of political imagery. In this context, I have to mention a third source of serendipity for this work: Darcy Grigsby's (2002) book *Extremities* provides a powerful demonstration of how imperial projects connect with those of compassion at the level of visual imagery and art. Paintings can become sites where "geographical extremities and bodily extremities articulated one another." Human bodies in paintings, and especially those visually demonstrating pain, can represent and reveal imperial pains. This triad between visual imagery, bodily pain, and world order will be one of the central points of focus of this book. I will review visual representations in order to discern the different traditions of political compassion. How are the pains of individual, nation, and empire represented so as to provoke compassion and consequent political actions? What are the means of representing the political violence and regressive political processes that have traditionally led to desired political mobilizations?

To simplify the task ahead, I am recognizing the authority of tradition and of the ways of remembering it, as, for example, in stories, schoolbooks, and works of popular culture. Some "bodies" are more strongly rooted in political imagery. They contain a gallery of striking memory images. In other words, there are some consistent themes and corresponding "bodies" that have been made significant through centuries of repetition in what is commonly referred to as "Western thought." More specifically, the bodies and corresponding skins I am tracing are the somatic/individual, the national/communal, and the imperial/hegemonic. We—in the form of one of these embodiments—see the skin and read or feel the movements of and on it. We are naturally caught by the sudden vortexes involving these bodies as they inherently instantiate and engage the "I" in one way or another—I as a Finn, as a European, or as a Westerner. I will go so far as to claim that there is a certain sense of unavoidability in this type of political feeling. Especially when the movement is a regressive downward one, I and we have our antennae up.

From this perspective, 9/11 was a deep shock. The planes colliding with buildings and the collapsing skyscrapers were sensed more than cognized, felt more than intellectualized. Many felt "world-order" pains, the sorrows of empire, and nostalgia for more innocent times. The images of nations and people around the world flying flags at half-mast, bringing flowers to U.S. embassies, holding candlelight vigils, singing the U.S. national anthem, following the TV coverage intensively, and voicing their worries in special TV and radio shows all tell of the strength and depth of the sentiments felt for the "body in pain." It is quite likely that this body was the world order itself—the hegemonic, hierarchical order of things that had defined post–cold war prosperity. It had many names besides the obvious one, such as "international community," "civilized nations," "the West," and "democracies." The object of the compassion and identification was the hegemonic power and, through it, the world order which that power maintained. In a sense, this worry over the order of things prevailed to a greater extent than compassion for the individual people who died that fateful day.

There have been other less pronounced occasions of worry and felt world-order pains. These hegemonic worries have been felt over Saddam Hussein's presumed weapons of mass destruction or over the nuclearized Iran. This body is at play also when we feel for our planet in imagery, as, for example, over global warming, avian flu, HIV/AIDS, or the Asian tsunami. Human polity, in its broad meaning, is turned into what may be called a body in pain. Its illnesses or regressions are intense. They resonate in all the bodies. Political pains become somatized and we can speak of politosomatics in much the same way as we discuss psychosomatic disorders.

Besides the world-order, hegemonic, or imperial sentiments, attention can also be focused easily on more intermediate established bodies such as nation and state. The derivates of these include the established attributes of a nation-state, most importantly, an ethnic group. Since this body is highly influenced in its present form by nationalism, I will refer to the accompanying political sentiment as "nation compassion." Violent regressions in the status of this type of "body" are easily registered and felt. Wars and conflict, even when one is not directly impacted, arouse heated debates. They are the objects of intense attention. For example, Israel's war with Hezbollah in Lebanon filled the airwaves. In the same way, the collapse of Rwanda caught the world's attention. Examples of such sentiments are endless. Remember the plight of the fleeing Kosovo Albanians in the face of the purge by Serb forces? These images moved the Western community to action and individuals around the world to loosen their purse strings and help those who had suffered. The famous photos of Bosnian Muslims in the early 1990s were as vivid as they were emotional in this political sense. Seeing the destitute and hungry men behind the barbed wire propelled the West into action in just a few days after years of inaction. The immediate reason was the wide outcry of anger and compassion. Even in the world-order-oriented cosmopolitan human polity, nation compassion is part of one of the most important bodies. Nevertheless, we are often numb with regard to this political feeling—for example, Rwanda at the start of the genocide or the plight of the millions of Iraqis fleeing to neighboring countries in the aftermath of the U.S. occupation. Sometimes, we feel for the distant others as individuals or nations.

Imperial-hegemonic and nation-state bodies and the related political compassions for world order and nation provide an important window into this book. However, the inherently political existence of an individual body should not be forgotten or underestimated. We are engaged with individual bodies other than our own. Images ranging from the plight of a starving person in Africa to a celebrity dying in a car crash move us. Gendered and racialized bodies provide ways of understanding the political existence of our individual bodies. "I"s are always part of political hierarchies even when they are deliberately excluded from them, as some singular cases of "terrorists" from the Unabomber to the shoe bomber show.

In the same breath, it may be said that by no means is this individual body ontologically "prior" in any hierarchical category of political entities. If we consider Aristotle's much noted dictum about "political animals"—and we will do this throughout this book—the political embodiments comprise the bedrock of our existence. Particular constellations of political embodiments—whether the individual, nation, or hegemony matters and to what degree—may be located through the answer to the famous question first posed by William James and later repeated influentially by the developer of frame theory, Erving Goffman: "Under what conditions do we think things are true?" Our embodiments change and fluctuate as do the answers to this question. This, nevertheless, does not subtract from the power of political embodiments to produce a sense of certainty. Three political embodiments—individual, national, and hegemonic—have an important epistemological dimension that have to do with the ways of gaining certain knowledge. The movements of these bodies and the sensations on their skins are knowledge and revelatory experiences.

Political epistemology—certainty produced by shifting power hierarchies—from a faint itch to extreme pain matters at different qualitative and quantitative levels. We feel in these bodies and have a sense that the things sensed are real. This "knowledge" compels us and holds us spellbound. The level at which this epistemological certainty is reached bears a strong family resemblance to what "we" and "I" are together with what various out- and in-groups are. For example, 9/11 made many people all over the world feel as if they were Westerners. The war in Iraq during the chaos of 2006 made former Iraqis feel they were Sunnis and Shias. The disintegration of the Soviet Union, or of Yugoslavia, made people feel they were of numerous nationalities, some of which were already forgotten. The extremity of the violence in Rwanda created the Hutus and the Tutsis. The flow of migrants across the rough seas separating Western Africa from the European Canary Islands creates individuals fighting for their lives. The vortexes of crises and extremity of violence blend and recombine political embodiments. Feelings of compassion run high. Depending on one's role in the vortex, whether participant, victim, or spectator, the sentiments and the resulting political movements are different. The Yellow or Red Scare was felt very deeply in the U.S. context. Cold war evening news bulletins transferred emotions through images of missiles, mushroom clouds, superpower summits, demonstrations, and other high drama and visual rhetoric. Rwanda was first externalized and then taken into the human polity when a wave of compassion and guilt swept the Western world. Somalia, Haiti, the bombings of Iraq, tension in the Middle East all of these were felt, if mainly as tensions at the level of the world order. Locally, as, for example, in the case of Israel – Palestine, they were matters of national suffering, justice, and security. Others felt for these out-groups. They felt nation compassion and identified with one of the belligerents. This world political feeling is an important subset of humanitarian sentiments.

Thus, the purpose of this work is the expanded understanding of the role of compassion for others in contemporary world politics. Clearly, humanitarianism as a sentiment for the suffering of others is a complex matter. This is often recognized, especially in the context of raging debates over its political versus apolitical and partisan versus nonpartisan nature. Sometimes, critical studies have reflected on the close connection between Western imperialism and humanitarianism. My aim is to expand the discussion to involve the various types of political compassion and their entangled histories. My more precise aim is not to introduce further dimensions of complexity, but to clarify issues by mapping out the environment in which humanitarianism, together with its collaborative and co-optive relationships with different political sentiments, exists.

There are various histories of political compassion. Only one, yet very prominent, trace leads to the enlightenment-era construction of the human polity as being composed of individual members. This often repeated historical story leads to an important achievement such as the abolition of slave trade and slavery in the form in which they were then known. However, there are other equally important traces of worry over the order and justice of things. The world-order worry in the Western cannon goes back to the "decline and fall" tradition coined by the historians of the Roman world.

This world-order worry has returned from time to time. The signs of imperial descent in particular—such as 9/11—have led to the sudden spread of these sentiments. The worry over the destinies of other nations has a history as old as that of nationalism. I remember being schooled in Finland and finding out how other nations felt for Finland when it was attacked by the Soviet Union during the Winter War (1939–40). I remember being touched by the recordings of Winston Churchill's passionate radio speeches, applauding the struggles of the small nation against its immense eastern neighbor. For me, Churchill's speeches felt for Finland. For him, it seems when I reread them now, his speeches illustrated the worries over the fate of Western civilization. Different political compassions overlap much in the same way as other sentiments such as anger and fear.

Before proceeding any further, it is vital to rehearse the way in which the history of humanitarianism is remembered and to point out the landmarks of humanitarianism as they are usually known. Humanitarianism, defined as compassion for distant others, is a multifaceted and historically sedimented practice. However, humanitarianism has its traceable roots. The concern for and sense of obligation to distant strangers and their communities derives from classical thought.

Another simplifying factor is that humanitarianism is often rather easily and unproblematically reduced to a liberal ethical version stemming from the French and British Enlightenments. I feel heavily indebted for Michael Barnett and Raymond Duvall from the University of Minnesota on illuminating to me the following account. From the late eighteenth century onward, humanitarianism opens up in a progressive narrative. It leads from the fight against slavery and the fight for the rights of minorities and women to the development of the laws of war and the establishment of such organizations as the International Committee of the Red Cross (ICRC). This progressive narrative is inherently modernist. It highlights the rationality and ethics of the humanitarian movement. Humanitarianism is seen as an intellectual exercise that has gradually defeated the forces of irrationality and blind aggression. Its Christian religious roots are often blended with the more universalist ethical underpinning of humanitarian activity. It appears in the form of neutral and universal activity that should not fall under any denomination or political machinations.

The generally accepted defining principle of humanitarianism is an inclusive entity of "humanity," or polity in the widest sense of human polity. The central idea behind this envisioned community is that in a human polity all individuals are of equal worth and, thus, deserving of assistance if in need. Underlying this humanitarian principle are presumably apolitical ethical commitments. These point to the need to go beyond territorial or civilizational boundaries. Human polity is the most extensive and inclusive of communities in its definition of who are deserving of being "like us." In this book, I will raise questions about such a universalist view and address tensions in the complex relationships between ethical humanitarianism and openly political considerations. I will also tackle the tensions between compassion as a sentiment, cognition, and strategy. More specifically, I will examine the multifaceted networks of international humanitarianism and their intimate connections with the changing faces of contemporary power politics.

The modern strand of humanitarianism became distinct in North America and Europe in the mid-nineteenth century. It has led to the emergence of what Hannah Arendt refers to as an institutionalized "passion for compassion" (Arendt 1990, p. 72). This institutionalized form of compassion may be distinguished from its close siblings: the institutional forms of charity, human rights, and developmentalism. Formal organizations emerged in a range of areas dedicated to the idea of providing relief to those in emergencies, or in immediate danger, whereas its siblings worked more with reducing the suffering of the masses and with eliminating the perceived "root causes" that place individuals in peril.

However, humanitarianism also materialized in more long-term political movements and mobilizations, including prison and child labor reforms as well as the international campaign against the slave trade. Other expressions of this humanitarian ethos were charitable and missionary work as well as the formation of the ICRC and international humanitarian law. However, the politics of compassion also involve political bodies other than individual ones.

For much of human history, polities—poleis, city-states, nations, states, and hegemonies—have been the primary objects of politically mobilizing bursts of compassion. Humanitarian movements and organizations became increasingly numerous and formalized during the last century, especially, since the early 90s. This makes for a vast humanitarian landscape in which states, international governmental and nongovernmental organizations, and transnational institutions form complex networks. These networks extend from the donor areas to the global south, employing a significant number of people and mobilizing resources of volunteerism. The scope of issues covered range from natural disaster relief to coping with man-made catastrophes.

It also includes fighting diseases and their impact, society and peace building, and participating in military humanitarian interventions. This network, which binds different human spaces and functions into a global fabric, provides one of the clearest examples of global civil society. From the perspective of the holistic vision of the world, this network community has to be taken into account because humanitarianism matters in contemporary world politics. However, the hierarchical hub-and-spoke structure of the contemporary world order is one of the constituent elements of the humanitarianism that prevails today.

The existing humanitarian framework provides a vital source of legitimacy in the present world order for all those who can tap into it. As in any order, the hierarchical element of the contemporary human polity designates those who benefit and those who do not. The legitimizing power of humanitarianism is at its most distinct in alleviating the sense of injustice stemming from such hierarchies. However, modern humanitarianism is said to aim to interrupt negative political processes by saving lives in order to reduce the quota of human sacrifices and to mitigate the harshness of the political world order.

There exist multiple tensions in the modern liberal humanitarian enterprise. Should humanitarian relief-organizations only save those whose lives are directly at risk? How independent and neutral they should be? Should the deeper root-causes be left to the responsibility of states? More development-focused organizations struggle to eliminate the perceived conditions that produce emergencies and cause vulnerability in the first place. In many cases, these perceived root-causes are located at the level of global structural imbalances and inequalities. Thus, many important transnational humanitarian campaigns have been directly aimed at the global power structures. Much of the scholarly research on humanitarian movements and NGOs has focused on their transformative role in making states redefine their interests and fixing the perversions of the centre-periphery circulations of (dis)empowerment. Recently, research has started to focus on how global power-hierarchies transform humanitarian actors themselves. Instead of being neutral rescuers or activist transformers, humanitarian organizations can be seen as creatures of world order. They do not stand outside of its power flows. In many cases, they contribute to the staying power and legitimacy of the present fabric of world politics. Moreover, they spread Western liberal governance mentality and its underlying values in ways that are often out of states' reach. Humanitarians, when successfully co-opted by powerful states and their hegemonic interests, can give a happy face to the underlying disparities and contribute to states' campaigns of winning the hearts and minds of people.

After this brief reminder of how humanitarianism is usually understood, I will return to the theme of the work at hand. Humanitarianism may equally well be woven together with the much older historical strands of political compassion. These traditions blend in the praxis of world politics, where compassions are felt and cognized not only for distant individual sufferers, but for nations and world orders. It is in the compassion-charged frame of war, conflict, crises, disputes, terror, genocide, ethnic cleansing, and other forms of political violence that humanitarianism in the modernist liberalist form may exist. Compassions are rampant in the polemic space of world politics. Thus, modern expressions of humanitarianism have a historical and political existence, and they do not work in a void. Every particular instance of humanitarianism interacts with other traditions of compassion. The complex relationships of co-option and collaboration are becoming even more distinct in the post-9/11 world, as civil–military relations are become increasingly underlined.

The dialectics of ethics and politics weaves complex networks of interaction and circles of emotionality between different actors and offers them various roles. When humanitarianism is approached from this perspective, it can be understood as an umbrella concept without any central fundamental strand that would exhaust it or run through the whole of its fabric. However, the complexities of humanitarianism have not been examined in a critical and historically conscious enough way, despite the recent flurry of studies concentrating on the interlinkages of humanitarianism with religion, security, culture, and trade.

I intend to contribute to the critical understanding of the rise of the current "humanitarian paradigm" and chart the patterns of co-option and collaboration from several perspectives. It is distinct in that it will analyze humanitarianism as a political performance. Because humanitarianism is based on the underlying imagery of dangerous regressive violence, I am intertwining elements from the classical model of regression. The model developed is noteworthy in that it integrates the flow of emotionality with the more cognitive aspects of the humanitarian frame.

There is a growing body of literature on humanitarianism, but it is often limited in two important respects. First, it has failed to adequately incorporate the role of the prevailing visions of world order in defining the meaning and practice of humanitarian action. Second, this literature frequently restricts the definition of humanitarianism to impartial, independent, and neutral relief to victims of conflict and natural disasters. This represents an important, but not the only, expression of humanitarianism in the modern world. The grounding premise is the claim that the understanding and investigation of humanitarianism should encompass the varieties of institutionalized and internationalized expressions of the goal to alleviate or eliminate the suffering of distant strangers. Seeing humanitarianism as an expression of both ethical and political considerations enables us to broaden our perspectives on how the ideas and practices of humanitarianism have evolved over time, in various areas of concern and in distinct cultural contexts.

Thus, the general objective of this project is the rediscovery of the various roots of humanitarianism that can enlighten our awareness of related contemporary political phenomena. One of the goals of this book is to move beyond the stylized humanitarian claims and to think about the complex operation of power in the relationship between the world order and humanitarian action, which can perhaps be seen to be simultaneously producing both ethical progress and political domination.

The structure of this book focuses on the themes expressed in the following questions: How do humanitarian practices reinforce and/or challenge the existing world order? What are the implications of the intimate connections between politics and humanitarianism? How are the complex relationships between humanitarian ethics and politics variously negotiated? How is power involved in the negotiation? What are the patterns of co-option between foreign policy considerations and particular ethical standpoints? How do humanitarian actors confront the differences between themselves and the objects of their humanitarian action, negotiate those differences, and critically reconsider their moral positioning?

The next two chapters develop the theoretical and methodological positions needed to disentangle the various strands of humanitarianism in order to appreciate the varieties of their entanglement. Two issues must be clarified here. One, there are sentiments that are first and foremost political—they are social and require a power hierarchy. It is easy to fathom what I mean by political sentiments if you close your eyes and think of various situations at your workplace. The power hierarchy or status differences that prevail at work translate into strong feelings of anger, humiliation, pride, depression, and stress. You may worry over the loss of your job, hope for a promotion, or scheme against another. Now, generalize from this to experiences between other political bodies in similar hierarchical situations. The political public moods—I separate sentiments as public emotions from psychologically understood emotions—consist of feelings for political bodies. Xenophobia, philanthropy, enmity, and humanitarianism are examples of political sentiments—I will use the word political emotion interchangeably with that of sentiment. They are partly cognitive in that they are based on articulated thought patterns and have belief systems. They are partly civil religious in that they contain a sense of reverence for something higher—to the schema of dogma and creed. They are emotional because of their ability to arouse quasi-conscious flare-ups, heightened charges, and synchronous behavior.

To reiterate, power politics has its own type of emotionality with its corresponding political sentiments.

Two, political sentiments spread. They move and intensify easily. My starting hypothesis is that what is generally understood as political movements are intimately intertwined ebbs and flows of political sentiments. Sentiments arouse, stimulate, captivate, and overwhelm. Sentiments beget sentiments. They are contagious. Sometimes, they lead to whirlwinds, to highly tense vortexes of emotionality. The vorticity of sentiments is self-feeding. They may spread horizontally, involving new groups of people, and deepen vertically, becoming more and more intensive.

The violent contortions of various political bodies have not been researched intensively in either political or social sciences. These pains are regressive processes. The customary scholar formulates his or her research agenda in a more progressive spirit. Light is shed on problems and solutions are sought. In all of this, the regressive direction is left in a void. However, in the classics of political science, intensive attention is paid to the tragedy of the human condition. The dynamics of the downward spiral have been discussed in detail. These influential discussions—from the ancients to the premoderns—form an important inheritance, a potentiality that has the status of an easily activated discourse or a language game. These discussions permeate popular culture as a background condition and form an alternative counter-strand to the more hopeful modernist visions. The regressive constructs paint a very determined and fixed image of the world. My intention here is to regard them as a language game, which, under certain conditions, has a great prescriptive force. I will read the classics as a source of wisdom, but not because they describe a preexisting feature of political life. They provide insights because of their ability to innovate and forge into being the very reality that they were and that you and I are breathing.

The "heavy" ontology of the theoretical approach is based on the following "playful" theme: The conditions under which we think things are true are not fixed. They vary. One such frame is provided by the common story stock of regressive narratives, such as cycles of revenge, stasis, genocide, and ethnic cleansing. When they are activated and you are engrossed by them, they are as true as they can get. The playfulness of the theoretical position should not distract from the seriousness of the theme. It is about the way in which political bodies feel tremors, become convulsed, and, ultimately, not only fall apart but become extroverted too. This is like a person pulling and turning a sock inside out. Friends are found from afar and the "nearest is the dearest" taboo is shattered. Former enemies are drawn into the communal split-mindedness. An anticommunity is formed, glued together by extreme hate, rather than the political friendship and justice that were so extolled by Aristotle.

The political message of conceptual configuration links with the theme of regression and with the classical treatment of violently regressive political processes. Usually, these writers point out the dangers or symptoms of regression. The mood of the writings is one of deep worry and even personal fear. The writers themselves feel a deep sense of compassion for those caught in the whirlwinds of intensifying violence.

A lesser known historian, Zosimus, offers a case in point. His account of the decline and fall of the Roman Empire was contemporary. One can assume that Zosimus himself became a victim of the decline-fall type of regression he was one of the first to formulate. His big work suddenly ends almost mid-sentence, as if he had become disembodied in the abyss of the fall. The same worry saturates the works of Thucydides, Plato, and Aristotle. Sweating, worrying, and empathy for the doomed political bodies saturate their writings. This charged emotional content is not there just to support the more intellectual argumentation. It is not merely a rhetorical ploy. Rather, worry and compassion, fear and horror, and humiliation and guilt stand out in these writings because they nag at us more effectively than the mere logical argument of the grand schema of things. Often, these moods are thematized by detailed and hyperbolic accounts of the extreme examples of lethal incidents. It is through this genre in history and political theory that sentiments and regressions become the co-constitutive building blocks of the still existing form of imagining how political communities become caught in the vortexes of violence.

The theoretical chapter will focus on Thucydides because the link between process or motion and emotion or mood is at its most vivid in his work. In his famous *History of the Peloponnesian War*, Thucydides describes how the war was one "grand movement" that expanded and deepened like a vortex, eventually engulfing the whole Greek world in its violent embrace. Among its rip currents, this "grand movement" contained the destructive phenomenon of stasis. While the war destroyed empires, the stasis inflicted destruction on smaller individual communities.

Thucydides brings disease into the same frame as the empire-war and the community-stasis submotions. The plague hit at the individual level. Its movement through the body from the head to the intestines portrayed the decomposition of what it meant to be an individual, a citizen. It affected somatic bodies by decomposing them and "moved the minds" of the people by causing erratic and incontinent social behavior. The "grand movement" was a three-headed monster, a hydra full of strong sentiments. While Thucydides makes explicit his compassion for the Greek world, for the smaller communities, and for the people, he sees that the sentiments are constitutive of the violent process. Thus, overall, Thucydides sees overlapping destructive political (e)motions impacting at various levels.

This culturally influential couplet of regressive political motion and emotion will work as the backbone of this work. It provides the context for humanitarianism understood as compassion for the distant other. Lately, humanitarian sentiment has become the mood affecting occasions of violent regression. Still, it is only one of the many political emotions influencing such situations. In the dynamic process, sentiments cannot be understood as separate from each other. They have valences. They connect with other sentiments. It is clear how compassion couples with antipathy and apathy. It is the counter-mood to the "not caring" about the distant other. It couples also with hate and its associated aggression. It tries to amend hostilities and bridge differences. Humanitarianism attempts to heal acute suffering and calm emergencies.

However, contextualizing humanitarianism among the aforementioned counter-emotions is not enough. Humanitarian compassion has to be placed among other political compassions to obtain a better idea about it and also about the myriads of couplings to which it can contribute. Compassion for the world order (a hegemony or hierarchy of some sort) provides one context for the mobilization of humanitarian sentiments. For example, the emerging post – cold war world order provided the backdrop for the Somalian intervention and also influenced the bafflement caused by Rwanda. Political compassion for a suffering nation or state provides another level that needs to be taken into account. Even when not recognized, these two political sentiments interact with the more individual-focused modern compassion.

2

Violent Vortexes
of Compassion

This chapter examines how the ongoing macro-level turbulence in world politics has radically recontextualized political compassion and, by definition, humanitarianism. Humanitarian mobilizations have usually been connected with single, isolated spectacles such as Rwanda and Somalia. My main argument is that this atomization of humanitarian emergencies misses much of the political compassion involved in cases such as Afghanistan and Iraq. Many of the largest recent humanitarian events are connected and better appreciated as parts of overall violent, regressive flows. A large part of political compassion in the age of "war on terror" is not only directed to the suffering of distant individual bodies, but also to the suffering of other political bodies; besides empathy for suffering individuals, this also denotes sentimental worry over the world order and compassion for suffering nations. The emotions felt toward political bodies constitute motions and vortexes, which can be viewed as one single process. It is presumed that, within this circle of motion, the sensing of flow is of crucial importance for the actors. The political emotions involved in this all-important sensing signal changes in the underlying power hierarchies and further intensify the agitation. Such unsteady flow models have impressive yet often ignored history in classical international relations tradition. This necessary background model, which connects large political movements with local crises and individual (e)motions, is reviewed through Thucydides's work.

Passions, Emergencies and Motions

Thucydides regarded the Peloponnesian War as the greatest movement in human history. He describes how this vortex of war engulfed all of Greece, causing strong convulsions in both big and small poleis.

The intensifying, regressive flow led to strong passions, which, in turn, helped to intensify the flow. Sudden emergencies such as the Stasis of Corcyra and the Plague of Athens, Thucydides claims, were emotion-laden submotions of the overall regression. I intend to argue that this model may be used to illuminate contemporary emergencies in Iraq and Afghanistan, which are part of the overall macro-motion since the collapse of the Twin Towers in New York City. Building on the Thucydidean model, I will claim that political compassion provides the foremost vector for intensification of the motion that holds different political bodies in thrall.

Compelling feelings for others is a multifaceted and influential, yet inadequately examined, political phenomenon. In the study of humanitarian emergencies, it is common to reduce compassion for distant others to mere modernist, secular, and liberal ethical visions, which derive from enlightened humanitarianism. However, political compassion may equally well be contextualized in much older historical strands, in the sentiments felt toward significant in-groups (e.g., nations and hegemonies or empires). Moreover, it is suggested that the more modernist version of humanitarianism does not work in a void. It interacts with other older traditions of compassion. These complex relationships of co-option have become even more distinct in the post-9/11 world.

It is argued that some contemporary humanitarian emergencies are not recognized as such for two reasons. First, they do not fit the humanitarian emergency paradigm that was created during the 1990s. Second, the term "emergency" does not capture the process-like flow of the highly compassionate events. My aim is to illustrate the inadequacy of present conceptualizations of humanitarian emergencies by examining the flow of events started by 9/11 and leading to perhaps the deepest humanitarian emergencies in Iraq in recent memory.

I intend to look at the flows of emotionality involved in the dynamic disintegrative processes of humanitarian emergencies. Proceeding beyond clear-cut, rational-cognitive imagery into one of political emotions, I will expand the idea that motions between communities and in the overall international setting are naturally unsteady. Unsteadiness of political flows reflects the constant possibility of vorticity, that is, the spiraling circle of inflicting and suffering pain. Within such a setting, the sensing of flows is crucially important for the actors involved. In a sense, emotionality becomes a constitutive element of agency in an emergency situation. It is fed by shifting power relations and positions in the hierarchy. The images of the emergency—for example, eyewitness accounts, news stories, and photographs—turn into triggers of complex emotional judgments: the images of suffering Kosovo Albanian refugees tell stories of the need to alleviate their suffering, but also about the labile nature of European security; the famous 9/11 image of a falling man contains a story of individual horror, but also the sentiment of the world order under threat; the haunting eyes of a child in a refugee camp in Darfur contain a strong charge of compassion, but also a reminder of stereotypical, religiously motivated violence between the West and Islam; tourists' videos of the Asian tsunami convey sentiments for the locals, but also for the emerging interdependent global order and for a world faced with changing natural forces. This emotional complexity can be better grasped by understanding the historically sedimented and culturally constructed traditions that come into play. In the search for this encompassing schema, I will first review the research literature concerning relevant modern thought on the "contagion of political violence" and on "diversionary war." The idea is that these contemporary research topics are closely related to the underlying neoclassical reading of Thucydides.

Many recent works have focused on progressive processes—for example, relief assistance, emergency aid, and community or state building— more in line with the overall modernization paradigm. The other side—the regressive linkages and processes—has been left mainly unattended. Therefore, it is not surprising that Huntington's (1965, 415) suggestion that when it comes to the disintegration of political communities, "perhaps the most relevant ideas are the most ancient ones," is still persuasive when looking for culturally significant models. When moving through the pages of Thucydides's *Histories*, it is very difficult to not be touched by the writer's deeply felt sense of compassion (Stahl 1966, 7). He seems to be suggesting that, for an observer, a sense of compassion is natural when faced with the hegemonic war, which he regarded as one violent, grand movement. He feels for the states—especially for the small poleis—that were engulfed by the maelstrom of the Peloponnesian War. Thucydides—together with his empathic reader—feels for the world caught in the tidal wave (Brunt 1967, 278; Monoson and Loriaux 1998, 285). I will argue that the sentiments of compassion were also among the most important driving forces of the regressive flow that engulfed Thucydides's world. The Thucydidean model was associated with emotional drama at the individual (the Plague of Athens), local (the Stasis of Corcyra), and macro (hegemonic struggle) levels. That grand movement is one total process that has to be considered in its totality if we are to understand any particular event of its flow. It is this emotionally fed dynamics that offers a helpful, culturally embedded model to enable us to understand the regressive grand movement initiated by 9/11. The unleashed political compassions help to explain the humanitarian relevance of Afghanistan and Iraq.

Humanitarianism as an Emotional Flow

The sentiment of compassion is an important part of the increasingly important humanitarian frame of world politics as ethics. In this sense, compassion can be regarded as an unusual social emotion because its object is other people's emotions and, therefore, it occurs only as part of dynamic social interaction (Clark 1987, 180). What are political sentiments? The starting point is that the motions inherent in any violent process translate into emotionality and these strong passions further contribute to the intensity of the violent flow. This definition, which is based on a classical topos, maintains that changes in power hierarchies cause individual emotions.[1] In her review of emotional content of international relations, Neta Crawford traces the origin of the English term "emotion" to "political or social agitation and popular disturbance" (2000, 124). Against this background, it is not a coincidence that the theories of political movements and political mobilization have been so receptive in including emotions in their models (e.g., Jasper 1998, 397). Research has concentrated on referring to such mobilizing events as moral shocks, frame alignments, and emerging collective identities. There are feelings in and around political movements (Jasper 1998, 397). At their minimum, movements stir the existing patterns of understanding what are positive and negative emotions, what should be expressed and hidden, and what constitutes adequate and inadequate responses. In related literature, emotions can be regarded in a positive light. They empower by translating influence and status into power, that is, into the capacity to produce intended and foreseen effects (Willer et al. 1997, 573). The emotions produced by power structures vary from negative to positive, from enmity to compassion (Kemper 1991, 330).

Wars—external and internal—have often been constructed as passionate movements. Sentiments ranging from disdain, superiority, hostility, and anger to compassion are equated with the movements and with the changing power relations signaled by them. The general idea is that changes in power hierarchies trigger emotions and stimulate participation in further flare-ups of collective feelings. The power-status differences are established, challenged, and reinforced by emotions (Lutz and Abu-Lughod 1990, 14). In this way, for example, the social practices of shame and mourning may channel angry situations into ones where factional or communal solidarity is strengthened (e.g., Durkheim 1965, 443). This type of channeling is quite common. In the language of terror strikes, the anger related to the immediate death of innocents in one's in-group is turned into resoluteness and open expressions of cohesion. In this way, emotions are formed in social situations.

A short review of contemporary research offers evidence that the motion–emotion pairing of the classical topos continues to be relevant. The connection between power and emotions has been examined by several contemporary thinkers. Kemper's studies (e.g., 1981) are refreshing for their emphasis on power hierarchy–related emotionality. In Kemper's model, emotions consist of actually or imaginatively existing social organizational or social relational conditions: "When these conditions are met, the desired emotions will flow of themselves, authentically" (Kemper 1981, 358). More specifically, the intimate relation may be based on a close connection between power relations and the primary, instinctive, or physiological feelings of fear, anger, depression, and satisfaction (Kemper 1987, 263).

Other theorists have put forth different models of emotionality flowing from social relations (e.g., Lewis 1971; Retzinger 1991; Scheff 1993). Common to several models of social emotion is the tendency to see emotions not only cognitively, but also physiologically. Social emotions can be seen as grounded in physiological changes—bodily movements and micro-expressions—rather than in cognitions (Summes-Effler 2002, 42). It is natural that such communication of emotion requires face-to-face interaction. A group of people has to be able to "see" in some way the bodily movements and facial expressions. Besides making a distinction between cognitive and more unconscious processes, the literature often points out that some emotions, such as respect and trust, linger on. These moods are chronic and recurring and differ from the shorter-term flare-up emotions such as hate (e.g., Jasper 1998, 402).

Humanitarian Emergency

In order to expand the nature of how humanitarianism is understood, it must be conceptualized in its paradigmatic form. The form of humanitarianism highlighted in popular culture and in scholarly literature derives from the world of the 1990s. What are the major characteristics of this by now already somewhat anachronistic humanitarian paradigm? Humanitarian emergencies are constituted by a complexity of issues and by a myriad of involved actors.

Despite the apparent complexity, humanitarian emergencies are often historically well-rehearsed activities. They have a history and contain a tradition. From a general perspective, humanitarian emergency is an exceptional, pain-laden event that suddenly surfaces for a relatively short time period and seems to compel some type of intervention by concerned outsiders. In an emergency, the sense of political stability changes to a sense of a fleeting and threatened existence. The emergency language

My aim is to claim that the apolitical machine has broken down partly after 9/11. Enormous humanitarian suffering goes unrecognized in places such as Iraq due to the inadequacies of the "individual as the sufferer" imagery. The failure to extend humanitarian sentiments to the refugees inside Iraq and the Iraqis fleeing to Jordan and Syria stems from the complexity of compassion. In many ways, the failure to fully appreciate the links between different types of political compassion has led to the bypassing of the flow from 9/11 to Afghanistan and Iraq.

Compassion for Other Bodies

Underlying the history of international relations, there are wide disagreements when it comes to what a "real" sufferer is or ought to be and what an "authentic" subject/body of compassion-evoking pain is. The producing of the sufferer as the subject depends on the constraints set by the different traditions of political compassion.

The significant suffering of others is commonly seen through the lens of a bounded in-group, a political body. More often than not, this in-group is equated with national boundaries (e.g., Reicher et al. 2006). The iconography of such suffering has a long and rich history. The suffering of a political body provides an important embedding for the humanitarian type of suffering: "Narratives of pain materialize an abstract entity like the nation-state to its citizenry, transforming it into a body that is symbolically connected to that of the individual . . . the frequency and intensity of the pain-filled language and the historical persistence of conflicts over sovereignty indicate that the wounds are spread throughout the body politic . . ." (Burns et al. 1999, 122). In this culturally significant genre of political pain, the whole polity may suffer. This suffering is a signifier of wider human suffering and, as a result, it often takes precedence over the individual's body in pain and provides the context for such suffering. It is appropriate for this type of pain that the sentiments of pity, compassion, and empathy have an object at the level of national political bodies. People feel for the Iraqi Kurds, the Kosovars, and for the people of Darfur. Visuals of individual suffering become contextualized in terms of a national or ethnic group's pain.

From the perspective of understanding the contemporary visual rhetoric of political pain, the iconographies of "ship of state" and "crisis at sea" become illuminating. The age-old "crisis at sea" imagery is expansive. It allows one to represent anything from personal to societal and state crises (Landow 1982). The variants of this imagery contain a shared sense of compassion, an acute need to help. The images are tense and emotionally charged. The time is scarce and the imagery implies distance. Although the castaways are in dire need of relief, they are hopelessly remote. The senses of sinking, being engulfed, and submerged combine with the theme of being cast adrift from the rest. The means of rescue are hampered by an unsupported existence that lacks connection to others and, symbolically, to the main trunk of humanity. The distance implied is social and emotional. The application of the imagery to a situation in which dangerous elements unjustly threaten a small, yet pious, nation or a religious or ethnic minority provides a case in point. Humanity's compassionate ability to connect with those in harm's way is accentuated by the inhumanity of the antagonist elements symbolized by the stormy high seas.

A paradigmatic example of the state/ship in crisis is available in the deep compassions aroused by Finland's perceived lone struggle in the Winter War (1939–40) against the Soviet offense. The general sentiment for a "nation in crisis" was eloquently expressed by Winston Churchill (1940, 273):

> Only Finland, superb, nay, sublime, sublime in the jaws of peril, Finland shows what free men can do. The service rendered by Finland to mankind is magnificent. . . . We cannot tell what the fate of Finland may be, but no more mournful spectacle could be presented to what is left to civilized mankind than that this splendid northern race should be at last worked down and reduced to servitude worse than death by the dull, brutish force of overwhelming numbers. If the light of freedom which still burns so brightly in the frozen North should be finally quenched, it might well herald a return to the Dark Ages when every vestige of human progress during 2,000 years would be engulfed.

Another World War II period example is provided by the scene famously portrayed in Picasso's *Guernica*, which depicts the atrocities committed by Franco's regime against the village of Basque on April 27, 1937. The bombing itself was mostly a cold test of new airpower technologies by the German war machine. The photographs from the massacre spread to the world media and caused an immediate reaction. May Day demonstrations around Europe became a public protest against the mass murder and for Spain's republican government. The objects of this type of compassion have lately involved different minority communities, as in the bullying of a small state by a big one (e.g., Kuwait in the hands of Saddam's Iraq or plight of the Kosovo Albanians during the 1999 war), the persecution of a minority community by the ruling regime, or the discrimination practiced against an ethnic or religious minority.

Related to the theme of a national body in pain, the imperial and hegemonic political body is often imagined as suffering. The various images of hegemonic decline are relevant from the perspective of the sentiment of compassion. For example, Plato's pedagogic myth concerning the submergence of Atlantis has a community suddenly caught in a violent deluge. The emphatic warning is that common sense is easily submerged by expressions of the darker side of human nature, by belligerence and avarice. The basic form of the related decline-and-fall imagery was later perfected by a historian of the Roman Empire, Zosimus, during the late fifth century (Goffart 1971, 412). The impassioned narrative states the reasons why Rome lost its sovereignty so rapidly, within a brief period of time. One explicated reason for the disintegration was overextension—"blind folly"—which resulted from the doomed attempts of one mortal man, the emperor, to control everything.

From this perspective, the immoderate greatness of the Roman Empire was a sign of its demise because it placed an unnatural strain on limited human resources. Edward Gibbon, the later representative of the imperial decline-and-fall tradition, agrees with this. Gibbon's interpretation of Rome's decline and fall highlighted the role of balance and moderation as arbiters of the empire's political health (Gruman 1960, 76). The excesses of power—for example, absolute domination and Christian immoderation—constituted the fatal breach of the bounds of prudence. Rome was submerged by its desire to control. This declinist imagery comprises an important locus for political compassion.

The particular character of 9/11's emotionality becomes clear against the declinist background. It can be claimed that the senses of abrupt convulsion, drama, and tragedy blended with that of surprise, suddenness, emergency, fear, horror, and sorrow. The tradition of hegemonic sentimentalism refers to the mobilization of compassionate movements that feel for, legitimize, and promote a particular kind of world order. From the perspective of this tradition, the suffering of a hegemonic power triggers compassionate sentiments. The mood enables a sequence of actions that fall partly under the rubric of just war and partly under the equally ancient theme of protecting "Christendom," "civilization," and "humanity" against different varieties of "barbarity." During these world-order moments, there emerges a galvanizing—although by no means thoroughly shared—compulsion to do something, to put things in order, to restore, spread, and perfect. This may lead to different levels of support and to varying forms of international interventions in the distant lands. The larger movement of decline combines with distant local regression. The collapsing towers of 9/11 led to a "compassionate" relationship with the failed community of Afghanistan and later with the failing state of Iraq.

Hegemonic suffering is easily associated with particular types of national and individual suffering. In the case of 9/11, political discourse came to be connected with strong identification by many with the hegemony and with the acknowledgement of its leadership. Immediately after 9/11, the U.S. government received numerous letters and messages of condolence from different governments around the world. These texts can be used as a measure of the different varieties of political compassion. I collected 44 such messages for the purpose of seeing how the body in pain was constructed and what the object of mobilizing compassion was.

The first clear cluster of texts reveals a high degree of bonding and solidarity with the United States. Phrases referring to the United States as a "state," "power," "leading nation," and "government" are highlighted. Fittingly, Tony Blair, the British prime minister, declared: ". . . I give [the United States], on behalf of our country, our solidarity, our sympathy and our support."

The immediate sense of 9/11 was that it was an attack against the United States, a state with the specific meaning of being a world leader, the lone superpower, or hegemony. The United States was recognized as a mighty nation, a world leader, and a state with a special role. At the same time, 9/11 brought forth the strong perception of a wider international community united in solidarity and unified in action. For a moment, it was as if the whole of known humanity was threatened by the "inhumane" elements who had managed to strike at the very center of Western modernity.

The messages of condolence revealed a strong sense of horror and shock in the face of a "common tragedy." The 9/11 attacks were seen as being inhuman, barbaric, monstrous, and mindless. The individual bodies were perceived as innocent apolitical victims. There was a strong sense of a community united in a shared tragedy. The strong sense of solidarity and compassion was further emphasized by a commitment to unified action against the attackers. The messages expressed determination and resoluteness in forming a common front against terrorism. The texts contained constant references to and offers of assistance in the struggle against terror, and 9/11 resulted in a tremendous sense of goodwill and empathy for the United States. It also gave it a relatively unrestricted hand when it came to the use of its right to self-defense and the right of the "international community" to defend itself and restore the "balance."

There were two other types of messages, which were less numerous than the first. The second discernible type of message condemned the attacks as criminal acts. Where the first type emphasized the sense of shared political community, these messages stressed that the attacks were normative violations. They were either criminal acts or morally reprehensible violations of international law and humanitarian values. The condolence messages that scored high on this factor contained reaffirmations of the importance of the international community in the multilateral sense of the term. Besides lamenting over the acts, these texts contained an implicit worry over the future of mutually binding norms and multilateral institutions such as the United Nations. The U.S. administration was not offered a free hand; instead, there were references to the international laws that bind everyone. It was notable that the United States was not identified as a state or a nation, but as a society of people. Numerous references were made to the suffering of individual people. The suffering body was constructed as an innocent world citizen having to face the horrors of inhumanity. The national membership of that individual was not considered more decisive than the membership of the generic human polity.

The third distinct message type highlighted the desire for political problems to be solved by political means. The associated discourse highlighted the extraordinary nature of the 9/11 attacks. They were an exception from the norm and meant to be treated as such. References were made to the meaninglessness of the cycles of revenge that might result from 9/11. These references can be read as an indirect criticism of the United States's own role in producing the attacks. Earlier U.S. foreign policy was seen as being among the root causes and the attacks were perceived as a blowback reaction to the United States's unjust policies or a boomerang effect stemming from that country's one-sided foreign policy. Much emphasis was placed on the need to stabilize the international order by avoiding strong counterreactions. Some of the clearest statements of this type originated from states with long-standing antagonistic relations with the United States. These included Libya, Iran, and Iraq. Libya emphasized the need to feel compassion for the United States, despite its differences with it. Iran appealed to world consciousness in its message. Iraq's response reminded everyone that the United States was reaping what it had sown. The idea of a blowback was explicated only in Iraq's response, which was delivered through the media. Syria and North Korea formulated their responses in terms of the need to fight all forms of terrorism. The phrase, "all forms," may be read as a reference to the state terrorism in which these states interpreted the United States—and its ally Israel—to be engaged.

Transferring Pain through Contagion and Diversion

It seems likely that there is a multiplicity of suffering bodies in international relations. The idea here is that international political violence usually evokes all of these multiple suffering bodies. In humanitarian emergencies, the suffering of the individual body is thought to take precedence. This is a normatively driven oversimplification. Furthermore, it leads to lack of recognition of those cases as humanitarian in which the other bodies are very salient. In the post-9/11 period, these cases are increasingly numerous and often interlinked. The politics of compassion should be expanded to involve these new types of humanitarian emergencies as well. However, in order to adequately understand the new types of humanitarian emergencies, they have to be placed in their proper conceptual "home." I will turn next to the various dynamics and schemata of understanding the push-and-pull factors involved in this extension beyond the "nearest is dearest" boundary and across various suffering bodies. I will locate these dynamics in the overall culturally constructed frame that has to do with the vorticity of compassion. More importantly, I will trace a model that is relevant to a compassionate connection that links hegemonic suffering to local-level individual suffering.

The morality drama frame of humanitarian emergencies is judgmental and emotionally intense. Its visuals stimulate and compel those far beyond the ground zero of the emergency area to intervene. This sudden "spread" of the sense of emergency should be given some conceptual substance. I will turn to two relevant theoretical connections. The following review of research on the contagion of violence and diversionary war is meant to introduce the importance of turbulent noncognitive processes from the perspective of emergencies. The overview will concentrate on the implicit models inherent in contagion-effect and diversionary war literature. The schematic models will then be contextualized in the Thucydidean classical thought concerning the intimate relationship between political upheavals, their wavelike spread, and the underlying flux of emotion. Indeed, it is suggested that the Thucydidean classical model looms large in the background of more contemporary ideas.

The term "contagion" refers to the idea that political violence in one location influences the possibility of violence in another location either by increasing its likelihood or by causing increasing immunity (e.g., Li and Thompson 1975, 63). Contagion often refers to the rapid transmission and spreading of violence throughout a region in a way that eludes "efforts to control its scope, speed and direction" (Koslowski and Kratochwil 1994, 215, 247). Furthermore, besides suggesting an external factor, the literature on contagion implicates some type of internal condition for the contagion to take hold. In addition to having external and local constituents, it is noteworthy that the dynamics of contagion depends on the varying political status. For example, Midlarsky et al. (1980, 272) define a hierarchy effect which makes terror contagious when "a perceived enemy of much greater size, power and force capability engages in what can be interpreted as the indiscriminate use of violence." In this way, violent acts by actors with high international status are more easily imitated by peripheral actors than vice versa. Highly visible violent acts lead to contagion from central places which have a relatively high status, into the more marginal areas.

One key finding seems to be that contagion has noncognitive qualities: it refers, in this sense, to the flows of emotional content or to the spread of a mood, sentiment, attitude, or judgment. Contagion can assume different forms. Besides the spread of technical mimicry, the transmission of symbolic-"performative" content is central to contagion. Implicit in much of the contagion literature is a presumption that violence spreads by social example rather than by conscious learning (e.g., Hill and Rothchild 1986, 718). The dynamics is often linked to human nature, which is regarded as essentially imitative of and responsive to other people's behavior (Govea and West 1981, 349). The literature on contagion makes constant references to noncognitive social learning (Rose 1976, 22; Hill and Rothchild 1986, 719). To describe contagion, terms such as "inspiration" and "stimulations" are used in the research literature. From the perspective of contagion, it seems that unconscious and habitual political disposition and dynamics matter (Mayer 1969, 294). There appears an often repeated assertion that contagion is possible if there are endogenous groups with at least the beginnings of identities conducive to political violence (e.g., Hill and Rothchild 1986, 720). These underlying or dormant identities can be suddenly reanimated as when the wave of nationalism spread around the former Soviet sphere in the first part of the 1990s. It seems that a latent group structure is the prerequisite for contagion to take hold: the more heterogeneous the in-group structure, the more room—or dormant identities—there is for contagion to take hold in some segments of the citizenry.

At the level of groups and group identity, the idea of diversionary uses of violence helps further clarify the push-and-pull dynamics of the contagion. The politics of compassion is an important ingredient of what is meant by specific types of political violence. From this perspective, it is important to examine the co-optive possibilities between different violent means to get a more adequate map of the related phenomena. An important form of co-option of modernist individual-centered humanitarianism consists of the wars of pretext. There is a long tradition of the state—both hegemonic and other—initiating seemingly legitimate humanitarian interventions for ulterior motives (e.g., Goodman 2006, 107). The image of "humanitarian rescue" can offer attractive opportunities for military aggression and a good frame for the safe expression of enmity.

Lebow's (1981, 23) pretext model of violence includes appeals for wide domestic support as well as signaling to other states the legitimacy of its actions against a target state. In terms of rational choice, the diversionary war model can be defined as follows: Leaders faced with domestic troubles, "who anticipate being removed," often choose to undertake adventurous foreign policies to create cohesion and to "divert attention from their domestic failures" (Smith 1998, 625) and to embark upon aggressive foreign policies and wars (Levy 1988, 666). The basic rationale of an actor engaged in such externalization of civil conflict stems from the belief that in-group cohesion tends to increase with out-group conflict. In this model, the existence of humanitarian argument lowers the pressure from other actors to stop the aggressive state from threatening with or engaging in aggressive use of force. Therefore, it is in the strategic interest of an aggressive state with in-group problems to argue for action on the grounds of humanitarianism.

Most formulations of the diversionary war dynamics tend to be rationalistic. Diversion refines the choices available to a political leader, different regime types are differently disposed to diversion, and different types of domestic conflict have different diversionary outcomes. Gelpi (1997, 256) argues that, when faced with internal problems, state leaders have at least three approaches from which to choose. First, they can appease the domestic opposition through dialogue and concessions. Second, they can repress the opposition by more coercive means. Third, they can try to restore a favorable status quo by cohesion-creating military activity abroad.

The depth of the regression affecting a state has implications for the likelihood of using any of these diversionary strategies. Some studies (e.g., Gelpi 1997, 262; Levy 1989;) have suggested that the likelihood of diversionary war increases with domestic nonviolent protests. However disruptive these protests might be, their consensual general form still signifies a degree of in-group cohesion. A foreign conflict and the accompanying "rally round the flag" effect may offer a solution to these early signs of in-group troubles. When the in-group troubles have escalated to the point of internal violence, foreign war may not seem a viable option. For a disintegrated in-group, anything "foreign" is already conceptually problematic. If systematic violence is an option, it is directed to close out-groups in the form of repression of minorities, ethnic cleansing, and genocides. On the other hand, these disintegrating "political bodies" easily become attractive targets for diversion-based outside intervention. Overall, it seems that there is a multistage and multiactor model of in-group failure explicated by the diversionary war schema.

Thus, in line with the argument delineated here, diversionary practices can be approached from a less strategic/rational perspective, which is more sensitive to the group's identity dynamics. It is notable that in the rationalistic models, the direction of causality is thought to be straightforward: In the words of Dassel and Reinhardt (1999, 56), ". . . domestic strife can encourage foreign aggression" and lead to a projection of force to external actors. Besides the push factor of the in-group problems, the pull factor of the site where the projection takes place is rarely considered. It could be equally likely that highly visible problems in some out-group communities stimulate or pull other actors into diversions in the form of humanitarian intervention. The pull factor of a failing political community caught in the vortex of spreading and deepening violence offers further insight into the practice of humanitarian intervention and to co-option between different actors.

The pull factor of failing states can be connected with contemporary humanitarianism, in which "emergencies" often deal with failing or failed communities. From this perspective, the co-optive practices are easy to understand since states and humanitarian agencies can become constituents of the same push–pull process. The largely noncognitive nature of the push–pull effect means that diversionary practices may become less strategic as states drift down the path of intervention enabled by various humanitarian agencies. These agencies, which tend to be on the "ground" first, formulate the legitimate need for an intervention. The use of humanitarian sentiments to legitimize military aggression can lead to mutual co-option or even to the co-option of the state's actions by strong humanitarian sentiments. Therefore, the state that uses humanitarianism as a pretext can learn to justify and understand its actions in a new way. The immediate actions become conditioned by different sets of considerations and the long-term behavior may change due to a new self-evaluation of the in-group as a do-gooder and an international example: ". . . framing the resort to force as a pursuit of humanitarian objectives, or adding humanitarian issues to an ongoing military effort, can reshape domestic political arrangements and the character of interstate relations . . ." (Goodman 2006, 109). The presence of emergency relief organizations gives an indication of where the pull is stemming from.

The Thucydidean Vorticity of Violence

Modern fragmentary thought on contagion and diversion illuminates the dynamics of emotional intensification of a violent flow. However, the classical models comprise a more holistic picture of the macro–micro association involved in changing power hierarchies.

Contagion-effect and diversionary-war literature indicates an underlying common dynamics. First, the local swirls of violence, which rapidly deepen, tend also to spread. Second, much of the spread is based on imitative and noncognitive processes. Third, violence tends to attract outside forces to intervene. Fourth, there are external—pull—factors and internal—push—factors involved in intervention, which are based only partly on strategic planning. Fifth, those outside forces that experience moderate in-group problems are especially prone to feel the push-and-pull effects. These effects intensify the emotionality involved, which can lead to the mobilization of political movements that makes interventions irresistible. What is at issue here is how different actors get caught in the vortex of humanitarian emergency and how it both intensifies and spreads. Next, I will contextualize this schema in the Thucydidean model of violent movement in order to clarify the underlying cultural dynamics.

For Thucydides, peace was a desirable political sentiment. Peace refers to a long-term mood defined by a state of rest or by a steady goal-oriented movement (e.g., Thucydides 4.62.2). The coming into being of the kinesis-laden hurly-burly of diverse movements led to the paralysis of this political mood and the steady deliberation it enabled. In Thucydides's work, kinesis and ekinethe suggest destructive types of "movement and instability" (Monoson and Loriaux 1998, 291). The ability to plan and maintain a chosen course of action was overwhelmed by the increasing complexity of the currents. In these large-scale kineses, categories—such as personal, state, and interstate—became confounded (Connor 1984, 7). The more confusing the currents became, the more destructive was their impact at multiple, increasingly overlapping levels. This deep "intestine" nature of war may be taken to have referred to deep societal movements resulting from and constituting the war whereby poleis and individuals lost their "reserve, the power to check their motion" (Monoson and Loriaux 1998, 292).

The political mood of peace is different from that of anger. The regressions, or offenses of personal honor, tribal filiations, and intra-polis bonds, were captured in the emotion-laden term, thumos (Kaziak 1999, 1068). Thumos was the general seat of emotions, a template which may actualize in several emotions. It was also the motivator of angry political actions against insult or injustice. It is important to note Aristotle's distinction between thumos, which is a special type of desire, and desires such as hunger or sex (e.g., *Nicomachean Ethics*, 1111b17-20). Here, thumos includes actions that are based on anger. What makes anger different, for example, from hunger is that the specific actions that follow are not predictable in the same sense: ". . . unlike the desire for food or sex, the general desire and fantasies of revenge do not determine what the angry man will do" (Rorty 1997, 647). Acts of anger are generalized, blind, unpredictable, and irrational. In this sense, one can imagine a general political mood of anger that corresponds to the fickle and erratic changes in the intra- and extracommunal power structures. Such changes in the political power hierarchies translate into the arousal of anger.

The spread of violence in Thucydides seems to refer to the ability of the overall violent vortex of war to transform into an intensifying flow. New sub-currents occur in the vicinity of war's rhythmic expression of energy. The vortex of war induces a sympathetic pulse, a current. The increasingly violent circular motion means that intervals in extreme pain production become progressively shorter: Violence keeps coming back in more intense spirals, circling round and back, again and again. The emotionality of this successive repetition is overwhelming for both the community's and the individual's self-continence. Furthermore, the local intensity compels the principals to intervene and participate in it, further fuelling a cycle of action and response. These moments accelerate what Thucydides sees as the normal periodicity of war—that is, the cycle of seasons. This natural periodicity shifts into a much higher rhythm when the participants, both big and small, are roused into mutually satisfying, yet extremely destructive, vortexes.

Thucydides's political ideas were greatly conditioned by Hippocratic medicine. It should be noted that this was a two-way street—the language of politics also permeated the medical thought of the time. To highlight this connection, some have suggested that Thucydides was moving even beyond the medical thought of his time by suggesting the dynamics of contagion. For example, Thucydides describes that the Stasis "ran its course from city to city" with steadily increasing intensity. However, there is an important distinction that is especially relevant for the model we are developing here. As Craik (2001, 102) points out, the "contagion" reading is an anachronistic interpretation of the *Histories*. Rather than referring to contagion, Thucydides was using a related, but different, idea of flux/flow. Violence moved from one community to another in the same way as the plague, which he describes as inflicting Athens, progressed deeper in the somatic body—starting from the head and progressing to a fatal intestinal condition—and vertically across human bodies. One significant difference between the more modern contagion dynamics and the Thucydidean flux was the ability of regression—for example, plague and stasis—to become more intensive as it spread. It is as if the condition mutates into a more serious form. Thucydides links this intensity effect partly to the fear aroused in people at the later stages, when they were more aware of the devastating effect of the flux (Thucydides, 3.82.4). There is an added horror in the acknowledgement of impending doom.

In Thucydides's time, "flux" was used to understand various political processes as well as in attempts to construe the realm of bodily physiological changes. This overall model found one expression in the Hippocratic medical thought, where bodily flux was thought to be the source of diseases (Craik 2001, 102). There was a close link across the soma–psyche boundary: it is important to realize that physical movements and the imbalances caused by them were thought to be the key to human emotions. Furthermore, the significance of multidimensional bodily movements found an expression in Thucydides's political thought. It is highly significant that for him, the war was one "grand movement," or kinesis megiste. The vortex and its various side whirls were referred to along with the concept of kinesis (ekinethe, kineo). The vortex model seems even more appropriate when its mythological connotations are considered—that is, the grand movement was set in motion by the sea power, Athens. In mythology, the coming into being of Athens was linked to sea vortexes. In the Homeric hymns, the sea swirls in confusion (ekinethe) at the birth of Athena. Thus, fluidity and flux and other Poseidonic qualities are abundant in Athenian iconography. On the other hand, it is highly suggestive that Plato, in *Statesman* (1995), uses the concept of "sea of diversity" when referring to existence outside or in the absence of a political community. The inter-poleis space—its ether—was imagined as a sea in flux. Fittingly, the "great movement" unleashed by Pericles's Athens is imagined by Thucydides as a "chaos, terrible flux, a destructive kind of motion" (Monoson and Loriaux 1998, 291).

It is highly significant that the macro-level movement did not spread only horizontally between political bodies. It also turned into increasingly deep vertical vortexes, or, as Thucydides descriptively frames it, into "intestinal disorders." On the one hand, according to Thucydides, these abnormalities referred to local-level factionalism and atomization (Monoson and Loriaux 1998, 287). On the other hand, this violent regression spread simultaneously into the individual level—both in the moral/psychological and physiological senses—as the striking subnarrative of the Athenian plague demonstrates. While the convulsions of the stasis atomized Corcyran society into factions and finally into violent, but extremely vulnerable, individuals, the Plague of Athens entailed a parallel story of bodily disintegration. This subnarrative highlights the influence of overall "movements" on human bodies as the loci of the soma and the psyche. The suggested direction of the dynamics is clear. The grand movement of imperial war gathers intensity and spreads downward towards smaller communities, which are thus set into disintegrative motion, and to the individual level, where somatic suffering—such as mass murder, disease, or mental incontinence, that is, rash actions, selfishness, and failure to obey sacred norms—takes place.

Thucydides sees violence (*bia*) as the intensifying constituent of the horizontal and vertical movements. The meaningless violence of the later stages of the vortex is very evident in the description of the stasis. Thucydides perceives stasis to be a regressive process which is common in times of a large war and which can strike any community: "During seven days . . ., the Corcyraeans were engaged in butchering those of their fellow citizens whom they regarded as their enemies. . . . Death thus raged in every shape; and, as usually happens at such times, there was no length to which violence did not go" (Thucydides, 3.82.2). As the vortex of war intensified and deepened, the smaller poleis were the first ones to unravel. However, it should be noted that these poleis did not only dissolve violently, they turned into what can be called anti-communities. The previously constitutive element of together-mindedness transformed into a "deconstitutive" element, into mutually felt animosity. Ironically, the shared hatred started to provide a "constitutive" form for the collapsed polis. In this situation, the stasis-ridden anti-communities directed their previously internal bonds outwardly, thereby actively attracting or pulling foreign elements into their internal struggles, so that the external war became internalized at the local level and vice versa. This violent kinesis was not only destructive within the engulfed community, it was also violently reactive, in a sense "contagious."

The process of stasis turns the pervasive sense of injustice felt by some in the community at its initial stage into increasingly hard doxa and a mobilizing force. The doxa expresses and legitimizes hatred and anger toward the in-group. Passions start to motivate judgment. The situation leads to shared and programmatic actions of expressed hatred. The programmatic nature of hatred points to an emergence of separate and incompatible communal value inventories:

> Dissatisfaction of itself is too unstable and reactive to give rise to the intellectual justification for remolding society anew. An underlying secession from a joint system of values to a separate set of values is necessary. The rage and animosity, which a perception of injustice engenders, gain permanence and direction only because they are organized and filtered through a new set of values. (Kalimtzis 2000, 119)

Thucydides notes this reversal of values: "Reckless audacity came to be considered the courage of a loyal ally; prudent hesitation, specious cowardice; moderation was held to be a cloak for unmanliness; ability to see all sides of a question inaptness to act on any. Frantic violence became the attribute of manliness; caution plotting, a justifiable means of self-defence. The advocate of extreme measures was always trustworthy; his opponent a man to be suspected" (3.82.8). The hatred-embedded values substituted the earlier deliberation with randomness and excess. The phantasms of revenge and retribution became excessive and arbitrary sources of pleasures (Kalimtzis 2000, 119-20). From this perspective, the appetite for retribution is even more against former political allies than it is toward strangers or outsiders, because hatred finds a more defined object in a former friend, whose agonies have more meaning than those of complete strangers. The "nearest is dearest" narrative turns into its antithesis and compassion is felt toward the distant others who are actively seeking to participate in the internal conflict.

For Thucydides, natural attraction existed between the principals of the grand movement—that is, the imperial warring parties—and the factions in the local unraveling communities. This mutual stimulation was based on growing internal agitations and movements, especially in Athens. The growing regressive vortex manifested itself in the incontinent, erratic behavior of the leaders and in rapid changes in the leadership. Edmunds (1975, 75, 81) detects in Thucydides two powerful sentiments that prevail under violent convulsions and which turn into desirable characteristics looked for in leaders: unreasoned boldness and rash quickness. According to Edmunds, the unreasoned and bold manner in which actions are taken contrast with the moderating "provident delay" that prevails under conditions of healthy polity. When political and physical death appears imminent, the primary mood favors decisiveness. The other decline- or stasis-intensifying mood is the inclination toward frantic rashness, which Thucydides—according to Gomme's translation—calls "the small sharpness of a little soul." When the rip currents of the overall conflict cut across a community, an appetite for quickness becomes the norm. Rapid reactions are valued because they have their own redemptive logic and retaliatory desire.

The Flow of the War on Terror

The Thucydidean model of political regression involves powerful emotional vortexes that spread, intensify, and overwhelm small and, eventually, even big actors. It is a model of mutual regression in which the compassionate connections provide the channels for constitutive emotional transfers. Caught in mutual regressive processes, the political actors are drawn to each other. Local hatred becomes the "cohesive" emotion, where outside actors are drawn through the compassion felt toward one side of the conflict. From this perspective, it is easy to see how both the Afghanistan intervention in 2001 and the Iraq invasion in 2003 were turned into clear-cut moral dramas in the United States. In Afghanistan, the so-called Northern Alliance was deemed to be the protagonist for good things, while the Taliban was treated as the enemy. In the same way, the Iraqi Kurds and Shias were seen as the bodies of suffering. The plight of these two groups was much highlighted in the administration's rhetoric and in media representations. These compassions stimulated the convulsion that the hegemonic power hierarchy faced on 9/11. Taken together with the compassion felt for the hegemony, the compassions comprised an overall vertically and horizontally spreading flow.

This macro-level regression was dramatically induced by the world-order shock of 9/11. The mobilization of that event for the purposes of restoring Western potency provided the background for the later events in Afghanistan and Iraq. These interventions further connected the United States to the local regressive flows in these failed or anti-communities. The dynamics of pull and push provided the context for the arousal of other political emotions. They also provided for the mutual contagion of political violence, that is, the suffering of different interlinked political bodies. It is in the frame of this flow that humanitarianism has to be recontextualized. The argument here has been that the interventions in Afghanistan and Iraq, with their subsequent humanitarian crises, have to be understood as one overall regressive flow. Ignorance about how the "war on terror" led to an intervention-inducing emotional atmosphere has led to considerable confusion over the status of the humanitarian emergency in Iraq. Much of the literature and humanitarian agencies are at a loss on how to understand Iraq. It does not fit the 1990s' prototype of humanitarian emergency as a temporalized, localized, and atomized event. Moreover, because of the existence of multiple suffering bodies, the humanitarian emergency in Iraq went largely unnoticed. Something else was thought to be at stake than the fates of the millions of displaced people.

It is clear that Iraq is not a typical humanitarian intervention, although it was partly justified as one (e.g., Mack 2004, 683). The just cause and last resort criteria were not fulfilled (e.g., Macfarlane et al. 2004, 977). Roberts (2006, 580) says Iraq should be put into the category of "transformative military occupation." His idea is that the United States made an effort to fix the failed Iraqi state and restore it from totalitarian rule. The consequences of Afghanistan and, more particularly, Iraq on the shape of humanitarian emergencies and interventions have been noted by many authors (e.g., Macfarlane et al. 2004; Piiparinen 2007). The main argument is that Iraq caused a moral vacuum in the arguments for an intervention. The underlying reason for this appears to be the pre-text nature of the intervention in Iraq. Iraq can be regarded as a self-interested military action, in which humanitarianism provided only pre-text or post-hoc reasons. I will argue that this argument is right in that it recognizes Iraq as a form, albeit deviant, of humanitarian intervention. The argument errs in not being able to adequately capture the sentiment of the world-order emergency involved in the war on terror. Moreover, the argument misses out on many of the compassions involved in Iraq and Afghanistan. It also fails to relate these to the root causes of the complex humanitarian emergency in Iraq.

In general, hegemonic powers externalize their internal in-group problems and smaller communities collapse, pulling the outside elements in. Thus, while the overall behavior of all the actors becomes whimsical and erratic, the big states can maintain themselves longer than the small ones. The regressive dynamics works itself through small actors in a sudden, highly visible burst. The small actors caught in the emergency become attractive or even compelling objects for the diversionary pressures of the principal actors. This holistic dynamics provides a frame for the understanding of the modern ideas about contagion and diversion. The dynamics also sheds light on the various processes involved in humanitarian emergencies: communal collapse, powerful mobilizations of compassion, outside intervention, and patterns of co-option.

Thürer (1999, 732) states a failed state is a cluster concept that "does not denote a precisely defined and classifiable situation, but serves rather as a broad label for a phenomenon which can be interpreted in various ways." The purpose of this paper was to point out the complicity of the nexus between macro-level turbulence and local-level failure for the regressive flows associated with state failure and intervention. Rotberg (2002, 90) uses the appropriate metaphor of "black hole" when describing a failed state: "A collapsed state is a mere geographical expression, a black hole into which a failed polity has fallen." This language is appropriate to the vortex model we have developed here. The disappearing political affinity has caused violence, which has turned the community into an anti-community. The additional property of this black hole like anti-community is the intense "gravitational pull," which it exerts on hegemonic power at the initial stages of political regression and which is still able to launch diversionary war.

The post-9/11 literature on state failure often evinces the argument that it is the special duty of the international community and its member states to rise and meet the responsibility of containing, managing, healing, and preventing political regression. The compassion for and worry over the world order are the sentiments mobilizing such interventions. State failures are regarded as implosions caused mainly by endogenous factors. However, foreign intervening powers play a more sinister role in state failures, which has rarely been examined. This article has given some substance to the notion that the contact between the hegemonic intervening power, the United States, and Iraq, which are at different stages of regression, could have led to a coupling phenomenon with a distinctive intensifying dynamics. In other words, external states do not only participate in helping people living in the territory of failing states, but also may act as catalysts of state failure and precipitate their own political regression.

Vorticity Model

Political, personal, and somatic "bodies" have to face the powerful currents of war and disintegration of political bodies (e.g., stasis) and somatic bodies (e.g., plague) at multiple levels. The influential medical ideas of Thucydides's time stressed the parallelism between different bodies, and between inner and outer movements (Padel 1992, 67). This topos still influences the discourses of political compassion. Movements at different levels influenced each other: the linkages aroused political emotions and linked them with personal emotions. Passions and judgments were connected to overall movements and, therefore, they could be properly interpreted only in relation to larger events and contexts (Young-Bruehl 1986, 6). The sudden movements at the level of international relations translate into public and private emotions that enable and constitute further macro-level movements.

The system- and structure-oriented field of international relations has difficulty in making sense of the motion or flow from one moment to the next. The meaning-carrying aspect of rhythm and tempo is often left untouched as difficult and idiosyncratic. Action in the form of progression of events and development of themes is required to cement the significance of what is happening. It is one such motion that Thucydides captures in his model of the grand movement of political violence. This movement was the current that electrified and animated events. Such a current unifies the different aspects of the political drama. The current unifies in the sense that we can then recognize the interplay between the various aspects of the political process as conductors of a single current that either spreads from one feature to another or flows through several features at one time. Among the layers of meaning in the spread of the violence dynamics are the macro-level power hierarchy (i.e., the American unipolarity), local-level political regression (e.g., the state failure in Afghanistan), and individual suffering (e.g., the jumpers of 9/11, Guantanamo Bay, or collateral damage). All of these bodies matter. However, they may be adequately appreciated only when seen as connected by the cultural mediated model of the flow of political violence. This means that although there are different variations of the themes of world-order turbulence, "ship of state crisis," and individual-under-plight emergency, it should be noted that their prescriptive forces are often triggered under the same circumstances, as parts of the same overall vortex.

My argument is that emotions are important constituents of violent motions. Political emotions communicate underlying changes in the micro- and macro-level power hierarchies. Emotions felt over there alarm and agitate. They mobilize further intensification of the regressive dynamics. Demagogues who exploit these sentiments are tempted to stir up and excite demos or particular factions of it. The stirred-up situation leads to what Thucydides calls the "morbid passion for what is absent" (Thucydides, 6.13.1). What is absent is in-group coherence and, increasingly, this is sought after by engaging in "rally round the flag" wars against distant enemies. In smaller communities, the desire for together-mindedness finds its perverse fulfillment in the slaughter of other factions. As noted, the parallel passions in big and small states can interlock. My attempt is to demonstrate how such a vortex might account for the overall dynamics of the post-9/11 world.

How the events flowed from New York to the mountains of Afghanistan may be understood through the Thucydidean vortex dynamics. The attraction to the Afghan landscape stemmed from an earlier grand movement in international relations, the cold war, and the Soviet diversion into Afghanistan. President Jimmy Carter stated in a speech on January 4, 1980, soon after the Soviet troops had rolled into Afghanistan: "Aggression unopposed becomes a contagious disease." Aggression was opposed and the larger macro-level motions fuelled local extremism, which, after two decades, reattracted superpower intervention in Afghanistan. The overall vortex has its own dynamic logic which is helpful in analyzing events at different levels as interrelated flows.

3

Vorticity in Action: Compassions, Stimulations, and Mutual Regressions

When on August 6, 2008, the Georgian forces occupied the capital of its secessionist region, South Ossetia, Georgia was using humanitarian claim to legitimize the military action. Similarly, when a day or so later, the Russians intervened, they used the language of humanitarian intervention. They were there, so the Russians said, to stop an imminent ethnic cleansing. There is nothing very noteworthy in these justifications of military action. They fit the emergence of the humanitarian frame in contemporary world politics. Similar claims have been made in connection with almost all military action taken since the end of the cold war. But they also fit a much longer pattern of state-led humanitarian action, which is centuries old. The intervention of a major power in the affairs of a smaller state with significant internal fractures and turmoil provides one trend in this long tradition. The political compassion of major states is often projected on such objects.

Thus, the Russia–Georgia nexus also illustrates the conceptual dynamics repeatedly underlined in this work—that the decomposition of different political bodies interacts dynamically. The participants are drawn to each other and galvanized by each other's actions. The Georgian state was in a state of virtual civil strife. The entire region, including neighboring Chechnya, was experiencing disorder and high levels of various kinds of political violence. World-order sentiments were also in play when Georgia, in particular, cried out that it was being targeted because of its democratic experiment and strong alignment with the West—that is, it had applied for membership to the NATO and was integrating itself more deeply with the European Union (EU). It called upon the United States to intervene on its behalf. The United States responded by sending military ships with the explicit mission of supplying humanitarian assistance. The chain of events was set in motion by a resurgent Russia, reasserting its own role in the region and in world politics. However, Russian regional stability in the Caucasus region was in doubt and the state of its society in its own territories, in Ossetia and Chechnya in particular, was cause for alarm. The way in which the political bodies at different stages of internal upheaval are drawn together is both tragic and intriguing. Much of the action may be explained through the vorticity model presented here, which emphasizes the role of political compassions.

The Thucydidean insights offer clues into a special, yet major, part of the regressive drawing together of political bodies: the large-scale "grand movement" between major players seems to be a combination of coupling between major states experiencing change and smaller states experiencing deep crises. In this chapter, I will continue the examination of this dynamism in the light of the neoclassical approach that I have adopted. How do political bodies connect? How do the movements in them and between them constitute sentiments? How does political emotionality lead to political motions? How do these motions turn into kinetic convulsions? As in the case of Georgia, these questions offer insights into contemporary individual–local–world interactions. I will concentrate on illustrating the theoretical configurations by drawing from the United States–Iraq coupling, which led to unheard levels of complex violence at its zenith in 2007, before calming down as a result of the combustible elements burning out and because of the larger U.S. military involvement. How temporary this relative lull in the violence will be, is a question I will raise.

Vorticity

One of the main arguments in this book has been that changes in the political power hierarchy constitute a particular type of sentiments, called political emotions. Specific stages in a dynamic continuum from political health to political failure translate into moods and, from there, into emotions. The mood that prevails in a healthy political community is very different from that in a political community that is witnessing emerging discord and split-mindedness. The regressive flow consists of changing hierarchies. The corresponding political emotions are stimulated, further convulsing the communal body. The crucial point is that such stimulation is contagious. Furthermore, its spread is likely to be at a much more accelerated pace under conditions of larger world political changes—the Thucydidean grand movement. Under these conditions, the changes in the power hierarchies at the local and world levels couple together. The emotions that are felt feed this coupling.

The idea is to trace the key concepts of the book—compassion, its co-option, and their connection to the violently changing local and global power hierarchies—back to their sources. The neoclassical argument used starts from the premise that the rediscovery of the conceptual roots of modern political phenomena can enlighten our awareness of the ways in which current world politics is constructed.

Violent slides to deeper and wider regression provide the link between the three bodies of this work: hegemonic, national, and individual. The earlier chapter reviewed how the wound first opens when interstate warfare disturbs the prevailing world order. This, in turn, leads to the emotional excitement of the whole political realm. The vorticity forms link between the hegemonic actors and the national bodies. The first points of further regression are the weakest communities, which have the most exposed internal structure—in the form of preexisting conflicts and factions. These failing communities attract major players to intervene in the name of legitimate right. Often, the bias toward intervention is due to the mobilizing power of compassion. The intervention is usually argued in terms of political compassion. It is done on behalf of a national body. When the conflict spreads further, it reaches the level of individual somatic bodies. I will discuss this in Chapter 5.

More nuanced examinations reveal an argument that communities at earlier stages of political regression are likely to externalize their internal conflicts and engage in so-called diversionary war. It can be further argued that in their externalization, these states may be attracted toward communities in the final stages of regression. Thus, different phases of regression are placed along a continuum that ranges from healthy political communities to stasis-ridden "anti"-communities and explains the "push effect"—for example, a state engages in diversionary war to externalize its internal problems—and the "pull effect"—for example, a faction in a failing state attracts external actors to participate in the in-fighting—at various phases. In this chapter, I will further examine and conceptualize this link between the world order and national communities.

Let me give one example of this type of approach, which is highly relevant for the theoretical underpinnings of this work: Does an international war link up with an internal conflict? For any theoretical examination of this question, it is relevant that war and internal conflicts are intimately related in their conceptual underpinnings. Evidence for the link is not hard to find. To begin with, Hobbes's paradigmatic description of the state of nature as a state of war owed much to Thucydides's portrayal of stasis in the city of Corcyra during the Peloponnesian War (Manicas 1982, 676). In a way, Hobbes, who translated Thucydides's main work into English, passed the classical construction of war into more contemporary times.

At least from this perspective, the lineage leading to the present-day image of war is related to that which takes place inside a single political community under extreme conditions.

At the surface of it, this type of approach goes against the spirit of modernism, which sees fundamental differences—discontinuations, gaps, and moments of emergence—between us and the classics. The potential implications of classical, historical, and conceptual imagery are often ignored. Contemporary political writing often focuses on progressive processes more in line with the modernization paradigm. The regressive linkages and processes have been left unattended for the most part. Therefore, it is hardly surprising that Huntington's (1965, 415) suggestion that when it comes to the degeneration of political communities, "perhaps the most relevant ideas are the most ancient ones," is largely accurate even today. The discursive materials of the "shadow" area of regressive processes in the classics are relevant because they focused on them and because the modernists ignore them as anachronistic anomalies in the grand progressive flow of history.

Humanitarians offer insights into these regressive processes. The object of modern liberal humanitarian compassion is usually a part of a failed or failing community. The visual rhetoric of humanitarianism paints the anguish and violence of such regression in vivid colors. Compassion for a nation plays a part in such imagery. It concentrates on the plight of a particular group of people under strain. World-order compassions are also involved. However, world-order anxieties are aroused only in the major cases. All three are involved only in some cases. For example, the perceived Serbian onslaught on the Kosovo Albanians provided an instance in which world-order compassion came into play because Kosovo was deemed to be a vital part of the emerging European security architecture.

I hypothesize that the process of political regression involves the coming into being of culturally meaningful sequences of reciprocal actions, which constitute self-reinforcing regressive trajectories. To uncover the regressive dynamics, I will utilize an approach that draws from the classical writings of Thucydides and Aristotle on the phenomenon of stasis. The reason why Thucydides in particular is relevant for the phenomenon of regression is that he presents the idea that the regression and failure of a political community is inherently tied into intercommunal warfare at the grand-movement level. From the Thucydidean perspective, a failing, stasis-ridden community increasingly directs its previously internal political bonds outward, thereby actively attracting foreign elements and powers into the internal cycle of violence and consequently fuelling both the external and internal aspects of the conflict. Thus, internal and external actors provide further regressive ingredients for the failing of troubled communities. Internal and external factors couple and constitute a single deepening and enlarging process.

At the level of political bodies, this vortex is lived and felt. This means that compassion for one's group, hatred for enemies, and friendship with the perceived enemy's enemies prevail. It is among these overall sentiments that compassion for the distant other and its co-optive patterns can be best appreciated. The vortex engulfs all the actors—or bodies involved—in a mutually regressive process from which it is difficult to disengage.

The Thucydidean notion of stasis as a disease-like contagious process of communal failure can be used to locate contextual embedding for modern imagery. For Thucydides, the process of a disease both inside a human body and between such bodies offered a template for understanding grand-scale political processes. In Greek thinking, stasis as a communal-level decomposition was associated with a plague (Kalimtzis 2000, 7). One of the earliest and most influential users of the term, Thucydides used it to describe the outbreaks of physical and political diseases in his account of the Peloponnesian War. The Greek root concept, "nosos," describes both the condition of political chaos/confusion and the outbreak of an epidemic disease. For example, Thucydides's account of the Athenian plague points to the resulting general lawlessness in the city in a way that closely resembles the account of the stasis that hit the city of Corcyra during the Peloponnesian War.

This classical template finds its match in the modern constructs of political violence. Political violence and its subcategories are often treated in terms of a disease (e.g., Spilerman 1970, 627). A case in point is offered by Zartman's (1995, 9) statement that "state collapse is a long-term degenerative disease." There are numerous such examples that equate extreme political violence with disease like a regressive process. Most and Starr (1980, 932) refer to "war disease" when they discuss the diffusion of war. Hamilton and Hamilton (1983, 41) state that the main paradigm in terrorism studies holds that "terrorist incidents may encourage further violence through a process of imitation or diffusion, giving rise to a dynamics of terrorism analogous to that observed in the spread of a contagious disease." It can be claimed that this way of formulating political violence in epidemiological terms revokes the classical language.

A third relevant example is that of the failed-state thematic, which became popular in the early 1990s. In Thucydides's account of the plague, violent bodily spasms are among the severest of the symptoms, but also the last of the symptoms. Matching this, his account of the disease of stasis involves violent spasms of the political body. The contortions, contractions, and involuntary movements of the political body are read as signifiers of an advanced regression. The widespread nature of these movements signals that the communal agency has withered away into an out-of-control situation (Kallet 1999, 232). The political spasms indicate the imminent end of community life. The last stage of the political disease involves isolation and "apart-mindedness."

The modern concept of extreme state failure fits well with the extreme form of stasis that, for example, fell upon the city of Corcyra during the Peloponnesian War: "During seven days that Eurymedon stayed with his sixty ships, the Corcyraeans were engaged in butchering those of their fellow-citizens whom they regarded as their enemies: and although the crime imputed was that of attempting to put down the democracy, some were slain also for private hatred, others by their debtors because of the monies owed to them" (Thucydides, 3.81). The term "failed state" was very prominent in the early 1990s, when it was thought to be one of the main concerns of the international community (e.g., Clapham 1996, 10). In the atmosphere of the generalized war on terrorism, the concepts of collapsed, failed, and failing states have gathered additional momentum. There exists a general sense that state failures lead to their territories becoming safe havens and breeding grounds for nonstate actors in the manner of Afghanistan (e.g., Rotberg 2002, 85). The terms "failing," "failed," and "collapsed" state refer to different stages of regression. "Failing state" refers to relative weakness in the functioning of the state authority. "Failed states" are regions that are "tense, deeply conflicted, dangerous, and bitterly contested" and where the central authorities have failed to function (Rotberg 2002, 85). "Collapsed state" refers to an extreme version of failure in which violent brutality is rampant and there is a total vacuum of overarching authority in the state territory, where an internal dissolution of the state has taken place, and where not only the regime, but all the functions of government have ceased (Thürer 1999, 731). State failure can be read to refer to the process whereby a state becomes unable to maintain its authority and, accordingly, the rule of law in its territory.

A fourth important point which the neoclassical approach brings to light is the practice of diversionary war. Stasis is accompanied by a process of extroversion whereby previously internal bonds turn inside out and stretch toward external surroundings. The external realm starts to draw the factions of stasis-ridden community. The political factions of the stasis-ridden community are attracted to foreign help in their internal struggle against each other. However, before the stasis reaches its final, devastating stage, the community's main faction tends to stretch its resources to battle outside elements in the belief that this will alleviate the internal situation. The community tries to externalize its internal problems and find cohesion through a common enemy.

Thucydides brings the theme of externalization to the forefront of his histories, for example, through the disastrous expedition of Athens against the Syracuseans. Athens was being plagued by private ambition, outright hubris, and conflicting factions when it undertook the disastrous military campaign against faraway Syracuse. Thinking further, Isocrates (436–338 BC.) illustrates what Thucydides had in mind. According to Isocrates, external warfare and war against faraway places results in together-mindedness at home (e.g., Kalimtzis 2000, 182). In this, he antedated the Roman saying, *Externus timor, maximum concordiae vinculum* ("The key to unity is to find an external foe"). Internal struggles are set aside when there is a common struggle against faraway enemies. Faraway enemies show domestic political enemies in the light of alikeness. For Thucydides, what Isocrates suggested was a symptom of the underlying disease in the political community. The need to externalize—that is, a diversionary war—was a symptom of the underlying serious slide toward more extreme forms of conflict.

Externalization of internal problems brings forth the crossing of distances and, therefore, necessitates the creation of distance. The acts of constructing and highlighting the themes of distance and foreignness are further signs of stasis. Externalization can be defined as projection to external places of things that are repudiated and intolerable in one's own place, such as conflict and disintegration. Externalization involves mechanisms to clear away things the community fears to find in itself. However, from the Thucydidean perspective, externalization makes external political events integral parts of domestic processes, thereby binding matters into difficult-to-control complexes.

Moving to the modern equivalent of the Thucydidean externalization, the concept of diversionary war comes first to mind. The use and significance of violence becomes a key component of group cohesion and sense of belonging. "Diversionary war" provides an additional element to understanding the spread of political regression. In terms of rational choice, the diversionary war model can be defined as follows: Leaders faced with domestic troubles, "who anticipate being removed," often choose to undertake adventurous foreign policies to create cohesion and to "divert attention from their domestic failures" (Smith 1998, 625) and to embark on aggressive foreign policies and wars (Levy 1988, 666). The basic rationale of an actor engaged in such externalization of civil conflict stems from the belief that in-group cohesion tends to increase with out-group conflict. It is notable that the direction of causality is thought to be straightforward: in the words of Dassel and Reinhardt (1999, 56), ". . . domestic strife can encourage foreign aggression." The influence of foreign "pull" and "attraction" in the form of a failed state is rarely considered. This is precisely the point on which the neoclassical interpretation throws light.

The modern diversionary war hypothesis concentrates on four factors: the choices available to a political leader, the consequences of a particular regime type, the role of different domestic actors, and the differential consequences of different types of domestic conflict. Gelpi (1997, 256) argues that when faced with internal problems, state leaders have at least three approaches from which to choose. First, they can appease the domestic opposition through dialog and concessions. Second, they can repress the opposition by more coercive means. Third, they can try to restore a favorable status quo by cohesion-creating military activity abroad. The depth of the regression affecting a state has implications on which diversionary strategy is used. There have been studies (e.g., Gelpi 1997, 262; Levy 1989, 26) suggesting that the likelihood of diversionary war increases with domestic nonviolent protests. However disruptive these protests might be, their general form still signifies a degree of in-group cohesion. A foreign conflict and the accompanying "rally round the flag" effect may offer a solution to these early signs of in-group troubles. When the in-group troubles have escalated to the point of internal violence, foreign war may not seem a viable option. For a disintegrated in-group, anything "foreign" is already conceptually problematic.

The Phases of Political Regression

With the help of the neoclassical approach, it is possible to bring otherwise disparate elements under a common framework. The regressive slide involves three important stages with a corresponding emotional environment: communal together-mindedness, sense of split-mindedness, and the mood of stasis. Next, I will review the signposts of political regression.

Phase 1: Enkratia

The precondition for any sense of healthy community is a commonly felt sentiment to coexist as a community. There is an air of common purpose, a reason to exist. This is the fundamental constitutive sentiment of any community. This prevailing sentiment has been given several names. For example, Aristotle formulated this sentiment as a just political friendship. For a political community to emerge, a capacity for mutual understanding and one's proper place in a community's hierarchy were needed. This pervasive understanding can be arranged according to numerous desirable and less desirable constitutive principles, such as aristocracy or democracy. Furthermore, there is an assumption that such understanding needs to be able to take care of itself and protect itself against internal and external pressures. It needs to glue people together, create a certain inertia vis-à-vis the whimsies of the moment and the hurly-burly that exists in the community. The existence of this elementary constitutive glue was the foundation of political health.

However, an additional important element is needed to have a healthy community. This is a mood for provident delay. The deliberative ethos and self-restraining attitude comprising a healthy polis are often associated with the Greek term, enkratia (e.g., Singer 2003, 84). Thucydides's ideal is an enkratic citizen "who takes care of his own body and property (6.9.2), who husbands his resources, and manages his own and the city's affairs with caution and restraint" (Wohl 2003, 180). The emphasis was on restrained and controlled behavior, which stood in opposition to the sentiments of haste and urgency.

Much of classical theorizing was Athenian in origin. It valued and evaluated democracy. In the democratic setting, a sense of together-mindedness manifests itself in the mood of shared love for one's community. The community itself may turn into an object of desire. This desire, however, is not whimsical. It affects, moderates, and steadies private impulses. A citizen becomes a lover and a community the beloved, and the relationship involves civil religious affiliation, a sense of duty, and the observation of a presumed, but ultimately mysterious, "sacred" code. Honor and duty were primary values and their imagery caused a sense of awe in the citizens who reflected upon the narrated past glories and visualized political architecture, such as temples and places of gathering. The role of the politician was to maintain the spellbinding, yet moderating, effects of the sense of something higher for which the community stands and for which its citizens were expected to make sacrifices. When one reads Thucydides in particular, the unavoidable conclusion is that an enkratic demagogue is one who, in a measured and controlled manner, speaks for the good of the community, instead of instigating and feeding their immediate impulses and desires. Thus, it can be claimed that the heart of classical politics was the ethical idea of self-restraint both in the individual and communal senses of the term (Barker 1960, 6). Private motions and interests were restrained by common interest and the communal sense of telos. Private emotions were integrated with the commonly sensed shared movement.

Thucydides puts the emphasis on the human nature of politics. By this, he refers to the realm over which humans, through their communal living, have a degree of control. The borders of this political space are, on the one hand, the hard facts that cannot be negotiated and, on the other hand, the accidental incidents that take place irrespective of human will. A healthy polis provides a locus for the maintenance and expansion of this political space. For example, a community would provide shelter against the hard fact of starvation when a crop had been lost due to the vagaries of the weather. Or, a community could protect its citizens against the harshness of external foes and the unremitting waves of the seas of anarchy.

Overall, healthy politics makes the community and its members immune from the negative effects of perceived nature's laws and from the unpredictable and fierce consequences of haphazardness. From this viewpoint, what Thucydides called "provident delay" is a primary sentiment of any healthy political deliberation. The stress is on this aspect of political space as a process that leaves time for argument and political prognostication. Thucydides's purpose was also diagnostic. He aimed to allow the community the time and the means to make the necessary corrections in order to stop possible regressive processes from taking their full effect. This, for him, was human space, and its respect was his compassion. He is full of praise for those, like Pericles, who managed to maintain and expand this human control.

For Thucydides, the existence of the skillfully managed art of memory was a further part of a healthy political community. It should be remembered that he opens his work as a book of memory. Thucydides's explicitly stated mission is to help people to remember so that they might be better equipped when the vortex of a grand movement strikes again. They should correctly remember the symptoms so as to pay attention to them and deliberate on them in time. It is noteworthy that the beginning of the regression, leading to the full-blown war, affected memory. The regressing mind may lose memory altogether by reducing it to a belief in the inevitable necessity of one's immediate interests, an accommodation of what is recollection to fit the immediate events and passions of the moment (2.54). In giving memory aids that are needed to resist these powerful affects of regression, Thucydides offers defense mechanisms for a political community and for the expansion of the human space.

It is curious and noteworthy that *The History of the Peloponnesian War* may be read as a book of memory. The art of memory is attributed to Thucydides's fellow Athenian, Simonides. The story of Simonides is less factual than didactic. The narrative of how he found the principles of proper public remembering is meant to educate the reader about the mnemonist aid of connecting images with a place. Soon rhetoric integrated the art of memory. Imagination—the Aristotelian inner eye—became a place for the devising of places and striking images, the strangeness and uniqueness of which were meant to help the correct things stick in one's mind. The art itself was deeply didactic. The Thucydidean theme was the place in the grand movement. War was the place. The destinies of remarkable individuals and the extreme violence of the ensuing battles became the images that were meant to make the grand movement unforgettable. From this perspective, Thucydides's description of the dynamics of war was a remarkable achievement in political architecture meant to contain the proper mind-set for both the leaders and the led.

Thus, for Thucydides, proper communal remembering recaps past horrors and mistakes. It reminds one of wars and their causes. However, the primary reason of memory is to enable the political community to function as an enkratic whole. In Thucydides's work, similarity in memories makes for the overall coherence of the political community (Cogan 1980, 168). The emergence of splits in communal together-mindedness signals loss of common memory and raises the possibility of unanchored future actions. From this perspective, it can be stated that rhetoric and the wider political deliberations are based on the existence and on the continuous rediscovery of the area of together-mindedness: "the mission of rhetoric is . . . not to persuade but to discover the persuasive element" (Entralgo 1970, 177). Similarly, Aristotle intertwines the creation of alikeness at the level of common opinions to controlling what is likely in the future (e.g., NE I, 1, 1355, b18). The idea appears to be that the degree of firmness both in the sense of the past and in the sense of the common future gives room, provident delay, for healthy political deliberation.

This political nature of justice is emphasized by Aristotle in connection with the strength of together-mindedness. He perceives justice as fundamental for a political community. All political decisions should arise from considerations and motives aimed at just solutions (Pol. 1253a37-39). Just politics aims at promoting the staying power of general political friendship in a manner that promotes the happiness of all (Kalimtzis 2000, 37). If the glue loses its adhesive power, political friendship loses its benign meaning. Aristotle's term, "living together," refers to the binding of conflicting tendencies into one overall, goal-directed process. Action within such a living together situation is a binding force as well as an expression of mutual cohesion and bounds. The praxis of common action is directly related to the staying power of together-mindedness. At the same time, this shared praxis represents what is meant by a healthy polis.

Phase 2: Akrasia

Approaching the subject under discussion from the general angle of the Hippocratic politico-medical perspective so pervasive in Thucydides, it is possible to say that akrasia was a diseased condition and enkratia was its cure. Roughly speaking, akrasia refers to the inability to prevent oneself from acting in a way that one knows is against one's better judgment, while enkratia refers to doing so. The loss of one's power over oneself, or akrasia, spells serious trouble for the provident delay and, therefore, for the staying power of the community itself. Akrasia produces actions motivated by immediate appetites, self-interested needs, temptation, and greed. The failure or the lack of will in connecting general reason with whimsies arising from particular contexts is the primary symptom of the akratic state of mind. The coming into being of individuals with cleavages between general communal reason and particular situations on the one hand, and between intentions and actions on the other, signals problems at the level of the political body. This close association between individual psychology and political ethos is entertained by Aristotle and Thucydides. Again we see the coupling of bodies. Psychology turns into politics and vice versa.

Growing and spreading anger, hatred, and a sense of injustice provide the counterforce to the staying power of any political community. For Thucydides and Aristotle, the beginnings of regression leading to stasis are at the level of the emergence of an individual's apartness and isolation from the political context (Kalimtzis 2000, 56). This constricts the political space with the result that the communities are increasingly exposed to the harshness and randomness of its environment. The term "akrasia" refers to the relative failure of individual and collective self-restraint. This phase involves an increasing number of individuals who are inside the bounds of a community's politics, but feel alienated from and untouched by its bonds of affinity and its bounds of proper behavior. At the communal level, an akratic community is a group of isolated and estranged people. Injustice is the fundamental reason for the growing number of akratics. The deterioration of the sense of political affinity between the members of the community involves a shift from political justice to a system which only resembles it and, eventually, which is dissimilar to it (Aristotle, NE 1134a24-30). One should keep in mind that this regressive slide from enkratia is especially alarming under the external conditions of general movement, or large-scale war.

Thus, the political state of akrasia refers to the weakness of the mind or will that results in incontinence (Aristotle, NE VII. 3, 1146a18ff). One acts in a way that one knows is not appropriate. Another example of akrasia is the failure to deliberate from abstract reason all the way to practical actions or vice versa (Rorty 1980, 208). Akratic people, who have failed in integrating cognitions with emotions, are in a constant state of having at least two equally likely courses of action open to them and, thereby, in a perpetual state of conflict. The objects of desire, which can override thought, include such things as victory, honor, wealth, and good (VII.4 1147b3ff). Behavior can lead to excessive desire of honor or self-interest. The strong desire to win—as in the case of the tragically unsuccessful Athenian expedition to Sicily during the Peloponnesian War reported by Thucydides—can make one do things that are contrary to what one thinks one and one's community should do. To further understand thoughts on akrasia, it is important to note the difference between what Aristotle calls thumos, a special type of desire, and desires such as hunger or sex (e.g., NE 1111b17-20). Thumos includes actions based on anger. What makes anger different, for example, from hunger is that the specific actions that follow are not predictable in the same sense: ". . . unlike the desire for food or sex, the general desire and fantasies of revenge do not determine what the angry man will do" (Rorty 1997, 647). Acts of anger are generalized, blind, unpredictable, and irrational. They decompose the provident delay underlying human space. To put it in another way, they constrict the political space and introduce anti-communal elements into it. Factions and cleavages start to emerge in an increasingly extreme and erratic fashion.

While narrating this sliding dynamic story, one cannot help but feel Thucydides's compassion for those trying to stop the slide. At this level, the book reminds one of the need for compassion for the enkratic and for the overall order in the Greek world. Once the big whirlwind of the grand movement has started, the smaller communities are particularly exposed to its grinding power. The sentiment of compassion is present. However, at the tragic level of individual political bodies, what is left of compassion is swept away by shared hatred for one's former compatriots, compulsion for externalization, and other anti-communal sentiments.

The failure to act within the bounds of together-mindedness, at this phase of regression, detracts from the staying power of the community by subtracting the number of possible actors who would act in concord and support with it. Simultaneously, the number of external actors who feel injustice and animosity is increased with potentially tragic consequences. A small number of these isolated, alienated, and distanced individuals does not constitute a full-blown stasis. At this akratic stage, the political community contracts into some type of governing plurality. Such contraction can even lead to a momentary positive bonding among the members of the ruling elite. It feels more coherent and stable in the short term. Much of expressive political behavior turns from a way of signifying communal bonds into a tool of representing plurality's cohesion and its rule's legitimacy. However, much of communal life is fixated by the increasing sense of cleavages.

It is important to note that there is an important threshold in the sociopsychological repercussions of akrasia. In the course of the dynamic slide toward increasingly desperate and violent times, there is a critical time point from which the regression can proceed to increasingly morbid forms or take a turn for the better. This threshold marks the point beyond which the community cannot engage in curative practices or even value them. Beyond this point, the in-group turns away from even attempting the reintegration of the growing numbers of marginalized people. They are treated with increasing hostility, which, in turn, gives these people a shared element and seeds for their bonding. Political cures become less and less obvious as random and erratic actions stemming from hate prevail and replace any unity of communal action.

At the later, more extreme stage of akrasia, the powerful spirit of general injustice offers an alternative to what one ideally thinks and does. Any demonstration of opposition is treated as betrayal by the in-group and as a dangerous apologism/moderation by elements hostile to the existence of the in-group. The margins grow and start feeling affinity in shared hatred and felt injustice. Through spread and intensification, the powerlessness can turn into a virulent type of empowerment, when these shared values and sentiments stemming from general injustice come into being. Akratics start bonding and identifying with their fellow akratics through programmatic bonds that are directed against the established faction—that is, the increasingly constricted, but "purified" in-group—and against everything that it represents.

At this later extreme stage of political akrasia, a sense of anticipation prevails. The general expectation make the time pregnant with the preparations for the final phase of regression, akrasia. Everybody is preparing for the violent expression of their "just causes." Anticipation mingles with a desire for an explosive demonstration of anger by the former in-group and those strongly opposed to it. This unusual situation is a catalyst for further akrasia because such an empowerment "rush" is unexpected and can release an explosion of repressed desires and a wave of extreme actions (Rorty 1980, 208). The overall resulting sense of political convulsions and movements may be infectious and difficult to resist. It can easily "ignite" the situation into one of generalized akrasia, that is, into that of stasis. The mood of expectation of a violent confrontation turns into a self-fulfilling prophesy.

At this point, the community loses all enkratic moderation. Provident delay turns into an appetite for almost any rash and extreme action. The akratic situation becomes particularly problematic when people afflicted with the condition acquire increasing power and rise in the power hierarchy. Akrasia spreads from the rank and file to the very top of a political community. It becomes the sign of a strong leader. Akratic demagogues stir up and excite demos or particular factions of it, creating strong movements that counter the former general telos of the community. The stirred-up situations lead to the "morbid passion for what is absent," as Thucydides puts it. What is absent is together-mindedness and, increasingly, it is thought that it can be reattained by engaging in patriotic wars against distant enemies. Distance here can imply geographical distance or increasingly "foreign" internal groups. In the smaller, less imperial communities, the desire for together-mindedness finds its perverse fulfillment in the slaughter of other factions. The "nearest is dearest" sentiment is turned into its opposite: One seeks to find enemies from near and friends from afar. Compassion for the distant other leads to strange combinations of actors under these conditions.

A further symptom of this stage is that the communal space is temporalized. Thucydides's account of regressive political processes captures vividly how the perception that one or the other political community is likely to end turns the attention away from together-mindedness and to the immediate fulfillment of narrower interests. The fixedness of time leads to the importance of doing something—of finding some "cure" and "relief"—immediately. Two extreme vices become manifest. Edmunds (1975, 75, 81) calls these "unreasoned boldness" and "rash quickness." The unreasoned and bold manner in which actions are taken contrasts with "provident delay" under conditions of healthy political friendship. The primary virtue becomes decisiveness. The temporally restricted situation easily leads to the conclusion that what is going to be done must be done in a bold and straightforward manner.

Phase 3: Stasis

In full-blown stasis, the continuing sense of injustice turns the beliefs of emerging political movements into hard, mutually exclusive doxas. Kinetic factors start to take hold of these groups as the in-group disintegrates. The common theme uniting any group is a shared anger toward other faction(s). In this way, passion motivates judgment and leads to shared and calculated expressions of hatred. The programmatic nature of hatred points to an emergence of a separate inventory of values and memories: "Dissatisfaction of itself is too unstable and reactive to give rise to the intellectual justification for remolding society anew. An underlying secession from a joint system of values to a separate set of values is necessary. The rage and animosity, which a perception of injustice engenders, gain permanence and direction only because they are organized and filtered through a new set of values" (Kalimtzis 2000, 119). The once prevalent inventory of values disintegrates into separate sets of values. These new values are designed to stimulate and fuel the extremity of communal infighting and hatred.

One of the most striking details of stasis provided by Thucydides is the way in which the prescriptive values lose their coherence and become the reverse of what they were during stasis:

> Words had to change their ordinary meaning and to take that which was now given them. Reckless audacity came to be considered the courage of a loyal ally; prudent hesitation, specious cowardice; moderation was held to be a cloak for unmanliness; ability to see all sides of a question inaptness to act on any. Frantic violence became the attribute of manliness; caution plotting, a justifiable means of self-defence. The advocate of extreme measures was always trustworthy; his opponent a man to be suspected. (3.82)

Thucydides continues his list in a way that highlights the extroverted nature of values. The values had changed from those instituted though previous interaction to those characterized by deep hatred and extreme violence. In the middle of intense rampant regression, popularity of the previous common values decreased as individual survival, best guaranteed by group membership, became the foremost concern. However, for Thucydides, the regressive slide does not stop here.

The increasingly rapid and violent process of stasis signals the hardening of akratic positions and the emergence of programmatic justifications for the entrenched hatred (Kalimtzis 2000, 119). The coupling of akrasia and stasis though the shared element of a widespread sense of detachment and spectacular rash actions creates a virulent atmosphere of insecurity and opportunity. Such hatred substitutes the communal logos maintained by phronesis with randomness and excess. Survival is not the bottom of communal values. Beyond it, the phantasms of revenge and retribution become the sources of excessive and arbitrary pleasures: ". . . the pleasure of punishment becomes unbounded and retribution may be out of proportion to the original, real or perceived infraction" (Kalimtzis 2000, 119-20). From this perspective, the appetite for retribution is even higher against former political allies than it is toward strangers because hatred finds a more defined object in a former friend, whose agonies have more meaning than those of complete strangers. As the actions in a properly constituted political community are defined by shared friendship, the same community under stasis comes to share hostility and hatred. The intensity of these phantasms of hatred makes the community inflicted by stasis as distinct an entity as the intensity of political friendship made it. Thus, at the extreme, a community just does not cease to exist; instead, it turns upside down.

The condition of stasis causes the extroversion of a political community: hatred becomes its "cohesive" factor. The above saying also shows up the degree of pleasure and excess that takes hold in the condition of deep stasis, whereby people can direct their diffused anger into common acts of specific hatred: "The fair proposals of an adversary were met with jealous precautions by the stronger of the two, and not with a generous confidence. Revenge also was held of more account than self-preservation. Oaths of reconciliation, being only proffered on either side to meet an immediate difficulty, only held good so long as no other weapon was at hand . . ." (Thucydides, 3.82). A symptom of this is that friends are found from afar rather than from near. The notion that the enemies of one's enemies are one's friends aptly illustrates the end of a political community built upon any version of together-mindedness. This curious yet horrifying alternative is present in Thucydides's (3.82) description of the Stasis in Corcyra:

In peace there would have been neither the pretext nor the wish to make such an invitation [to call in foreign help]; but in war, with an alliance always at command of either faction for the hurt of their adversaries and their own corresponding advantage, opportunities for bringing in the foreigner were never wanting to the . . . parties [of stasis].

An additional stasis-intensifying value is frantic rashness, which Thucydides (in Gomme's translation) calls "the small sharpness of a little soul." The phrase echoes the narrowness, especially in terms of interest, represented by such actions of frantic rashness. In the case of boldness, those who demonstrate moderation are easily regarded as enemies: the hatred prevailing under stasis leads to repulsion for those who advocate the restoration of together-mindedness. When the constitutive element has turned into a shared "disconstitutive" element of repulsion, quickness becomes the norm. Rapid actions are valued because they have their own redemptive logic and retaliatory desire: Act or be acted upon, kill or be killed. Paradoxically, the failed stasis-ridden community has an element of together-mindedness in that it is held together by shared hatred.

The Internal – External Nexus

When the community crosses the threshold beyond which in-group coherence ends, a sort of anti-community emerges, which is defined by full-blown stasis. What were previously internal bonds making the community cohesive are now links that are outwardly directed. The external bonds react freely and erratically with external forces. These failed communities attract and stimulate external actors and factions in them to launch diversionary wars. It can be argued that the appeal is especially irresistible for external communities in the initial phase of disintegrating together-mindedness. These actors still have sufficient coherence and the means for labor- and resource-intensive projections of military force.

The neoclassical approach can further distinguish between different scenarios of vorticity. One can subdivide the split-mindedness phase into two. During the first regressive phase, the community is still capable of healing activity. The primary argument is through the shared medium of gaining back a lost sense of political cohesion. However, the methods of restoration and revival used at this stage of regression can easily be the constitutive elements of further regression. The discourse of this phase is characterized by securitization, hardening of the attitude toward deviance, externalization, projection of force, and growing suspicion. The situation leads to increasing individualization and "desolidarization" (Thürer 1999, 734). In a related context, Dassel and Reinhardt (1999, 60) paraphrase Samuel

Huntington's famous remark: "Each group employs means which reflect its peculiar nature and capabilities. The wealthy bribe; students riot; workers strike; mobs demonstrate; and the military coup." Such a contested situation in which commonly respected rules disappear is prone to lead to diversionary war (Dassel and Reinhardt 1999, 81). The heightened sense that something is seriously wrong may be projected outward to the perceived foreign hostility. Political communities at this stage cannot easily resist the temptation to embark on foreign wars and interfere in the internal affairs of other communities. These externalizations are launched in the name of defending the cohesion of the domestic community.

During the second regressive phase, the community is incapable of common actions and turns increasingly inward as the political environment is pregnant with the anticipation of an intense outburst of violence. Political infighting gains ground and programmatic factions, composed of akratics, come to define political life. The community starts to appear ambiguous and becomes an increasingly erratic amalgamation of disparate groups. It is difficult to tell who is in charge, to discern recognizable organization, and to tell what are the respective identities and capabilities of people. The infighting and "internal" projections of force are increasingly violent and easily spiral out of control. Rather than being capable of externalization, the factions "internalize" against each other. This second phase is characterized by language games of mutual distrust, hardening of the attitude toward moderation, and an inclination toward marginalization, temporalization, haste, boldness, and unreasoned actions.

The community is also prone to be indirectly or remotely influenced by foreign powers. Thus, the process of further failure is intensified both for internal and external reasons: "And the trend toward violent disorder may prove self-sustaining, for war breeds the conditions that make fresh conflict likely. Once a nation descends into violence, its people focus on immediate survival rather than on the long term" (Mallaby 2002, 34). In the infighting, the political factions easily resort to foreign assistance. In this way, the factions in communities in the second phase of regression are prone to turn to communities in the first phase for allies and resources. This process of coupling is reinforced by the push effect of externalization, which characterizes communities in the first phase.

The communities in the first phase can engage in curative practices when the first symptoms of possible regression emerge. Curative ability means that the spread of contagion elsewhere leads to further immunity in communities in the first phase. From this perspective, it can be argued that the process of contagion is mirrored by a process of spreading immunity. The caution of the communities in the first phase and the externalization of those in the second phase comprise attempts to find a cure, to immunize oneself. The communities in the first phase engage in the method of externalization mainly to get rid of the internal causes of political regression. However, while the methods of the communities in the first phase are genuine and phronetic, the methods of the communities in the second phase are often methods of cohesion in name only.

Black Holes in World Politics

A black hole is a body in space with extreme gravitational pull. Failing states and political communities that are collapsing inward provide an appropriate analogy to these physical bodies in world politics. Thürer (1999, 731) quotes an elderly woman from Georgia, who connects the themes of in-group cohesion and state failure: "If a country is attacked from the outside, the people draw closer together. In an internal conflict, the beastly nature of people is revealed. They turn out to be able to kill children." Drawing from the neoclassical model, she could have added that the factions of civil strife turn out to be able to draw in outside forces. Literature on state failure often evinces the argument that there is a special duty of the international community and its member states to rise to meet the responsibility of containing, managing, healing, and preventing political regression of the civic type. The argument is that civil strife—for example, the paradigmatic case of the Rwandan genocide—may lead to the most extreme types of political violence. Moreover, it often seems that the world order is at stake when the members of its hierarchy collapse with the result that an intervention by a major player becomes necessary. State failures are often regarded as implosions caused mainly by endogenous factors. They stimulate a governance type of mentality of external actors who are drawn in, at least explicitly, to demonstrate their duty, legitimacy, and compassion.

However, it is possible to argue that the foreign powers or the international community also has a more implicit and sinister role in state failures, which has rarely been adequately examined. This chapter will give some substance to the notion that the contact between states at different stages of regression can lead to a coupling phenomenon with a distinctive dynamics. In others words, external states do not only participate in helping the people who live in failing states through the sentiment of compassion for the distant other, but may also act as further catalysts of state failure and, in so doing, precipitate their own political regression. The resulting coupling leads to a dynamic nexus that can initiate a new vorticity or feed a preexisting one.

Thürer (1999, 732) further states that a failed state is a cluster concept that "does not denote a precisely defined and classifiable situation, but serves rather as a broad label for a phenomenon which can be interpreted in various ways." The purpose here is to point out the complicity of the external/internal dynamics for the regressive political flows associated with state failure and collapse. Rotberg (2002, 90) uses the appropriate metaphor of "black hole" when describing a failed state: "A collapsed state is a mere geographical expression, a black hole into which a failed polity has fallen." In the language of the neoclassical theory of regressive political processes, the disappearing political affinity causes violence that turns the community into an anti-community. A failed community just does not cease to exist. It acquires a new violent form in which together-mindedness is not the constitutive element. Mutual hatred provides the key to the understanding of such black holes. Moreover, the additional property of this black hole–like anti-community is the intense "gravitational pull" that it exerts on other states in the initial stages of their political regression, while it is still coherent enough to launch a diversionary war, usually under the humanitarian banner.

The emergence of such a situation and the corresponding flow of events depend on the existence of linking elements in both the external power and the failing state. The in-group cohesion model that defines much of the conventional diversionary war hypothesis begs the question why diversion takes the direction it does. What factors that influence externalization seem to be more important than what is the precise form and target of the diversion? My claim here is that the answers to these two questions are strongly linked. What type of external actors stimulate and inspire the search for in-group identity by a state able to launch diversionary actions? The answers to this question are various: Historical animosities between states, cultures, or even civilizations can become important ingredients of the "diversionary war projection of force" type of imagery.

Material goods and resources may also explicitly induce diversionary behavior. For example, the existence of large oil reserves may stimulate a leader pondering the possibilities of a "rally round the flag" policy. However, perhaps the most important source for stimulation comes from the presence of an imagined foreign element. This object can be a foreign state. This distant object target can be framed as hostile for historical, cultural, or accidental reasons. For a state experiencing identity problems or so-called in-group troubles, the distinction between "us" and "them," together with that between "domestic" and "foreign," becomes complex. This further increases the significance of the various remaining "aliens," "illegals," and "foreigners" inside the state's territory. The external foreign state is somehow seen as connected with groups inside a diversionary state. The distant, yet linked, aliens are precious for the purposes of a diversionary war and for the desired unifying effect.

The creation of such "distant" groups—that is, distancing—is a process that almost instinctually takes place at the same time as in-group problems emerge. These groups offer a kind of safety valve for a political community to reunite. This could happen, for example, by foreign policy debates that threaten national unity. The factional cleavages, splitting, and splintering then move on to external policy. This would lead to the creation of enemy images in tandem with the overall internal conflict whereby some internal groups become associated with external power. The reverse takes place as well when the in-group actively acquires foreign "friends." This could, in turn, trigger the distanced group, now at the margins of power, into deepening their bonds with the external actors.

It should be kept in mind that an actor who is capable of diversionary behavior is a bigger actor. According to the vorticity model, such actors participate in the grand movement. The smaller actors, who become the targets of the diversion, are linked to the grand movement only through the major actors. The major powers regress slowly, whereas the object states may fail in a rapid sequence of events. Thus, even if the political regression starts at the same time, the objects of diversion manage to reach deeper levels of regression more rapidly than the major actors.

The regressive dynamics that couples external and internal political bodies includes three key phases. First, moderate political regression couples with extreme regression somewhere else. This may take the form of an intervention argued, for example, on humanitarian grounds. The overall effect is likely to maintain and further induce a mutual process of political regression.

Second, because all of the political bodies experience regression, their identities are increasingly confused. On the one hand, this means that the accompanying diversionary war is an improvised—a work in progress— rather than mechanically executed task for solving a problem. The target, a failed or failing state, on the other hand, is a labile, complex, and ambiguous phenomenon.

Third, the extreme overall dynamics has a paradoxical result. As the targeted external enemy becomes associated with internal elements, the whole domestic/foreign distinction becomes harder to sustain. This result is contradictory to the pronounced aims of the initial externalizing motives. The failure to bring about a "rally round the flag" phenomenon brings the initial enemies—both domestic and foreign—into an increasingly confusing and complex situation. This extreme, or, in neoclassical language, stasis, may result in outbursts of the most violent kinds of kinetics.

The Soviet Fall – Afghan Stasis Nexus

The start of the Soviet doom narrative started in the late 1970s. It included a worry over the resurgent Soviet Union. The context was one of confluence of events. Different processes, which evolved according to their own distinct reasons and methods, participated and mingled in the single political consciousness. These perhaps disparate events came to be interpreted as one meaningful sequence. The perceived spirit of the time seemed to point to the powerful Soviet Union extending well beyond its immediate orbit. In the last years of the 1970s, the United States was still suffering from its losses in Vietnam, the Iran revolution had overthrown the United States–backed regime in that country, the Sandinistas had assumed power in Nicaragua, and the Soviet troops had occupied Afghanistan. This confluence of factors, from the U.S. perspective, signaled dangerous loss of power. The Soviets were on the move. In response to the confluence at the end of the 1970s, Brezezinski formulated his vision of the "arc of crisis." This arc referred to a number of states existing along the shores of the Indian Ocean, which were strategically important, yet within the reach of the Soviets. This confluence led to increased allocations for the U.S. military budget and to new initiatives such as the Star Wars.

The Soviet experiences in Afghanistan and its eventual imperial collapse provide one of the most important sources for today's discourse on imperial demise (e.g., Cordesman and Wagner, 1990). Its memory is still vivid. It provides a precedent and a benchmark for the unexpected spread of regressive sentiments. Lieven (1994, 218), for example, regards the demise of the Soviet Union as instructive in its "parallels in the history of the decline and fall of other empires." From this point of view, the prolonged Soviet occupation of Afghanistan was an instance of imperial overextension. The social learning that spread from Afghanistan to the other regions represented a contagion of political regression. This regressive flow was so virulent that it helped to deconstitute the whole Soviet frame. The true believers in the Soviet experiment could not control the gravitational waves radiating from Afghanistan, which was amplified by the events in Poland and Chernobyl. The moderates, like Mikhail Gorbachev, came too late to have any meaningful role other than overseeing the collapse.

The events in Afghanistan were a culmination of a series of Soviet military adventures that had taken place during the 1960s and 1970s in the Soviet sphere of influence. The attempts to disengage first failed and then came too late. The apparent meaninglessness and futility of the violent occupation provided a new way of framing Soviet power. This frame portrayed the infallible Soviet Union in terms of an anachronism waiting to be buried under the burgeoning wave of (re)emerging national sentiments. The wider dissemination of this understanding had ripple effects in many areas, which subsequently proved to be crucial in the fall of the Soviet Union. The prolonged conflict and ultimate defeat led to "profound doubts, both at home and abroad, about Moscow's military capabilities, strategic vision, and political will and judgment" (Graham 2002, 12).

The Soviet occupation of Afghanistan may be regarded as an engrossing political spectacle, which sent an impulse of imperial decay through the empire. Michael Dobbs tellingly titled his article in *The Washington Post* (November 16, 1992), "Withdrawal from Afghanistan: Start of Empire's Unraveling." His wording is echoed in Sarah E. Mendelson's (1993, 338) review of the environment surrounding the Soviet withdrawal. She sees the events leading to the withdrawal as signaling the end of the pre-perestroika Soviet Union. Mendelson points out that a sudden withdrawal is very difficult and politically costly. Starting a war, especially one with diversionary intentions, may make the in-group—the ruling elite and the true believers—stake their interests on the success of the war (e.g., Mendelson 1993, 347). With the stakes being high, policy reversals are generally not favored and there is strong pressure to continue pursuing a military solution. However, as demonstrated by the Soviet decision in 1985 to delay any withdrawal for a year, persistence can easily lead to an escalation of violence and major military setbacks. The stakes got increasingly higher.

This growing need to do something, to stop the paralysis of the imperial heartlands, made Afghanistan appear to be a good way of reversing the paralysis and preventing the danger of imperial decline. The stakes got higher for the Soviets as time wore on. The threshold for withdrawing and for letting the communist government in Kabul collapse was high. Through the processes of social learning, the collapse could have led to political instability in other Soviet client states, strengthened opposition forces in the Soviet sphere of influence, and created a spillover of Islamic militancy in Central Asia and the Caucasus region. Furthermore, ideological defeat would have been demoralizing and humiliating, and the Soviet capabilities of military domination would have depreciated greatly (Daley 1989, 496). The imperial overstretch was intensified by the ensuing game of chicken. So much value was incrementally invested into the foreign occupation that in the end, staying in the game was justified, not because victory would have been likely, but because this was a battle for all that the Soviet empire had come to stand for—its core principles, values, and prestige. At the end, the withdrawal, which could, in other circumstances, have been a mere symptom of possible imperial decline, suddenly came to mark the beginning of a fateful disintegration and imperial fall.

It can be argued that Afghanistan was not only an interlude to, but an essential trigger of, the Soviet collapse. Domestic political health became compromised at least partly due to the failure of the Soviet diversionary strategies in Afghanistan (e.g., Deudney and Ikenberry 1991). This message was then further accentuated by other contemporary disempowering spectacles, such as the Chernobyl accident and its handling. The overall message of the flow of events was clear: It pointed to the accelerated tempo of signs of decay. The role of the Afghan war in demonstrating that the Soviet Union was disintegrating has to be considered. In the eyes of both foreign and domestic audiences, it was a symptom of the dysfunctions inherent in the Soviet system. The sudden collapse of the Soviet Union between 1989 and 1991 was noteworthy because of its relative bloodless-ness (e.g., Hollander 1999; Wohlforth 2000). One reason for this may have been that it was deemed futile to use force and coercion to their fullest extent in a situation where the empire's universal mission had already failed irreversibly. The social learning, spreading from military disasters such as Afghanistan, led to the complete failure of the underlying Soviet political religion. At the end, there were no serious in-group true believers left even to put up a last stance for the Soviet empire. With the vanishing imperial political religion, any acts of imperial restoration became frivo-lous as the brief coup by the Soviet leftovers in 1991 demonstrated.

The Soviet Union was participating in the grand movement of the Cold War. Because of this, it was already under enormous strain and predis-posed toward externalization. The compassion that the Soviet leaders felt toward the communist regime in Kabul gave it a proper cause to project its power through the occupation. Its actions were rash and rushed. They indicate the growing akratic condition inside the state body. Afghanistan was much further down the regressive slide. It was still coherent enough a society to draw in foreign help. Its factions were clear enough for the Soviets to find and make the object of their compassion and of the inter-vention that followed. The stasis in Afghanistan drew in the Soviet Union, which was still in the first phase of the increasing akrasia. The coupling of the akratic Soviet Union (in the first phase) and the stasis-ridden Afghanistan (in the second phase) could only lead to an even further regressive slide. The other factions in Afghanistan attracted the help of first Pakistan and then the United States. By the mid-1980s, the equation, where the spreading grand movement was coupled with the deepening local sta-sis, was very much in force.

In some ways, the present Western intervention in Afghanistan can be seen as a part of the continuum started by the decline and fall of the Soviet Union. The present grand movement, the war on terror, was stimulated by the world-order anxieties caused by 9/11. These compassions "compelled" intervention by the Afghan factions. The presence of the Al-Qaeda in Afghanistan was a constitutive element of the full-blown stasis in the country. Can the West then be considered an akratic actor? Or the United States, for that matter? In sev-eral ways, the domestic politics in the United States have been very partisan, with very strong, emotional, value-based issues. The war in Iraq may be regarded as a diversionary conflict, which was aimed at demonstrating the power of the Bush administration domestically. It caused a short-lived "rally round the flag" phenomenon. These features are symptomatic of an early akratic polity. However, the U.S. polity still has a significant degree of together-mindedness when it comes to the importance of fighting the war on terror in terms of Afghanistan. There is no splitting or splintering on this issue. It remains to be seen how many diversionary wars—coupling with external failed polities—the United States can handle before its borderline enkratic–akratic condition worsens to a clear first-phase akrasia.

World-order compassion provided the impetus for both superpowers to intervene in the same failed anti-community. The Soviets were concerned about the bipolar world order turning into a unipolar one. The U.S. military support for some factions in Afghanistan—much the same ones that it confronted on 9/11 and after—was propelled by the same world-order compassion. There were growing sentiments among the Americans that the United States was losing ground to the Soviets, who were about to gain strong foothold in a part of the world considered vital to U.S. power. The compassion for and anxieties over the existing world order were also at play when the United States decided to install its own governance in Afghanistan in 2001.

The anti-community in Afghanistan has stimulated much of the world-order concerns during the past 30 years. The various factions of the Afghan stasis have been able to lure foreign powers into the internal power struggle. The shared hatred that maintains such a community has also been a source for other types of compassion for the distant other. The worry over their nation and their nationality and factions has mobilized the Afghan people against the Taliban and some for the resistance by the northern rebels. At the level of modern liberal humanitarianism, compassion has been felt over the plight of women in Afghanistan, for the refugees inside the country and those in Pakistan, and for the horrors the people have faced in dealing with the land mines left after the Soviet withdrawal.

Degeneration as a Site of Generation

Before concluding this chapter, it is important to consider the creative and innovative chaos created by imperial decline and fall. A formulation of the basic underlying argument is that dynamic changes in hierarchies are felt and lived through political sentiments. Much of what takes place in political bodies under such labile conditions may be understood as dimensions of intense emotionality. So far, I have considered mainly one aspect, the regressive political process binding internal communal upheavals and war through sentiments of compassion and hatred.

However, more positive sentiments are also bound to political and local upheavals in the world. Liberation and moments of identity creation reveal another aspect. Vorticity may act as an engine of innovation. New identities are created and old ones made active. The case of the Soviet empire's fall, coupled with the stasis in Afghanistan, may be seen as such a generative moment. Many identities, both previously existing and totally new, were created. Many of these were national in character. Much nation/state compassion was felt from Estonia to Afghanistan. The Eurasian map mushroomed with newly independent states professing their vitality and rich histories.

Thus, shifting hierarchies under a strong vorticity may lead to sentiments that are more generative and creative than the ones described so far. This link has a powerful prescriptive force. The sentiment of creation has been traditionally linked with imperial twilight. This is partially conscious as many national projects see their opportunities knocking when the lability of the world order is felt. The narratives linking imperial collapse with the emergence of creativity and with the renaissance of cohesive identities are old and commonplace. Even a quick glimpse into literature reveals sentimental nostalgia for the doomed order. However, it reveals also a deeply felt sense of excitement over what is let loose and an anxious anticipation of the new world. Historical evidence is always admittedly anecdotal. Some cases in point are offered by Jewish culture, which experienced periods of growth in tsarist Russia, and also the Finnish politico-cultural golden age during the period of the fall of the tsarist empire.

Minority cultures are attracted and/or compelled to rising empires with initially strong leading cultures. From a generative perspective, various minority and diasporic groups find refuge inside empires. The loosening of the central authorities and the general imperial decline may offer them room to forge their own communities. The straightening of these often ethnic, religious, national, and political mobilizations is one aspect of the regressive process. In a way, they contribute to the increasing factionality. They may also offer objects for opportunistic distancing and externalization by the in-group, which senses trouble. They may be turned into "fifth columns" and "enemy aliens." At the same time, these emerging groups offer opportunities for outside powers to form alliances. However, the emerging groups may also be left alone in the heated confrontations of the communal fall. These narratives perceive decaying empires as settings for creativity. This narrative stock, which centers on the argument that crisis and creativity are connected, is often echoed in public discourse: "War as a forging ground of nations" or "Within the orbit of empires, there exists creativity". Crises open up a strongly kinetic field of contrary forces of collision, separation, and, therefore, generation. This is the other side of the degenerative/regressive story.

The pains of a political body can create a new sense of awareness. Emergency may lead to the emergence of a new, mutated political consciousness: "On the social as well as the individual plane, it is the sick organ which creates awareness, and it is in moments of crisis that men are most aware of the enigma of their presence in the world" (Goldmann 1964, 49). The decay of imperial political bodies stimulates the political imagination. The sense of tragedy, as a deconstitutive element of imperial doom, is associated with the presence of birth. The main sentiment of imperial fall as a moment of cutting loose has a long history in Western Judeo-Christian thought. The Israelites escaping from an Egypt plagued by pestilence offers one such stock story repeated to most Westerners through their schooling and popular culture. Narrative templates exist and they may be made active by the intensive emotionality of the decline.

The ability of the rising empire to digest and assimilate—that is, to function as a melting pot—has its opposite in the imperial fall's political convulsions and revulsions. Napoleon is said to have stated that empires die of indigestion. As previously pointed out, this intestinal side of political fall was highlighted by Thucydides as well. This political imagination comprehends imperial decay in terms of cultural rebirth and identity proliferation. Arrested assimilation is constituted by outside and inside pressure toward increasing acknowledgement of (re)emerging identities. On the one hand, the imperial in-group—the leading identity—directs mounting hostility, persecution, discrimination, and violence against the new identities. On the other hand, the in-group cohesion of the new groups is reinforced by countercultural movements in the shadows of the empire. New identities give a sense of power to the marginalized people and also provide a cohesive and unified world view. In other words, imperial crises turn (re)emerging groups in on themselves (Aberbach 1997, 136). And, in comparison with the disunity of the dominant in-group, these new identities hold increasing appeal. From the perspective of this influential stock narrative, these dual pressures create a demand for cohesive identities.

4

Compassion as a Morality Drama at the Profiled EU and U.S. Borders

Spatial patterns, or inclusion and exclusion, as any other criteria for belonging to humanity, comprise the heart of humanitarian occasions. It appears that the changing international order from a bipolar balance to a United States–led hierarchy has made international borders hyperbolic in a qualitatively different sense from before. They have changed from relatively horizontal political geometry into limits comprising the current political power hierarchy. Those international borders that coincide with the layers of the global hierarchy are especially sensitive toward bursts of political sentiments. In this chapter, I will review the dramas involving the boundaries of the EU and the United States.

The international borders in a hegemonic world order are increasingly differential, and at the same time, selectively more flexible; for some, borders are nonexistent, for others, simply impenetrable. One common feature is semipermeability, which refers to the selective ability of different people to move across a border. Occasionally, the processing dramas at the borders turn into tense morality plays or rituals of acknowledgment that allow the world order—together with the states and communities comprising it—to demonstrate its continuing efficacy and usefulness. From this perspective, knowledge about contemporary border practices is often inadequately contextualized. I will show how the drama of the processing of the world's people at its political borders is related to wider political imagery in the United States and in Europe. In the European border spectacles, this efficiency is related to controlling unwanted and illegal migration and preventing the "abuse" of asylum policies. Although the same imagery is present in the U.S. border dramas, they are saturated by the image of a militant Islamic terrorist. In this chapter, I will attempt to map the frames of border drama in the EU and the United States.

The crux of the argument is building a case for the importance of these representational-emotional frames. The border dramas that occupy the front pages of European and U.S. newspapers and everyday popular political discussions are becoming more frequent. Legal and illegal migration arouses emotions and seems to touch people's perceptions of their political bodies. The legitimacy of the bodies, from individual, communal, all to the way to hegemonic, is evaluated and in flux in the border dramas. Security is easily translated into the ability to uphold the limits between the different levels in world hierarchy. For the political individual, this means that the ability to cross these limits may lead to better possibilities to pursue his potential. For a nation or state, it means that its identity and prestige become dependent on its existence inside of the hierarchy. For the hegemony, the maintenance of its structure is everything. The flux and vexing of the limits of its structure result in highly emotional border dramas, in which all of these bodies are at stake.

Borders as Lived Life

The starting point is that border experiences matter: The socially shared and often personally lived experiences at international borders greatly influence the way in which people understand their belonging and nonbelonging to diverse overlapping national, local, and global communities. Borders as lived life contain a political pedagogy based on selective processing and filtering— that is, profiling. Airports, border crossings, seaports, and other crossroads supply not only the physical, but also the imaginary templates for acknowledging the logic and authority therein of separating people into various entities—for example, into states, communities, nations, ethnicities, cultures, and civilizations—and of crafting hierarchies from them.

The didactics of political border experiences have always been at the heart of state sovereignty. Because a sovereign state's power can be said to be at its most definitive and explicit at the international borders, the recent change toward an increasingly well-structured, hierarchical world order has had wide ramifications. The change in "what is learnt at the border" is indicative of the deep qualitative transformation of the international system. My intention here is to examine these changes. What are the new frames? What is the flow that maintains the suspense of the border dramas? Who are the main figures in these dramas? I aim to examine the central stock figures and the underlying dramaturgy of the border spectacles and to trace the landscape of the contemporary world-order imagination. To accomplish this, I will chart and contrast the border dramas in the United States and in the EU.

During the twentieth century, the spread of the universalistic ideal of citizenship partly replaced the older more particularistic and elitist notions. Border practices were, at least nominally, based on a system of random checks, whereby most, if not all, people were inspected for travel documents and for security. But the fledgling international hierarchy after the cold war bipolarity has brought about a marked change in this tradition. After the seminal event, international borders are increasingly defined by a perceived imperative to classify and differentiate the flows of people. Individuals are classified, their movements differentiated, and their flows slowed down or stopped. Pronounced and consequential spirals of suspicion and trust saturate the atmosphere. This personally experienced vortex of danger, fear, anxiety, boredom, ease, and hate provide an effective setting for politically relevant learning, for the contemporary spectacles of power.

The fact that most people have personally experienced the crossing of borders gives border-related memory images and stories a high degree of relevance. Such heightened importance makes it understandable that the prevailing hierarchical world order saturates the "semiosphere" of border crossings. At these places, people experience, learn, and memorize the effectiveness and status of the order. Is the border "leaking"? Who are the suspicious types? Who is authorized to move smoothly across borders? What types and backgrounds are standing in the long queues? Who are the privileged and preferred ones? How thoroughly are people being checked at the security check? What were the different lines at the passport control? Who were checked more closely than others? How was I treated? Who were allowed to board first? Who were the last? Who looked like immigrants, illegals, drug smugglers, prostitutes, or terrorists? Who can fly and who has to swim, run, or dig? Who has to hide and conceal identity and places on a camp? These questions and doubts are reinforced by popular culture—for example, movies and evening news—which provides the visual rhetoric needed for memory and storytelling.

Profiling defines a practice whereby people are reduced to figures in a hierarchy of types based, for example, on their skin color, clothing, background, religion, ethnicity, region and state of origin, socioeconomic status, and spending habits. My argument is that the micro-level border practice of profiling is inherently linked to macro-level world-order and security-related demands. An individual at an international border crossing becomes a personified abstraction, which derives its meaning partly from the global U.S. mission in the war on terror and partly from the specificities of the more regional dynamics.

Frames of Border Dramas

The frame-theoretical conceptualizations developed by Erving Goffman provide the theoretical support for understanding current border dramas. The frame offers a way of understanding world politics as a form of specific politico-cultural performance (e.g., Goffman 1974, 10). Here, the notion of frame may be defined to refer to an "organized and bounded social entity most immediate to the individual's experience" (Gonos 1997, 854). Public acts that gain their power from the sacredness of in-group boundaries involve heightened and engrossing dramas and spectacles. These public events tend to be tense, emotional, theatrical, and spectacular. Public drama creates a sense of having its own specific type of reality, which suspends the way events normally proceed. Frames produce a sense of realness and enhance their participants' sense of solidity of meaning. In this sense, they offer a clear gallery of figures which allows both the spectator and the performer "to conjure up a desired self-image" (Fine and Manning 2003, 46). For example, the spectacle of rounding up people on the shores of Spain offers solidity for the performers—the Spanish authorities, the Schengen officials, and so on—and security for the average viewer of the evening news.

The gallery of figures—or, the subjects—of the border dramas become meaningful on a stage. These dynamic "frames" address the question, "Under what circumstances do we think things are real?" This question has quasi-cognitive status (James 1985, 352). This means that the frames are acknowledged rather than rationally known, authoritative rather than freely chosen, and emotionally appealing rather than cognitively satisfactory. In any particular polity, such frames are multiple, overlap, and are seldom free of contradiction. For example, what is known as a human smuggler might appear as a compassionate helper from the perspective of a humanitarian frame. In these cases, the question of realness becomes a function of specific types of attention, as Goffman (1997, 150) points out while quoting from William James: "Each world, whilst it is attended to, is real after its own fashion; only the reality lapses with the attention." The question of realness turns into one of attention: How is attention captured and encapsulated? Familiar frames and the shared experiences they contain are fundamentally forms of fixing the trajectory of acknowledgement.

Thus, it seems that the less than cognitive or almost religious-like experiences have a fundamental impact on the way meaning and certainty are comprehended. This appears to be even more true when communities' or polities' boundary conditions are at stake. These border dramas highlight the role of noncognitively gained preconceptual revelations over empirically verified objectivity. Individuals are turned into types, flows of events into mythical community forming narratives, and outcomes into signifiers of security. Next, I will turn to the political mythology that gives substance to today's frames and flows regarding borders both in the EU and the United States.

The Declinist Frame

An environment in which people's reduction to types intertwines with the worldwide production of security is often anxious, tense, charged, and even dramatic. At their most dramatic, the occasions of profiling are highly publicized spectacles. No-fly lists, red flags, diverted or stopped flights, and intercepting fighter planes accent these captivating stories.

CNN carried the following news on May 12, 2005: "U.S. authorities have released a passenger and his family detained after their transatlantic Air France flight was diverted to Maine Thursday afternoon when the man's name matched one on the U.S. 'no-fly' list, federal officials said . . . . A federal official told CNN that the man's date of birth matched that of a person on the watch list, and the names were a 'nearly exact match'. But he was allowed to continue on his way Thursday evening after being questioned, a U.S. Customs and Border Protection official told CNN." Such presumed "close encounters" stimulate and excite the security-related imagination. Such dramatic situations are easily turned into morality plays: Morality plays at the border involve fights by the protagonist—often presuming the guise of all humanity—against the bad minority of rogues and socially "unintegrable" people such as terrorists.

The figure of the "rogue" is one of the foremost descriptors of the sources of worry in the contemporary world order. In the 1990s, the term "rogue state" came to signify illegitimate existence outside the international community and its accepted behavioral norms. Etymologically, "rogue" derives partly from the medieval term "ragamuffin," which referred to a demon or devil, and later to a ragged and disreputable person. In the same spirit, Darwin (1859, 1: 32) used the term "rogue" in a reference to a plant that deviates from the "proper standards" in horticulture. The important role played by the rogue figure in the cultural imagination was noted by Jung (1973, 10), who generalized that a rogue in the figure of a trickster "haunts the mythology of all ages." In this light, present-day rogues may be detected in the world political discourse as "evildoers," "enemies of freedom," and "axes of evil." The way one talks about the scheming Iranians, the devilish Saddam Hussein, or the deceptive regime of North Korea offers ample evidence that Jung's statement may be valid in the mythology underlying the current world hierarchy. Moreover, the root of the term highlights both "devilishness" and "ruthlessness" (Spitzer 1947,

90). These connotations of the term evoke the figures of an "infidel" and "heathen." These meanings capture well the contemporary politico-religious definition of illegitimacy in international relations. Whether in the form of a state, terrorist organization, or individual person, the rogue figure seems to share common features.

In modern popular culture, "rogue" defines a continuum along which there exists a whole variety of types—for example, illegal immigrants, economic opportunists, asylum abusers, drug smugglers, suicide bombers, and Islamic extremists. The protagonists of these dramas include such stock figures as watchful aircrews, alert border guards, efficient security agencies, reporters who "dug out the truth," and politicians "who did their job." Other stock figures that are detected by the racially charged eye at the border include tourists, Third Worlders, business travelers, people of color, and, increasingly, the fuzzy category of Muslims.

Rogues stand in opposition to the protagonists. From a general perspective, morality plays involve a communal verdict, a passing of a judgment about the moral status of the participants. Morality plays can be said to put the limelight on the actors' moral characteristics and their ability to make correct choices. In many ways, morality plays stage events in a manner that highlights the sense of being at a crossroads. The main question becomes how well the actors choose: Do their choices reflect progressive or regressive moral characteristics? Questions of this type are answered at tense, critical moments. From that moment onward, there is a strong sense that events can continue either negatively or positively. Another way of looking at morality plays derives from the iconic Western notion of the Protestant ethic. It can be argued that one major way of doing morally virtuous labor in contemporary times is by sweating over security concerns. The perspiration connected with the feverish agitation of the globalizing world provides the setting for the staging of the border-related morality plays. These morality plays contain a stern moral lesson about the disastrous consequences of laxness and lack of vigilance. In this respect, the morality plays are not so much focused on the punishment of the wrongdoers as on teaching correct behavior, and the virtues and values of the "proper" figures.

It can be argued that the ambiguity between vices and virtues provides the background for staging pedagogic morality plays. On the one hand, there is a sense that what is taught as vices can still be taken by some as virtues. The age-old saying that "one's terrorist is another's freedom fighter" captures the essence of this nervousness. The committing of acts of terror can readily be construed as acts of justice and their inherent rationale may hold dangerous appeal to people. This presumably "devious" and "strange" appeal of vice is compounded by the perceived dangers inherent in leniency and tolerance. On the other hand, although good and evil are each illustrated by different and distinct figures, there exists a tense atmosphere of surprise. It can be suggested that this intense mixture of opposing elements is tightly related to the ambiguity between vice and virtue. For example, the essentially virtuous figure of the cosmopolitan businessman is nevertheless a figure with mixed content. This figure is often evaluated against the background of idleness. Comfortable first-class seats, privileged access, and top-level hotels can indicate excess and overindulgence. The Western wealth represented by the international business traveler is potentially both sinful and virtuous. In a similar way, border guards can be alert or lax/corrupted, airport personnel caring or unsympathetic, and politicians good or self-serving. The stage is set in a way that the central figures in the border-related morality plays are very human-like, torn between things and composed of varying particular characteristics. Thus, the drama turns into a telling gauge of polity's underlying conditions, which is read with mythic lenses. The tension puts the emphasis on the moral worth and judgment of the respective actors. The set of figures becomes Manichean: those trying to do their utmost to stop the looming doom and those who contribute to the decay of the world community's moral character.

In an important way, the unforgettable dramaturgy and visual rhetoric of 9/11 has set the stock plot for subsequent plays, especially in the United States. Although striking, the elements of this drama are as familiar as they are ancient. Deviant figures managed to hijack and pervert the sacred icons of modernity—airplanes and skyscrapers. The visual rhetoric of the images was one of distortion and collapse. The inversion of icons portrayed the image of a disintegrating world. The theme of sacred symbols turning into their opposites is an old practice in morality plays—for example, sheep and wolves—that points to the disintegration of reality. The anxiety deriving from transgressed and violated boundaries provides another related ingredient for the plays. They become the setting for attempts to maintain and restore wholeness. At the level of polity, the dramatic tension is one of a fight against the decline and collapse of the presumed sacred essence of the community.

Thus, in the border dramas, the nervousness and anxiety is framed by what can be called declinist images.[1] A prototypical case in point is offered by Samuel Huntington's worry over the dilution of the American creed under the influence of the Hispanic influx (2004). Another example is provided by Robert Kaplan's (1994) notion of overwhelming criminal anarchy, which spreads from the Third World. In contrast to these conservative declinist visions, the liberal formulations highlight such concepts as "blowback" and "boomerang effect." These liberal visions stress the lone superpower's tendency to contradict its own norms and rules—for example, Guantanamo Bay, prisoner abuse, and torture—rather than submergence and dilution. The source of the decline is regarded as internal rather than external. Decline is caused by the consequences of the superpower's incontinence. In the staging of the border-related plays, the various forms of "declinism" have their uses. These separate images of decline, regression, and disintegration set the dramatic tension of the world-order morality plays that take place at the international borders.

It can be argued that the theme of submergence, which has been broadly influential under the United States's neoconservative ideological trends, leads to specific self-fulfilling expectations inside the border-drama frame. Even a quick review of declinist literature reveals a stress on the world community's creed, that is, on its moral, religious, and cultural underpinnings—for example, the "American way of life" or "Western values" (e.g., Huntington 2004). From this perspective, it is often thought that the primary sign of trouble is the disregard of civic virtues and of the underlying civil religion. The causes of this are easily associated with foreign elements: the civil character becomes diluted when the hegemony of the preponderant actor turns into its opposite, into submergence, by the excessive assimilation of the dominated elements. The thoughts that connect a world power with the constant fear of submergence may be interpreted as a significant cultural narrative that dramatizes contemporary morality plays. This means that the world-order morality plays are meant to demonstrate that the core element—the top of the hierarchy—is not going to be submerged and diluted.

The geopolitical imagery of these dramas takes on an explicitly hierarchical form, which differs greatly from the anarchical geopolitical visions of classical international politics. The hierarchical imagery points out the differential place of various nations, ethnicities, regions, civilizations, and people. In this spirit, it is often argued that the diligent maintenance of the hierarchy's divisions—the new international borders—is the best guarantee against submergence by the wave of "terrorist" anarchy (Kaplan 1994, 124). Border guards stand in a very different place from where they stood only decades ago.

Besides the theme of the worry over dilution, it can be suggested that the border-related morality plays are celebrations of "rule following" and the power of good examples. They point out the importance of faithfully following proper practices in international and domestic political behavior. Furthermore, they demonstrate the negative consequences of any deviance from the sanctioned norms. The smooth flows of international life, which are represented at border crossings, are read as signifying the health of the underlying political order. These interpretations reassure you against declinist interpretations. In the context of the world-order morality plays, the term "rule following" takes on a civil religious meaning and shifts the pedagogy from the cognitive to the noncognitive level. Social rule following can be interpreted as the acceptance of something as a guide and giving it allegiance. In the post-9/11 world, much of the political rhetoric is based on the premise "don't debate, act"—that intellectual argumentation does not provide the necessary sense of firm grounding of the world order that needs to be instilled in people. In this prevalent rhetoric, the nuances and complexities of intellectual political deliberation are de-emphasized. Instead, their place is taken by political rituals of acknowledgement. In an important sense, the rules being followed at the border are grounded on the authority derived from the ritualistic acknowledgement of the central political sacredness.

Thus, border dramas set the protagonist apart from the antagonist, while leaving room for a range of more ambiguous figures. The flow of events is easily interpreted and evaluated in comparison to the conservative submergence and liberal rule-accordance declinism.

Next, I will examine which are the more nuanced figures and narrative flows that are involved in these plays. What follows is an examination of the rituals of acknowledgement inherent in the morality plays that are staged at the EU and U.S. borders.

Visual Rhetoric of Civil Religious Sanctity

The contemporary border dramas contain different characterizations of how one should feel. The political emotions attached to the EU and U.S. border dramas are related, yet they derive from different visual backgrounds. 9/11 provides the most striking image of present-day world politics. The most stereotypical image of 9/11 contains a bird's eye depiction of planes exploding into the World Trade Center towers. Debris, fireballs, and smoke fill the air. The skyscrapers are exploding, burning, and collapsing. Besides the iconic view from afar, there are several culturally supported ways of remembering this seminal event—firemen hurrying to a drastic, but fatal, rescue, the disbelieving faces of people, and the running away from the debris and smoke of the collapsing buildings.

A political—dealing with power relations and the (im)balances therein—reading of such images provides a window to the theme of hierarchy in world politics. These images contain a theory of legitimacy in world politics. They are by no means static. These images are "agentive" in that they actively remind us of 9/11 and rearrange our sense of legitimacy and right. They come into play as a vital background condition when certain actions are taken: for example, the bombing of Afghanistan in the name of the war on terror sometimes involved what is termed as "collateral damage." The power of the Western imagination to legitimize the interpretation of such occasions depends on the images and their political heuristic. You are actively reminded of what the images of 9/11 stand for. This remembering rearranges the disparate "facts" of the day to fit the inherent sense of truth.

A photograph or a visual representation comprises a visible scene. This visible scene is full of clues on how to interpret what is going on. Its physical features embody keys to a polysemic, more invisible scene. This background heuristic is polymorphous in that it involves the interaction of multiple levels of meaning. Despite the complexity, the invisible scene may leave no doubts about the meaning of what is going on. The power of the heuristic to stimulate and inspire action may be equally compelling. No sense of hesitation is felt. Especially when international security, order, and justice are at stake, the clarity of the drama takes precedence over any apprehension of inherent complexity. Things start to stand for something. For example, the bird's eye vision of exploding skyscrapers starts to stand for something clear and clarifying. The background condition can be referred to as those things under which we think things are real.

However, if asked, clarity is generally much harder to come by. It seems to be resistant to exact formulations. Cognitive clarity disappears. It is difficult to answer with a single sentence that would be part of a coherent intellectual schema, if asked, for example, what 9/11 was all about. The background is noncognitive to an important degree. It reveals rather than explains, shows rather than says. It conveys sentiments, rather than passing on something more intellectually satisfactory. One way of putting this is that the highly revealing images of world politics— for example, the refugees in Darfur or the starving, fly-infested child in Ethiopia—clearly demand recognition. Nevertheless, turning this clarity into documents and other means of political definition is not an easy task. It is at this level that the power of images is at its highest. It is also here that many opportunities for co-option occur.

Pictures are not accidental. When they are abundantly available, some of them come to represent events in a way that stands for the apparent order of things in world politics. However, such images are revelatory. They are felt to reveal something essential of the politics of their day. To repeat, it is important to note that the way in which events are pictured is not a coincidence. Rather, the present is in a constant dialogue with the past through memories. Memory images condition and are conditioned by current events. For example, 9/11 is usually imagined from a distance. The drama takes place above the ground and in the air. To reiterate, perhaps its most common representation is from afar, just at the moment when the towers explode, when the second plane is just about to hit, or when the towers collapse. The scene is one of explosion with the knowledge of imminent doom. These representations seem to capture much of the iconic aspect of 9/11.

The perspective of the political sacred seems to capture additional aspects of this scene at the horizon. Two previously noted terms coined by Mircea Eliade (1959) in his cross-cultural studies of religious anthropology are relevant here. First, kratophany; kratophany is an aspect of the sacred that refers to an event at its most tense moment. It mixes awe with horror. The fear of witnessing something unheard of blends with a strange sense of attraction and fixates the attention. This attraction–repulsion theme is present in much of the visual rhetoric of world politics, ranging from the images of 9/11 and the dying children in Kosovo to the images of the precision bombing of buildings in the Iraq war. These images convey a profound question at the moment of life and death. The kratophantic quality provides the dramatic tension needed to frame these moments in a tangible, engrossing, and captivating manner. The spellbinding drama of public death and the resultant appeals to the cult of sacrifice lead to powerful and catching political emotions. Something must be sacrificed, whether monetary donations or men in immediate military action.

The power of kratophany to produce a charged field of drama and tension depends on the existence of meaningful power. Kratophany refers to the ways of demonstrating legitimate power. However, such legitimacy can exist only inside a particular spatial imagination as, for example, performances of authority or effectiveness exist inside a frame. Eliade's concept of hierophany sheds vital light on this spatial aspect of the political sacred.

Like kratophany, hierophany also provides an important ingredient of the invisible scene. Hierophany establishes the more specific conditions of profound meaning. It starts from the idea that the sacred consists of an acknowledgement of the aspect of communality by a group of people. It is the moment in which a lasting sense of community is created, maintained, or restored. At the level of the invisible scene, it refers to those practices that celebrate and honor the communal aspect. It is crucial to note here that these moments contain a political architecture and temporal expectations. Hierophantic architecture structures the community into one of hierarchy with a center, periphery, and an outside. For example, 9/11 reveals a center in the form of a superpower being attacked. The center is acknowledged in the numerous acts of compassion and condolence around the world. The periphery is defined by the states, nations, and groups of people that recognized the event in seemingly the same way. The outside is defined by those who celebrated the "chaos" brought about by the seminal event. Temporally, hierophany opened up a zone of expectations consisting of American or Western actions to restore the world order. It legitimized certain military actions and delegitimized a host of activities connected with terrorism.

The hierophantic charge of images offers a way to enhance the politico-psychological sense of a particular shape of a community among those in it. This is especially true of the images that arouse world political sentiments from compassion to hate. In his *Sacred and Profane*, Eliade (1959) refers to hierophany as the "sacred" code that reveals and brings to light the perceived higher realm in a profane world. Perceptions of world order can be thought of as belonging to the "higher level" (Eliade 1971, 10). So, the question becomes how the scenes in the profane world bring to light "American hegemony," "conflict of civilization," "evildoers," "axes of evil," or "the fight between freedom and its enemies." The underlying political architecture may be monistic, dualistic, or pluralistic; unilateral or multilateral; hierarchical or anarchical; progressive (revivalist) or regressive (declinist). These "higher notions" give things and events "their reality, their identity, only to the extent of their participation in a transcendent reality" (Eliade 1971, 16).

This politico-religious sacred offers some content to the power of the invisible scene that was embodied, made visible, in the images of 9/11 and many other recognizable dramas of world politics. Besides the kratophany and hierophany of world politics, there is a sense of the mystery, rituals and practices of (de)contamination (Aaltola 2008, 40). These aspects, which are highly conditioned by Christian culture, determine the different aspects of polymorphous space. As a method, they offer a way to the "hierarchization" of various codes. They provide clues to figuring out the underlying "code" and how different codes interact: how different levels—that is, incongruous elements and heterogeneous materials—are tied together into one coherent whole; how various things—signs, emblems, flags, buildings, background— become objectifications of the higher code.

Despite their seeming factuality and correspondence with "what happened," there were several alternatives to the iconic 9/11 images. The morning after 9/11, newspapers around the world did their best to convey what had happened. They carried huge visuals across their pages. There were two common alternatives to the most stereotypical image—firemen running at their own peril to rescue people and puzzled, horrified people watching the unraveling of the fateful day. A fourth framing—the notorious image of a "falling man"—was shown, but soon disappeared due to numerous complaints from newspaper readers. The image was that of a jumper who tried to escape the inferno of the Windows on the World restaurant, located at the top of the North Tower. The image was considered too graphic, too disturbing. Readers and viewers complained vociferously against its depiction.

In terms of political compassion, the falling man would have framed 9/11 in terms of the individual's predicament. The decision of whether to burn or jump to death was the choice faced by many of the people in the burning buildings. The emotional content of the image is an unnatural, tortured, and petrified individual whose body is in free fall upside down. He is tangling, twisting, and turning in the air. This body in pain could have offered a framing device adequate to the act of terrorism, which usually targets innocent individuals. The chosen framing device was not the individual fall; instead, it was the image of collapsing buildings that became a reminder of 9/11.

However, the act was framed differently and the individual was not the target or the symbol of the suffering. The target of compassion was the nation or state of the United States. Moreover, the scale of the attention paid to the United States and the hyperbolized atmosphere around the world cannot be adequately appreciated without taking into account the existence of world-order compassion. It seemed as if the roots of the world order had been shaken. The horror of this convulsion was captured by the images of the buildings exploding and collapsing, taken from afar. These pictures only imply individual suffering; they do not show it. In actual fact, images do not exist of the bodies that fell or were burnt. The fact is that a pervasive air of world-order compassion has characterized the post-9/11 world. One has only to consider the nonexistent images of the U.S. war casualties of Afghanistan and Iraq. Individual bodies do not frame world politics as they did, for example, in Vietnam. Imperial nostalgia, fear of Western decline, and the sentiment of restoration are the prevalent contents of the humanitarian compassion for the human polity.

The spread of political emotion from the epicenter of ground zero and its intensifying ripple effects soon became evident. They changed the American polity and formed a new, more openly hierarchical and Western-led version of human polity. The emotionality of this hierarchy and any changes in it were felt intensively. The run-up to the war in Afghanistan and the polemic before the invasion of Iraq were part of what was started by the collapsing Twin Towers. In a way, the explosion image contains a political theory that was later realized to its fullest potential by an intensifying vortex of compassion and hatred.

The neoclassical reading of Thucydides (Chapter 2) also points to the differential consequences of such a grand movement at the world-order level. At the intermediate level, the side currents rip through smaller political entities. The impact of this stasis-like condition has been felt in Iraq, Afghanistan, Pakistan, and, to some degree, in Palestine, Jordan, Morocco, and Egypt. The model also expects repercussions at the individual-somatic level. Although 9/11 was not a frame from the individual perspective, the world-order anxieties which resulted from it can easily be somatized at the social and psychological levels. Global fevers such as SARS and avian flu can be the direct embodiments of such anxieties. These pandemic diseases, which were largely based on scenarios of impending doom, may have been interpreted as individual-level manifestations of the underlying grand movement.

At the beginning, the other levels—of the smaller community's and individual's suffering—were discounted at the expense of the political sentiments of patriotism and being a member of the same civilization. The image of the jumper contained nuances that differed from those of the prevalent explosion image. Its focus on the body of an unknown individual brought forth individual suffering and doom. The loneliness of the individual falling contrasted sharply with the images of collective suffering that came to saturate the meaning of 9/11. The corporeal body of a human being and its suffering was quite different in terms of cultural history than was contained in the explosion image. If the jumper images had come to prevail, the meaning of 9/11 would have been constructed differently. Furthermore, the potential for different actions and implemented policies would have been strong. The world as we know it—the future of 9/11 in which we live today—would have been transformed.

The images that came to represent 9/11 were not random. Rather, they were serendipitous, set up by the complex yet flowing dialog between memory and the present. This was reflected in the fictitious anecdote attributed to President George W. Bush immediately after the event, which claimed that he said: "Through my tears, I see possibilities." This leads to the obvious question concerning the memory of the explosion image—that of association conditioned by knowledge about cultural history. It consists of finding correspondences that might inform one about the images. What types of images typify such occasions of destruction and confrontation? Is there a particular Western genre that contains a political heuristic, which also came to play in the explosion image of 9/11? What are the different variants of the image? Can we find similar images in European popular culture? What about the different levels of political compassion? Do they have their own historical strands at the level of "artistic rendering"? The scene of 9/11 can be thought to be about a clever enemy penetrating the defenses of a surprised protagonist. It is about the disturbed boundaries of a community, it is about communal outer limits. As such, the image bears a resemblance to a large number of scenes present in the Western gallery of iconic representations. For example, the painting by Raphael in 1521, *St. George and the Dragon*, is an analog of the explosion image (Figure 4.1):

Raphael's painting is about a community, the presence of which is denoted by the church tower in the background. The church—the sacred essence—is at the center of a community in this particular genre of Western painting. The scene itself—the confrontation with the dragon—takes place at the margins of the community. The power (potentia)—the circular perimeter emanating from the center—of the community is being shadowed by what the figure of the dragon represents. Dragons usually stand for pestilences that follow the presence of sin in a community.

Figure 4.1   *St. George and the Dragon* (1504–06) by Raphael.

Death, war, famine, and plague follow from civil irreligiousness. The fiery breath of a dragon can be read as foul air. The presence of contaminated air is also indicative of the cave from which the dragon surges forth. The atmosphere of a community has been poisoned and has become poisonous. The correspondingly poisonous communal sentiments are embodied in the rogue figure of the dragon. The act of communal exorcism involves sacrifice and restoration of the pious communal creed.

There are numerous other examples of this genre of politico-religious paintings. They are meant to arouse compassion and point to the dangers of civil irreligion. They also provide an expression of remedy: Restoration of the communal external and internal boundaries can stop the decline and eventual fall represented by the four pestilences—War, Famine, Death, and Plague—as shown in the painting in Figure 4.2:

Figure 4.2   *Der Krieg* (1896) by Arnold Böcklin.

Even when the apocalyptical themes are stripped away, this 1896 painting by Arnold Böcklin represents the same theme as Raphael's from a few centuries before. The burning community in the background is being ravaged by the pestilences. The city gates have been broken down and chaos has been introduced in the political community. The simultaneous presence of death, famine, war, and plague ties them together much in the same way as in the neoclassical model being delineated in this book. The painting seems to also contain the message of a spreading vortex. The horsemen are hurrying on from the collapsed city to its neighboring ones. Böcklin's painting lacks the triumphant revivalist tranquility of Raphael. The armies of violence are on the march. The grand movement is convulsing the civic nature of *civitas terrena*. The genre has acquired a declinist variant of doom and gloom, of decline and fall. If this painting of Böcklin blends intra- with intercommunal violence, his other powerful painting, simply called *Plague*, points to the other dimension of violence—the impact of communal disintegration on individual bodies. The transposition of these terms is much in line with the neoclassical vortex model presented here.

Moving on to a concrete example of how this genre has been used in world politics and, more particularly, in a nation's foreign policy, look at an illuminating example from the period of the Finnish independence struggle. Eetu Isto's *Attack* (Figure 4.3) is one of the best-known paintings in Ateneum, the Finnish national gallery.

This painting was meant to provoke strong nationalistic sentiments and worry over the destiny of the nation. The Maiden of Finland is under attack by the monstrous double-headed eagle, which embodies Russia. Finland was formally an autonomous part of the Russian empire at the time of the painting. Russia was going through prerevolutionary turmoil and had imposed strict censorship in Finland. Arts became the primary means of expressing politics in a coded manner. From Sibelius's symphony *Finlandia*, and Akseli Gallen-Gallen's illustration of the mythological Kalevala to Eetu Isto's nationalistically oriented work, artists tried to convey political sentiments to the nation's elites. These works borrowed heavily from the aged genre of artistic representation of a community under attack, the same genre that came into play in the visual rhetoric of 9/11.

Moving toward understanding the modern European variant of the community under attack genre, take a look at Gericault's *The Raft of the Medusa* (1819), which provides a signpost of such a mode of representation (Figure 4.4).

Gericault's work is part of the traditional genre of crisis on the high seas. This genre may be thought to complement many of the themes present in the

Figure 4.3   *Attack* (1904) by Eetu Isto.

communal crisis genre epitomized by Raphael, Böcklin, and other painters such as Isto. However, the emotional charge is markedly different. The raft and the horror faced by those in it are meant to provoke sentiments of compassion. The true story—of people cast to the mercy of the sea—behind the painting underlines the emotional effect of this "news-painting."

Figure 4.4   *The Raft of the Medusa* (1819) by Theodore Gericault.

The coded language of the scene has a wide span. It may be read to represent anything from personal and communal to national and state crises. Ultimately, the task of interpretation is not to choose between these levels to see how these levels blend and enhance each other. The deepening and enlarging vorticity of political violence assists in the polysemic—or, multidimensional—reading. The "ship of the state" and its crisis themes are present here. However, it is important to note that the community of people on the raft represents, rather than a group of victims, a community of refugees of some kind. Their background is saturated with a common story of injustice. They are an unjustly treated and persecuted group, or community, of people. The horrors they have faced—for example, forced cannibalism—accentuate their position at the very margins of humanity. The political emotion provoked by the painting is one of compassion for the distant other, one of humanitarianism. These people are at the periphery of what was then the French empire. The distance implied is not necessarily physical, but also social and emotional. The image conveys a sense of injustice and of dangerous masses unjustly threatening small, yet pious, minorities. The raging sea is a signifier of disproportionate and illegitimate violence by the many toward the few. The agent images are meant to compel immediate action for the defense of the persecuted and for the reaffirmation of the boundary conditions of belonging to humanity. The distance also implies the utter hopelessness of the governance of the empire. Its extremity was one of emergency.

Irrespective of the wider ramifications, the painting contains a sense of acute and desperate need for help. The emotional engine—that is, its system of agent images—is as tense and dramatic as possible. For those cast adrift, time is extremely scarce. The situation is highly temporized. The fate of the people is hanging by a thread. As in Isto's painting, the rough and stormy high seas imply emergency. They imply political storms at the extremities, the outer periphery, of a declining empire. In this painting, the castaways are in dire need of help, but they are hopelessly remote and distant. At the same time, they are represented in such a way that turns this peripheral position into a central one. In this sense, the raft is at ground zero, where the world political macrocosm gets condensed into a tense microcosm. A frame is set that is extraordinary, yet at the same time paints the ordinary events of its time in familiar sentimental colors.

The political schema and the source of the inherent dramatic tension in this painting may be read to belong to the submergence type of declinism. From this perspective, the scene is a submergence morality drama. The sea is an enormously powerful political metaphor, anchored in the Western political imagination. The vortexes of it are at the center of the painting. The senses of sinking and being engulfed and submerged combine with and accentuate the theme of being cast adrift. In a metaphorical sense, the means of rescue are hampered by an unsupported existence that lacks connection to the solid trunk of humanity. In this way, the painting contains an expression of the perimeters of the colonial world order. It paints the perimeters of the world hierarchy, where monstrous horrors still exist. The painting highlights the theme of submergence through overextended extremities. It also contains a call to arms: it demands action to do something for these horrors at the margins. The call to arms is two-dimensional: the humanitarian mobilization combined with one of imperial reform.

The Beginnings of the European Profiling Drama

The visible scenes—common representations of world politics—are full of clues over how to interpret what is going on. It embodies a key to a polysemic, more invisible scene. It is polymorphous in that it involves the interaction of multiple levels of meaning. The complex invisible scene pervades, leaving no doubt about the meaning of what is going on. The clarity of the drama takes precedence over the complexity. Things start to stand for something. The background condition can be referred to as those things because of which we think things are real. However, if asked, this clarity is much harder to come by. Cognitive clarity disappears. It is difficult to answer in one sentence that would be part of a coherent intellectual schema. The background is, to an important degree, noncognitive. It reveals rather than explains. It contains sentiments, rather than something more intellectual.

The emerging and increasingly hierarchically ordered global space contains different images, which revolve around the morality plays of rule following and submergence. Before proceeding to examine profiling in the heartland, that is, in the United States, it is instructive to review the beginnings of the European profiling practices to understand the broader differential change that is taking place.

In the context of the enlargement and deepening of the EU, there is a constant search for an understanding of the nature of the emerging union. It can be hypothesized that the plays at the border offer a tool for a self-image. The key term "profiling" has profound implications because it includes what may be called a normative proto-theory about the proper nature of a political community, that is, about the inherent order of things. Profiling determines who are allowed to cross borders and, ultimately, who are considered polity's trustworthy members and how they are hierarchically related to each other. Indeed, the primary aim of developing profiling policies is to establish conditions that ensure healthy political communities in a specific culturally constructed sense of the word. From this point of view, the way in which a border functions is indicative of the underlying conceptualization concerning what should constitute a well-ordered political community.

When trying to figure out the nature of the European profiled border and its wider implications, a description of the relevant frame, flow, and figures is analytically useful.

Frame

While Europe has long experience with political violence and terrorism, the type and scale of terrorism witnessed on 9/11 has never been encountered here. However, the train and subway bombings in Madrid and London demonstrated the relevance of the issue and reinforced terrorism-related measures. Although this is true, many popular interpretations have placed the blame on the blowback consequence of U.S. foreign policy. The Madrid terror strikes particularly were associated with the Spanish government's pro–United States foreign policies. Consequently, such specific European experiences have given substance to the frame of border dramas. Terrorism matters in the EU, but it is interpreted against a different historical and political background and in connection with different issues such as the worries felt over the deepening and widening union.

Besides and in some respects over the discourse of terrorism, the most significant template for the European profiling is the perceived rise in legal and illegal migration. This significance is due in large part to the enlargement of the union and to the hierarchy created through differential deepening of the integration (for example, the Schengen and Euro areas vs. rest of the union). The change of the union to a de facto political community of immigrants—which was driven by the end of the cold war, the German unification, enlargements, lifting of internal boundaries, and the attraction of its economic prosperity—has meant that the issue of terrorism is easily blended with that of migration (Muus 2001, 31). This relationship between security and the movement of people is further reinforced by job insecurity in countries where unemployment levels have reached well over 10 percent in stagnant economies. It can be argued that the recent developments and their constitutive narrative dynamics have increasingly turned border-related morality plays into dramas of submergence. This means that the legitimacy of the EU and its effectiveness is at stake on its southern and eastern borders.

Although the main impetus for the recent transformation of international borders both in Europe and the United States has roots that go well beyond 9/11, that fateful day opened a window on pronounced policy changes. It is important to trace the seeds of the more recent policies. Various ad hoc policies, processes, and institutions, such as those associated with Trevi and Interpol, preceded the 1985 Schengen agreement and the establishment of the Europol (Baldwin-Edwards and Hebenton 1994, 138). Common policy coordination and cooperation across internal boundaries were well under way during the 1990s. However, before 9/11, there had been deep suspicion and resentment against any supranational European police within the EU (Bigo 1994, 162). The rationale and impetus for such an establishment came to appear more justified after the 9/11 attacks: the European Police Office (Europol) was given extra powers and 2002 also saw the establishment of the Eurojust, which member states can request to investigate criminal activities.

The frame is further defined by the anxieties felt over the lifting and shifting of the EU's boundaries. Judging from the internal discussion in many EU member states, border management is mainly an issue of controlling unwanted and illegal immigration and preventing the "abuse" of asylum policies. It can be argued that in the EU, the banishment of the "illegal immigrant" and the "abusers of the asylum system" signify the safety of European integration and alleviate the anxieties felt toward Eastern enlargement and the proposed membership of Turkey in the EU.

Flow

The flow of the EU border dramas stems from the need to address problems that the citizens perceive as important and to avoid a nationalist

however, this was not primarily caused by 9/11. It can be argued that the anxiety stems rather from the vast eastward expansion of the EU, as the following quote from the Brussels Council, October 16-17, 2003, suggests: ". . . Council stresses that with the forthcoming enlargement, the Union's borders are expanding, and recalls the common interest of all Member States in establishing a more effective management of borders, in particular with a view to enhancing the security of their citizens." The more recent council conclusions contain such expressions as "intention to pursue rapidly," "speeding up," "set up swiftly," "to swiftly examine," "at the latest," "as soon as possible," and "a new approach is needed." It is clearly believed there is a constant yet narrow window of opportunity. This offers also an additional way in which terrorism relates to migration: Anxieties are growing and the terror scares and strikes are feeding the conventional sense of urgency.

The sense of urgency also applies to European profiling, which involves the idea that distinguishing illegal migrants from legitimate ones should be as quick and efficient as possible. In addition to the profiling at the points of entry into the EU, a lot of effort is concentrated on "accelerated," "rapid," "streamlined," and "efficient" procedures.

Keeping this in mind, there are a number of new devices at the disposal of the protagonist. The Schengen Information System (SIS) and the new SIS II are the main instruments for policy enforcement in Europe. At the practical level, the lifting of the internal EU borders is linked with the harmonization of border controls, visa policies, and police and judicial cooperation. The development of an effective SIS system at the EU's external borders has been viewed as a way to establish the free movement of people, mentioned under Title IV of the EC Treaty. However, it is significant that the free movement of people can also be seen in terms of Article 93 of the 1990 Schengen Convention, which regards the maintenance "of public policy and public security, including national security" as the main purposes of a harmonized system.

The 1990 Schengen agreement led to the creation of multiple, common border control measures. SIS II, the Visa Information System (VIS), and the Customs Information System (CIS) comprise the crux of recent European developments. The basic idea behind these measures is to create a centralized platform that will provide identification measures a uniform format. SIS II differs from the earlier system in that the list of data sources is extended to include items such as credit cards, visas, and residence permits. Future plans encompass more ambitious EU passports and identity cards that include biometric data. The database of asylum applicants, which is based on fingerprinting (EURODAC), has been operational since 2003. There is also a plan to develop a system based on the digital facial images of those who apply for residence permits or visas (Van der Ploeg

1999, 295). Particularly after the 2005 bombings in London, there have been discussions about a Europe-wide database of criminal records for terrorist convictions and confiscation of property.

The Privileged Foreigner

There are gray-area figures that fall between the protagonist and the rogue. Some foreigners have rights due to their high socioeconomic or professional status. The EU and its member states try to attract as many highly trained experts as possible to gain a competitive edge and to avoid brain drain, especially vis-à-vis the United States (Mahroum 2001, 27). At the same time, since 9/11, the lure of U.S. education and professional careers has diminished somewhat. These developments have led to a situation in which a few foreign workers are being accorded privileged treatment. The position of these people is legitimized because they are thought to represent an essential ingredient of global economic competiveness. Most of these people come from other Western states and from the educated elites of the developing world, such as India and China. These people do not arouse submergence-related nervousness. They are treated very differently from their less fortunate compatriots in the border-related plays.

The Illegal Immigrant and Asylum Abuser

The gallery of deviant figures offers a prominent role to "an abuser of European hospitality." With respect to political asylum and immigration policies, the presidency conclusions of the council meeting in Laeken express the need "to maintain the necessary balance between the protection of refugees . . ., the legitimate aspirations to better life and the reception capacities." The concept "reception capacity" can be interpreted to refer to a political as well as organizational and logistical problem. In the EU texts, too lax an asylum system is often viewed as a source of political disorder, the reason for the electoral successes of the nationalist far right and for the failure of the attempts to streamline the European decision making in key national referendums. The term "reception capacity" provides a coded common definition, a point of convergence. It is also the term that comes to play in the border-crossing morality plays. The dramatic tension between the protagonist and the figures of the illegal immigrant and the asylum abuser takes place in the threshold where there is a common perception that the reception capacity of member states is under threat.

Thus, in the EU context, immigration is often linked with the concept of over-pressure, which refers to the point at which the pressure posed by the external flow of people is no longer tolerated and interpreted as legitimate by the locals (Nicholson 2002, 436). Although there has always been a link between culturally distinct minorities and security, the past 20 years have allowed the relinking of migration with national security and, more precisely, with a certain understanding of terrorism (Weiner 1995, 10; Lodge 2002, 41). While following recent debates, it is easy to get a strong impression that the bulk of the European antiterror measures after 9/11 have been aimed at refugees and asylum seekers. At the level of policy and political communication, terrorism becomes a tool to address reception capacity. The less permissive and more restrictive policies lead to a sense that something is being done to alleviate the concerns of the citizenry, while at the same time indirectly reinforcing these anxieties (e.g., Edwards 2001, 159).

So far, rather than concentrating on single individuals, the EU's attention has been focused on the management of the larger flow of people across its external borders. As might be expected on the basis of these policy aims, the profiled European borders are considered much more efficient in capturing unwanted immigrants than terrorists. Likewise, it is not surprising that in the European discussion, the flow of asylum seekers is mostly not connected with terrorism, as indicated for example in the following quote from the council conclusions: ". . . in practice, terrorists are not likely to use the asylum channel much, as other channels are more discreet and more suitable for their criminal practices."[2] However, much of the border-related discussions still concentrate on the figures of illegal immigrants and asylum abusers.

The Dublin Convention of 1990, which set up standards for the evaluation of asylum applications, allows for an accelerated procedure for the "manifestly" and "deeply" unfounded asylum or human rights claims. These cases are excluded from the 1951 Geneva Convention's protections, and they apply to those on the terrorist list or those who have terrorist or criminal affiliations. These people are not granted access to asylum procedures at all and can be immediately turned away or arrested at the border. This profiling is, for example, based on the designated "safe country" status of the asylum seekers' origin or on the fact that applicants renew their application after being rejected from another EU state. Those who are allowed to access the asylum procedure are subject to ever more rapid decisions that are increasingly based on taking the applications at face value.

The Hooligan, Troublemaker, and Antiglobalist
The European gallery of rogues includes the figure of the aggressive troublemaker and, more specifically, that of the football hooligan. There is a common infrastructure and tools of border control at the disposal of the protagonist, which enable the placing of temporary and geographically specific restrictions. The new extensions of SIS include profiling based on a list of individuals with histories of violence (Lodge 2002, 50). These instruments have been used in cases of violent anti-Europe and antiglobalization

demonstrations in connection with major international meetings. Those on the list are prohibited from traveling to certain places or events during certain periods of time. The aim is to stop potential troublemakers in major traffic hubs from reaching their destination.

The Illegal Worker and Foreign Prostitute
Those whose rights are based on an often illegal employment relationship with a single employer, for example, foreign prostitutes, have few rights (Muus 2001, 42). Although they have some purchasing power and exist at the level of consumers, they lack political or even human rights. Furthermore, they are often viewed as dysfunctional outcasts from the perspective of the community. If they are not defined as victims, they are viewed as social problems in the popular culture. For example, there is the stigmatic broad notion of "disease" associated with prostitution and illegal workers are sometimes thought to be the cause of the high unemployment in many of the member states. In the European border dramas, the figure of the foreign prostitute is not only a source of contamination, she is also an abused figure who needs special protection by the protagonist. The figure of the human smuggler has emerged in this connection. A human smuggler is perceived as a deeply deviant figure undeserving of any empathy.

EU Refugee-Monsters-at-the-Gates Drama

The compassion contained in the visual rhetoric is expressive in two ways. First, the suffering of people is made tangible by the presence of immediate death. Second, the dangers to the empire are made concrete by the desperate condition of the people at its periphery. In many ways, the second sense can become the primary one as the compassion for the efficient political order starts to frame the feelings for the individual sufferers. The destiny and future of the political order of things is represented by the sufferers, whereas their future turns into an issue of secondary importance. Gericault's work offers clues to the submergence dramas of today. Such dramas are especially used in the European media and popular culture. Although the buzz has been about American submergence writings, à la Huntington, the European political imagination may be said to be submergence fixated. The representations of flows of people or illicit activities prevail in the European imagination. Perhaps the roots of the imagery go all the way to Zosimus and to the fall of the Western Roman Empire at the hands of approaching "barbarians." The conventional visual representation of the fall is portrayed through arrows and dates pointing to the pattern of the Empire's collapse. This imagery is often reproduced in the modern map of migration. For example, a look at the web page of the Office of the UN High Commissioner for Refugees (UNHCR) reveals diagrams in which the underlying message of Europe under attack or siege is reinforced. The imagery reminds you of the depictions of the fall of the Roman Empire, with arrows signifying the approach of different "barbarian tribes." The invisible code present in the visual representation is telling. Something alarming, threatening, and sinister appears to be going on.

The drama of the migrants trying to reach the shores of Europe echoes these representations. In recent times, various pictures of desperation and defiance of death reach living rooms and breakfast tables across Europe. For example, the images of migratory flows to the Spanish Canary Islands have been widely seen. They are reminiscent of Gericault's high drama on the sea. The faces of the drowning people denote something at the individual level as well: The immediate language into which they could be translated is one of compassion toward the individual. However, due to the existence of the coded language of the submergence of Europe and its civilization, other interpretations come into play. They are filtered through different traditions of political compassion. The faces may start to remind Europeans of the multitude of people waiting at its gates. Although sentiments are felt for them, they turn into embodiments of different types of monstrosities. They stand for the overflow that manages to get as far as the shore of the Canary Islands or to the different reception centers inside Europe, such as the infamous Sangat refugee centre in France.

The individual does not stand for himself. Nor do the desperate people at sea stand for the desperation inflicting their background communities— high unemployment, famine, environmental degradation, epidemics, and military conflicts. They start to stand for a security threat and their potential ability to reach their destinations symbolizes an emergency for Europe. These people cause worry as much as compassion. The compassionate element is embodied in the form of the human trafficker and smuggler who have duped the people to take the high-risk journey to the Canary Islands. Bodies in pain—that is, the face of a drowning man—usually demand action in the form of an intervention. However, the body in pain is not that of the man himself; it is actually felt to be that of Europe or of its individual member states. When what one sees is this, the action demanded is one of closure and to secure the "leaking" points of access.

Inside the EU, there has been a lot of talk about the urgent need for international cooperation in stemming the "tide" of immigration. The submergence-related fear of being overwhelmed and the washed-out discourse prevails in the media and popular talk. In newspaper headlines, vigilant gate-keeping is emphasized and demanded. Politicians foster and reframe this type of sea imagery. The people seeking entry are seen as strangers at our gates: the attached media representations are striking, frightening, and ominous. They evoke memories in the Europeans of the decline and fall that have been intensively practiced at places of education. The "tide" of migrants causes different EU member states to demonstrate their efficacy by such steps as starting satellite monitoring and diplomatic offensives. New embassies for the EU and camps for potential migrants are set up in Africa. In these public representations, Europe is framed as a miracle that attracts migratory flows. Headlines count the numbers of those who drown en route to Europe. The voyage, which is motivated by the lure of economic gain, is seen as one of peril. The effectiveness of the border patrols is demonstrated by the crossing over journeys that start even further down the African coast. As a result, the journey becomes longer and even more dangerous.

It is not only the EU, but also its member states, that demonstrate their ability to act. One form of this is accusing other member states of their ineptitude. For example, France accuses Spain of inaction and Spain hits back by pointing to the recent French riots in the suburbs of Paris. The primary tone of the accusations is directed against the laxness of other states' immigration policies. Other states are seen as causing trouble for all by purposefully creating jobs and benefiting from the flows of illegal workers. Attracting workers from sub-Saharan Africa is seen as problematic when the challenges of integrating the workers into the host societies are considered. This type of framing is in line with the submergence thematic.

Africans desperate to reach Europe are now setting out from Senegal and from other Western African locations such as Mauritania. They have almost 1000 miles of rough seas to cross. Spain's government, which is in control of the Canary Islands, is treating the wave of immigrants as a policing problem. It is seen as a humanitarian problem at the level of individual bodies. However, those at sea and those being detained are not treated as refugees. Their origin is not recognized and they are not identified as members of any particular group. Their desperation is generally not justified in the media as a group of people fleeing political hardship. Consequently, while camps to detain potential immigrants have been set up by the EU, they do not operate like refugee camps.

Thus, horrific events involving overpacked, capsized boats and drowned people shock media audiences in Europe. However, the sentiments they feel are not those of compassion toward the victims, but of horror at the face of the flows that the drowned are made to stand for. The desperation of the immigrants and the fact that half of them did not make it to Europe are symbols of battle for the European identity and the purity of its creed.

Meanings are passed by in selecting certain stories to tell. The rogue figure of the human trafficker plays an important role. For example, the media is fixated on the exorbitant fees Africans are made to pay to get to the Canary Islands. It presents a reminder that the "crosser-overs" are also victims, not a cause for insecurity. They are given a human face. They are only recognized through the stereotype of being naive victims, ultimately of their own economic wants. Spain sends signals that it needs help and solidarity from the other EU members. Alarms are sounded and a state of emergency prevails. The EU is seen as forced to stem the tide of African migrants. Frontex, the EU's external border security agency, sends emergency coordination teams to the Canary Islands. Frontex notably appeals to all 27 member states for equipment such as aircraft and vessels. These political sentiments legitimize the previously unthinkable. Large-scale repatriation flights and reception centers are set up in the transit countries (Senegal and Mauritania). The EU develops its structures as a response for the seen demands. It sets up a maritime policy and perfects its control over its airspace and land borders.

Media stories emphasize the economic aspect also in their "root cause" stories. The reason for the wave is that other, shorter routes to Sicily and through Morocco have been closed off. Access to the Spanish and, ultimately, to the European economies is seen as the background condition. The Canary Islands is a favored route because the Spanish industry, particularly its construction sector, relies on guest workers to a large extent. Newscasts summarize the situation in many of the Western African countries, telling stories about unemployment, etc., to explain why so many are desperate to make it to Europe.

U.S. Finding-the-Needle-in-the-Haystack Drama

The European border dramas closely follow those in the United States. They offer a useful point of comparison and contrast. Arguably, the morality play at the U.S. border has a much more visual frame, a more distinct flow, and a different set of figures than the European ones. One of the most noticeable differences between the EU's and the United States's border-related morality plays has a lot to do with the spectacular, visual nature of 9/11 and its effect on the dramaturgy of U.S. world politics. A further argument could be made that the pedagogic function of the U.S. morality plays has much to do with their sheer visual power. Such research concepts as the "visual rhetoric of sanctity," "visualization of moral life," and "visual spectacles" become descriptive of this setting.[3] The visual nature of the politics and the robust use of public iconography greatly enhance the simplification of the interpretative act. The emphasis has shifted away from the nuances of the 1990s to the world-order pedagogy and from subtle and complicated specifics to the brute force of the striking visuals. In this context, the iconic is blended with the striking details in morality plays that are increasingly mythic.

Related to the simplification of the interpretative act by a strong pedagogic function, political action is prioritized over deliberation: a strong sense of situational complexity, relativity of perspectives, and drawn-out argumentation is considered increasingly illegitimate. The need to do something, the sense that time is scarce, and the fear of an imminent terror attack create a bias toward dramatic action. However, it can be argued that a particular type of complexity has remained, even though much of it exists only to accentuate the sense of instructive drama.

The U.S. border-related morality plays revolve around accurate identification of figures. What makes this task harder is that, in the U.S. morality plays, the deviant figures can take on pretense: In the official documents, it is often claimed that they can manipulate their appearance, deceive the innocent, and hide their true faces. The drama is one of careful and watchful confrontation. The case of the so-called Dirty Bomber, who was captured at Chicago O'Hare Airport on June 10, 2002, is a case in point. The Attorney General, John Ashcroft, issued the following lines in his dramatic announcement: "Once again, I commend the FBI, the CIA and other agencies involved in capturing Abdullah al-Muhajir before he could act on his deadly plan. Because of the close cooperation among the FBI, the CIA, Defense Department and other federal agencies, we were able to thwart this terrorist. To our enemies, I say we will continue to be vigilant against all threats, whether they come from overseas or at home in America. To our citizens, I say we will continue to respect the rule of law while doing everything in our power to prevent terrorist attacks." The border drama was one of the accuracy and timeliness of the U.S. action. It was meant to signal the viciousness of those who "hate the American way of life" and the "goodness" of those who are staged as fighting for their country and, by extension, for Western civilization.

It can be argued that a degree of uncertainty and ambiguity is instrumental in achieving the required engrossing dramatic tension in the U.S. border-related morality plays. The audience of these contemporary morality plays is asked to remain on their toes because things might not be what they appear to be. The deviant figure is a deceiver requiring complex systems of profiling to detect its essence under the pretense. The play aims at getting to the bottom of things, securing them. But the dramatizing uncertainty remains whether this is achieved in a lasting way: one may be left wondering whether the sense of security is deceptive. Such uncertainty- and ambiguity-related questions saturate the modern world-order morality plays. Connected with the ambiguity is a sense of central authority. Governmental authority is declared and adherence to it is demanded.

Evidence is held secret for reasons of national security. The validity of specific cases—dramas—are turned into questions of governmental authority, rather than evidence-based argumentation.

Frame

The context of the U.S. border-related morality dramas is a contest between the good and the deviant. The situation is tense, dramatic, and open-ended. The theme of coexisting contradictory forces is further reinforced by the pervasive and unremitting religious aspect, which is signified as civilizational—either one between civilizations defined by the "high" religions or one between the Western moderates and the Eastern extremists.

Because of this religious charge, the concept of kratophany describes an essential feature present in this type of setting. As stated earlier, kratophany describes dramatic tension at the most critical moments. Kratophany may be taken to refer to a charged field of attraction and repulsion. This is especially tangible at the scene of an international border, where not only different, but also incompatible, elements are pictured as coexisting.

A strong sense of kratophany was present in the stock U.S. morality play, 9/11. The scene of planes flying into landmark buildings intertwined the ultimate evil with striking acts of heroism and blended horror with a strange sense of captivating fascination. It can be argued that this kratophany provides a valuable background narrative for the staging of the post-9/11 U.S. border-related morality plays. In other words, there is a tendency to concentrate on sudden and striking events at the expense of events that have a longer duration.

It can be argued that the setting of the border-related drama between the protagonists and the deviants has at least partly to do with the notion of a civilizational clash. The discussion concerning profiled borders is often based on cultural givens—for example, American character—and on the firm sense of the higher value of the Western civilization identified with it. In this context, Samuel Huntington's ideas concerning civilization clash have been influential (e.g., Kreutzman 1999, 255). It is not difficult to argue that the perceived solidity of Western civilization compounds the sense of nativism and essence, and inevitably turns the attention to the issue of foreigners and incompatibility. The kind of migration, which brings incompatible elements together, is easily defined as a destabilizing, corrupting, and submerging factor (e.g., Huntington 2004). In this context, migration appears as a great danger and a potentially revolutionary movement, which might dilute the United States's national essence and its creed. Following from this logic, the practice of profiling for terrorist "types" turns into a way of screening for civilizational fitness and filtering out incompatible elements, or foreigners who are too alien.

What are the incompatibilities present at the staged border? Huntingtonian morality plays draw from the American civil religion, from the so-called American creed. Huntington famously identifies immigration as a source of potential decay in a political community (e.g., Huntington 1993, 22). Of particular concern are those immigrants "from other civilizations who reject assimilation and continue to adhere to and propagate the values, customs and cultures of their home societies" (Huntington 2004, 141). What make this source of decay even more potent are modern forms of communication. Previously, once immigrants crossed regional and continental divides, they largely lost contact with their native landscape. According to Huntington, contemporary forms of contact do not cut immigrants' umbilical cords in the same way (Huntington 1997, 38). Links and contacts remain, turning people coming from different civilizations into sources of decay and erosion—into what could be termed as "fifth columns" and "enemy aliens."

It can be thought that the defense of a civilizational way of life involves a search for constancy in its various defining characteristics. Constancy allows for the making of predictions based on ethnic, religious, cultural, and national features. Palumbo-Liu (2002, 111) traces the roots of the project of finding this kind of constancy to the birth of American studies in the 1940s and to Margaret Mead's attempt to distil the national character. The central idea in these studies was that culture could be approached in an anthropo-logical manner to define the national character. Thus, culture as a mode of being and as a way of life became definitively and inseparably connected with the identifying concept of Americanness. This idea of constancy and primor-diality resonates well with Huntington: "In conflicts between civilizations, the question is 'What are you?' That is given that cannot be changed. And as we know, from Bosnia to the Caucasus to the Sudan, the wrong answer to that question can mean a bullet in the head" (Huntington 1998, 71).

The existence of civilization begs the question of its borders and composi-tion. What is Western civilization in U.S. profiling? The general starting point is offered by President Bush's ontological definition of terrorists as evil people "who hate [the] American way of life." Incompatibility with the American way of life can examined through the differential practices at the border. For example, the Visa Waiver Program (VWP) allows the citizens of several coun-tries to travel to the United States for as long as 90 days without a visa. It is telling of the U.S. object of identification that in 2006, of the 27 countries on the VWP list, 22 were European.[4] The citizens of these countries are likely to enjoy entry and exit to the United States without the unpleasant hassles expe-rienced by the rest.[5] The list of states is based on the refusal rates of U.S. visas.[6] It is, therefore, indicative of the overall preference patterns of immigration into the United States. The program is reciprocal in that the states on the list grant the same privileges to U.S. citizens. It can be claimed that this kind of reciprocity forms the presumed "hard core" of Western civilization; it exemplifies the supposed nonthreatening elements that can be integrated into the model of modern Western societies.

The definition of a constant national character and especially the one connected with the United States/West has implications for people wanting to cross international boundaries. Combining culture with national identity and with a way of life leads to an imperative of integration designed to prevent the feared dilution of national character. When relevant and redefined borders are made to stand for hierarchical cultural distinctions, an individual crossing them is expected to be willing and able to undergo a profound change. This suggests that civilization as a signifier is also a measure of the ability to adapt and integrate into its constituent geographical locations; a Westerner is able to adapt to the worldwide modern cosmopolitan culture, whereas a Muslim is seen as able to adapt only to Muslim culture. The civilizational distance becomes an important device which helps in the deciphering of the morality plays: the sense of drama is triggered by the presence of high incompatibility with such strange habits and alien looks at the border crossings. These differences are turned into politically relevant coded language.

Flow

As compared to the EU border-crossing morality plays, the main difference in the U.S. practices is the history of immigration to the United States. Due to historical reasons, the American public debate on immigration is relatively different from the European one. The United States is a "nation of immigrants," in which "immigration policy is a highly institutionalized process and in which pro-immigrant groups have a legitimate, entranced role in policy-making" (Joppke 1998, 272). Against this background, the profiled borders of the United States explicitly aim at filtering out terrorist types and identifying "dangerous individuals" from the vast stream of cross-border traffic. The needle-in-the-haystack flow of the morality play revolves around a filtering process: the dramatic tension and suspense is created by a culturally resonant manhunt or chase type of situation. The vigilant protagonist is out there to catch the individual terrorist and terrorist cells.

The detection and identification of the terrorist demonstrates also the identifiability and solidity of the American character. It can be argued that, from this perspective, the catching of the terrorist is tightly connected with the maintaining of the boundaries of civilization. In the context of globalization, international transactions being a necessity, the concept of trustworthiness and verifiability have become vitally important. The different conceptions and measures of trust decide who can move across borders. In practice, trustworthiness is often equated with identifiability. The term "background checks" is revealing because it implicitly brings the notion of civilization, as a cultural, religious, and historical concept, into tangible issue. The amount of detentions, delays, and waits at the border are directly related to one's background and, often, to civilizational membership. The "smoking them out" and "hunting them down" type of language reveals the search for the true essence of people. From this perspective, it can be argued that the solidity of the American character is allegorically reaffirmed through finding and confronting the truly evil people who can no longer hide under their pretence.

Figures

The Protagonist

Whereas the EU's manifest protagonist draws from secular, cultural resources, the United States's protagonist is a more moral figure, a custodian of principles (Demerath and Williams 1992, 170). In contrast to the EU's pragmatic arbiter, whose task it is to turn various moral issues into practical ones, the custodian of principles converts the content of everyday politics into fundamental moral issues. In the morality plays, the custodians of principles emerge during times of crisis, offering to remedy a threatening course of events. They offer hope of restoration and return to fundamental values. They do this by applying culturally embedded visions of right and wrong, which often have an overtly Christian tone. The legitimacy of the custodians of principles ultimately depends on how they promise and manage to alleviate the crisis and heal the situation. A stock example is offered by President Bush's appearance and speech in the ruins of the World Trade Center. It can be interpreted that he and similar figures (such as New York City Mayor Rudolph Giuliani) managed to give meaning to apparently senseless acts of terror by being in the middle of the vivid landscape and successfully using the visual rhetoric of sanctity. These custodians of principles appear to stand in guard of Western civilization and the American way of life. The presence of figures akin to these custodians is felt at the profiled U.S. borders and their authority flows from every act of dramatically catching the bad guys.

As a stock figure of the U.S. morality plays, the custodians of principles are regarded as visionaries who lead their people forward. The custodians of principles actively require faith in their mission from others. Rather than being rationally convincing, they persuade through powerful images and appealing visions. It can be suggested that these arbiters of morality stress the belief in the general moral way of life of the community. They mediate between "testimony," drawing from the perceived fundamentals of American culture—that is, a healthy life, religious liberty, and the pursuit of happiness—and from the noncognitive revelation of visions for the future. For the modern American custodians of principles, it is the moral efficacy of the political community that provides the primary fundamental and the source of moral borders. The custodians of principles draw from emotions and feelings in creating inspiring and visionary political performances.

Another important type of sacred becomes relevant in the context of the quasi-religious U.S. border plays. As said before, hierophany refers to the spatial aspect of sacred space. Furthermore, it also reveals the hierarchy of this space and, therefore, its center. It refers to the central political figures as interpreters of powerful and extraordinary meanings. These sacred meanings cannot be comprehended only through the cognitive method. They require more revelatory awareness, which is provided by the "inspired" interpretations offered by the custodians of principles.

The American protagonist in the border-crossing morality plays signifies the preemption of terrorism. Terrorists have to be stopped before they commit their acts or manage to reach U.S. soil. The preventive figure is armed with the necessary tools to uncover hidden identities and suspect backgrounds. An illustrative case in point is provided by the experimental project with the iconic name of Matrix, which was dismantled in the spring of 2005 because of privacy concerns. Matrix, short for Multistate Anti-terrorism Information Exchange, was supposed to speed up the access of police to people's records through the use of parallel processing of data on numerous sources. Matrix included a proactively inclined statistical program that could scan available records to measure an individual's propensity for acts of terror, the so-called terrorist quotient (TQ). The evaluation of the likelihood was based on statistical methods developed by a private company, Seisint. The method is based on scores derived from basic factors such as ethnicity, nationality, age, and gender as well as more derived ones such as credit history, past criminal activities, professional licenses, property records, bankruptcies, business affiliates, and "hot" addresses used by terrorist suspects and their associates.

Another criticized and partly changed, yet revealing, program is the Department of Defense's Total Information Awareness program (TIA). TIA draws data from many commercial data-collecting sources. Because of the "big brother" implications, the term "total" in the name of the program was changed to "terrorist."

There are various other existing and often overlapping systems for automatic profiling in the United States. They differ from the controversial programs in that they are less based on using speculative means, such as TQ. The Computer-Assisted Passenger Pre-screening System (CAPPS) was first utilized by Northwest Airlines in 1994. During the late 1990s, this system was adopted by the whole aviation industry after being recommended by a U.S. government commission. The development of the system stemmed from the bombing of the Pan Am flight over Lockerbie and gained further momentum after the TWA flight crash in 1996. The overall profiling program that is being developed in the United States by the Department for Homeland Security is called the United States Visitor and Immigrant Status Indicator Technology Program (US-VISIT), which started in January 2004. US-VISIT is an automated entry/exist system at air and sea ports which aims at making international travel speedier and at filtering out those individuals and groups that intend to do harm.[7]

The Transportation Security Administration (TSA) maintains the "no-fly" list and a list of people that require additional screening. The inclusion of individuals on these lists is officially based on secret criteria. The system will assign passengers three color codes—green, yellow, and red—signifying the level of risk posed by each type of passenger. More than 90 percent of the passengers will get a green code. The rest will get a yellow code, meaning they require further screening. The iconic red code will be assigned to a few passengers, who will be prevented from boarding and possibly arrested. The assigning of the color codes depends on the correlation between travel data and the data concerning known terror suspects and incidents of terror. Important past travel data include the city of departure, destination, traveling companions, and the manner and date of purchase of the ticket. Airlines will send the passengers' full name, date of birth, address, phone number, and travel itinerary to a centralized data-processing facility. Passenger Information Records (PIR) contain all the information that airlines demand on each purchase of a ticket, such as name, departure and return flights, possible special requests by the passenger (e.g., special meals or medical conditions), frequent flyer number, and credit card number. PIR also include the passengers' place of residence, travel agent information, and emergency contact name and address in the case of non-U.S. passengers. All in all, the PIR can contain about 60 items of information, the exact nature of which depends on the airline. The data will be matched with data from private data-collecting companies.[6]

The Businessman and the Good Consumer
The morality plays at the U.S. border involve the figure of the vigilant and law-abiding citizen. It can be argued that this figure highlights the role of the consumer and consumption. For example, in the airport morality dramas, these figures revolve around the types of international businessmen and U.S.

tourists, whose work and consumption fuels not only the airport duty-free shops, but also the U.S. economy at large. One example of the importance of these figures is offered by the so-called Smart Border Plan, which was started in 2002 between the United States and Canada. The explicit aim of this program is to increase border security, while speeding up legitimate travel for business and pleasure. To qualify as a legitimate traveler for the program, one needs to fill out an application and pass an interview. The application includes personal details, past work history, and places of residence during the past 5 years.

It is indicative that in the post-9/11 environment, consumer habits are used to provide one of the most important indicators of passengers' identity. The role of consumption is increasingly important for the legitimacy of a modern state such as the United States. Spending and the "American consumer" has become the focus of state building and communal civic culture (McGovern 2003, 68). National identities are increasingly fused with consumption as a way of life. Moreover, consumerism is intertwined with the notion of civilization. It is, therefore, not surprising that the PIR data contain information of the passengers' consumption habits.[7]

It may be said that the implicit argument behind these profiling practices is that the values and practices of consumption constitute a binding force that produces constancy and predictability in people's lives: "Consumerism and modernism are joined at the hip because consumption is an indispensable part of the civilizing process. The process of consumption, of expressing our identity through tastes and possessions, changes the entire field of interaction. It makes possible new kinds of social identity" (Sznaider 2000, 297). Because the relationship between salaried work and the desired material and nonmaterial products is made through credit, people are tied to their jobs to maintain a certain lifestyle and quality in life. Regular payment schedules to creditors create the much-desired constancy. The ability to keep a record of this valued constancy is an additional benefit of the credit system. The recognition of who is who in the system is made more efficient by the quantification of associated types based on credit records. When it comes to the actual capture of terrorists, however, the evidence is fuzzier. The affluence and family ties of the 9/11 terrorists indicate "relatively high levels of education, socio-economic status, and stable family ties" (Hoffman 2002, 305). The inability to differentiate terrorists using these characteristics turns profiling into less than science.

The Terrorist
The figure of the terrorist represents the rogue at its extreme, the most dissolute behavior imaginable by the post-9/11 mind. The figure of the terrorist emerged from the defining defiling act. The terrorist became a complex consisting of determinate and detectable signs. How is this figure

recognized? It is not surprising that in the aftermath of 9/11, immigration offenses became the primary tool for detaining suspicious people. The process was based on profiling groups of people—men from a Middle Eastern background—and using minor offenses to detain and deport them. One such sign of a possible terrorist, very much in the foreground of the public discourse, is the overstaying of visas.[8] In the U.S. discourse, overstayers of visas are regarded as exploiting the country's hospitality. This sign is related to the European language game of "asylum abusers."

At the point of entry, a person's name may become a signifier of a potential terrorist. The name itself is important because it provides the basis of what is called "name profiling." For example, the United States's most wanted list includes individuals with common Arabic names. If the passenger's name corresponds with or resembles any of those on the list, he cannot proceed without first being cleared. In this way, names like Ahmed or Mohammed can result in further questions. The number of false positive alerts, checks, and arrests is lower with names that have their origin outside of South America, the Middle East, and Southeast Asia.

One further identifying feature of the figure of the terrorist is the supposed disposition toward passivity. It is considered that a member of a terror group has a tendency to submit to an in-group's or its leader's will and an inclination to be indoctrinated. The characteristic of submission is combined with a tendency toward societal dissociation. The image is of an individual empty of individual personality and full of in-group mentality. The *Weekly Bulletin* (May 19, 2004) of the Federal Bureau of Investigation (FBI), which warned about possible suicide attacks in the United States, provides further examples of the type of people who could be terrorists. These characteristics range from people wearing bulky jackets on a warm day and smelling like flammable liquids or explosive chemicals to people whose "fists are tightly clenched." Besides these measures, the bulletin raises the possibility of disguises: copying methods used in the Middle East, terrorists can look like pregnant women or wear police uniforms. Antisocial passivity stands in opposition to the U.S. sense of spontaneity.

Borders as Political Spectacles

International border crossings provide a setting for the expression of the underlying values of being a citizen, European, American, or Westerner, besides expressing numerous other shades and variations of identities. In the case of the European identity, the border morality plays are meant to provide a locus for a sense of mixture of people united in their diversity. This sanctioned sense is achieved through contrast with the figures of the abuser, illegal immigrant, and the human smuggler. For an American, on the other hand, the crossing of an international border provides a sense of belonging to a great civilization whose way of life is being celebrated by secure and efficient travel along the arteries of the world. Where the European experience is based on a careful balance and sensitivity for each member state's perceived social harmony, the U.S. emphasis is on reaching decisive clarity and identifiability, and on the ability to eliminate threats. At the personal level of the individual traveler, the eye equipped with the respective political imaginations is on the lookout for different things. At the EU border, the imagination focuses on human traffickers and illegitimate asylum seekers, whereas at the U.S. border, one looks for possible terrorists who might hijack planes and turn them into weapons.

The figure of the rogue is mischievous, cynical, unfeeling, and utterly controlled by its evil predispositions (Perelmuter 1979, 820). Part of the rogue figure's social construction is its important moral and pedagogic function. It is meant to teach the bad consequences of illegitimate behavior. Thus, in the border dramas, the figure is continuously running into trouble, pain, and injury. From the infamous shoe bomber, Mexicans swimming across Rio Grande, dead Chinese in lorries crossing the channel, to the desperate attempts by Africans to reach the shores of Canary Islands, TV images contain an important lesson. This pedagogy is not about compassion for the distant other and humanitarian sentiments. It is about the consequences of evil, about the sanctity of borders, and about worries concerning foreign elements. The political compassion contained in these graphic dramas is for political bodies: the nation, state, community, civilization, and, ultimately, the world order.

Through the recent changes in the world order, borders have become the loci for the morality plays of a transformed world order. Through the morality plays of rule following and submergence, reassurance, security, and certainty are conveyed. The morality plays at the border signify the sovereignty of the imagined political community and its secured existence. The whole political community is both literally and symbolically present in the physical halls of international entry and exit. However, the place is largely imaginary, a politico-cultural artifact meant to produce a sense of a community that has strong borders. The profiled border, as it is expressed in the uneven and differential flow of people across borders, creates an imagined landscape for a community of people. From this community, those beyond its gates—the unwanted elements—stand apart. The question of how real the threats actually are is not as significant as the question concerning the status of the morality plays where those threats belong. They are allegories aiming to instruct people about the legitimacy of the underlying sanctity of the political community.

5

Compassions at International Airports: The Hub-and-Spoke Pedagogy of the American Empire

In this chapter, I will argue that airport hubs, together with their interknitted networks, have an important bearing on the formation of what is meant by the international extension of the individual body—for example, the international community, the Western community, or the world community. The argument is that an airport, as a gauge of undiluted and consistent world hierarchy, provides for a connection between the individual's experience, when he moves through the hub-and-spoke structure, and the world order's transformation, which has been characterized lately by the war on terror and the rise of the power of the United States. It can be hypothesized that airports teach people the central rituals of acknowledgment that are needed to navigate in the Byzantine structures of the modern hierarchical world order. The "aviopolis" provides a place for the production of appropriate imperial categories (e.g., Westerners, Third Worlders, and terrorists) for the measuring of modern virtues, and the demonstration of constant vigilance is directed to the political wholesomeness of the imagined world community. The striking reminders—for example, suspicious strangers, auditory and visual warnings, memories of past terror attacks, metal detectors and security checks—placed throughout the airport frame are meant to drive home the fact that survival is at stake in the post-9/11 world. As in the case of international borders, the affirmation of political health takes place against the "declinist" images of dilution of important hierarchies and failure in following the central norms.

It may be argued that the increasingly extensive resolution of the relationship between individuals and their layered concentric political embodiments is at the forefront of the new era in world politics. The airplane is an important symbolic vehicle mediating between these political bodies. The individual sitting in an airplane belongs to a larger infrastructure. The geographically extensive nature of this network turns it into a direct experience with the hierarchical world order. Post 9/11, much public attention has been fixated on air safety as a broader indicator of the hierarchical world order's status and health. My argument is that movements through an airport and airspace have a pedagogic dimension: the meaning of the hierarchical world order is passed on to an aggregation of people caught in the aviopolis frame and flow.

Political Revelations at the Aviopolis

The bridgehead to understanding the political pedagogy of international airports is epistemological. The pedagogy depends on how certainty is felt at the aviopolis. In a sense, airports have to do with the foundations of knowing in world politics—with postulations and presuppositions of the very validity of the world order. However, instead of presupposing that knowledge is based on rational, intellectual, and empirical criteria, emphasis can be placed on what may be called airports' political epistemology: the knowledge acquired may be understood to depend on there being a community that acknowledges and recognizes the knowledge as legitimate. In this way, airports are places where authority is recognized and instructions for making "proper" judgments and acknowledgments are given. It can be hypothesized that airports teach people the central rituals of acknowledgments that are needed to produce the modern hierarchical world community.

Many of these rituals of acknowledgment have to do with interactions between sign technology and human flows. In various places in its internal architecture and in the links between major airport hubs, the emerging world order is envisioned and embodied. Perhaps, this vision of the world is at its most distinct at the board of arrivals and departures, where the status of the global space can be evaluated at a single glance in the words "on time," "delayed," and "cancelled" in connection with the names of world cities. A telling example of the board as a status indicator was 9/11. The unprecedented act of suspending all flights in U.S. airspace had a dramatic effect on the board of arrivals and departures. For a moment, the board, indicating the status of the global space, went blank. From this perspective, terrorism constituted an act disturbing global airspace and a flagrant act of sacrilege against the values signified by the modern hierarchical world order. It is important to note that the didactic vision of the world is simul-taneously an image of one's own home and one's identity in that world. It can be said that an airport is an important part of the communication of the praxis and ideals of hierarchical globality: interpretations of a particu-lar type of world are made visible to the global traveling mind through arrangements of airports' political architecture.

Crang (2002, 571) argues that "of all the spaces of a globalized world, air-ports may be the most emblematic." In the feverish agitation of the booming global space, airports provide one of its truest signifiers (e.g., Dodge and Kitchin 2004, 195). The contemporary political imagery of the world includes two major focuses—economy and security. It can be argued that the introduction of jet aircraft in the 1950s, its wide-bodied version in the 1970s, and the emergence of major international airport hubs changed the praxis of political economy and national security. Airports and air-traffic infrastructure are often thought to be crucial if a state or region wants to be a part of the global zones of pros-perity (e.g., Garcia-Zamor 2001, 415). Bigger and better airports are considered necessities for survival in the global markets, in the free trade competition, and in the tides of technological innovation. Bottlenecks in the demand and supply of landings per hour are thought to negatively affect the economic development in the surrounding region and turn vital investments elsewhere. The security impact needs to be considered when the global space of the post-9/11 world is examined. In several ways, the war on terror is engrossed with airplanes and air-ports. The economic function of an airport to distribute global wealth has been blended with the need to defend against "terror."

An important change is inherent in the now omnipresent danger that people with illegitimate intentions can use the vital arteries of the global world to get through to the heartlands of the West—that the imperial borders differ from the customary boundaries of sovereign states. An illuminating comparison can be made to imperial Rome's territorial imagi-nation (Lintott 1981, 65). The limits of the Roman Empire were not precise. To an important degree, the limits of Rome were its roads and various access routes. It may be argued that the increasing transformation of the contem-porary world order to imperial arrangements is predisposed to rediscover and reformulate this old "imperial" meaning of boundaries. When the space becomes global, it loses its meaning as something to be secured and rein-forces the need to secure the access routes connecting the imperial vastness. At least, it is worth exploring the implications of the argument that the main arteries of the globalized world have turned into the boundaries of the empire led by the United States. Airports' security implications are height-ened because they provide access routes to the centers of political power. It is argued that because of this, it is not surprising that substantial experiences take place on the routes to the centers of power as the security stakes get higher. It can be hypothesized that the revelatory nature of these experiences fosters and educates people in the ways of the contemporary world hierarchy. The movement in the airport frame, from an important perspective, crystallizes the macro-level political architecture. This means that the "person at the airport" is put at the foreground of what will be called airport morality plays. These plays need an engrossing frame to provide a drama thick enough for revelatory experiences.

Imperial Morality Plays at the Airport

Stemming partly from the conflicting demands of economy and security, the airport political space is tense, nervous and, occasionally, highly dramatic. By its very nature, an airport is a crossroads. The notion of a crossroads contains a critical element of danger and confusion. Although the distant other is met in a highly controlled manner, there are anxieties involved in travel through international airspace. It can be suggested that one of the central reasons why people feel anxious at international airports derives from the process in which they are profiled and reduced to types. Exposed to this reductive process, people at the international airports are nervous for different reasons. Often, people are anxious about flying and about losing their valuables or passports. Another often cited source of anxiety stems from the quality of service. An airport is a place where tangibles, reliability, responsiveness, assurance, and empathy are recognized and evaluated by tourists and business travelers while they themselves are being profiled. This brings about an economy of evaluation in which the true identities of the respective actors—ranging from individuals, localities, and ethnicities to the status of the world order—are revealed.

However, there are other causes for sensing anxiety, which range from being an asylum seeker, a member of a religious or ethnic group or a person with a minor immigration violation against his name to being a member of a criminal group. Placed on the airport space, people who have a reason to fear being discovered, also have a reason for uneasiness. Although for an average Westerner, they are a nuisance or a reassurance, the airport exposes people to drug dogs, X-ray machines, metal detectors, mandatory searches, tight restrictions on movement, security inspections, and intense screening. Staring customs officers, tight questioning, metal detectors, bio-identifiers, computerized facial recognition, and other technological marvels are meant to produce an environment in which people's intentions are "revealed" and suspicious behavior is recognized. As the National Report on 9/11 suggests (2004, 548), to terrorists, "international travel presents great danger, because they must surface to pass through regulated channels, present themselves to border security officials, or attempt to circumvent inspection points." The anxious yet revelatory character of the aviopolis is a crucial part of its political architecture.

Thus, the airport frame is full of suspense ranging from mild irritation and fits of boredom to a thick sense of drama.[1] With this in mind, it is suggested that the international airport has an important performative dimension. Distinct acts in it—ranging from cancelled flights, diverted flights, significant delays and security alerts to the catching of a drug smuggler or a terrorist—may be regarded as dramatic, theatrical, or spectacular. From this perspective, the notion of the "psychological frame" offers a way of understanding the airport as a politico-cultural performance.

The theory of sociopsychological frames, developed by Erving Goffman (1974), offers a methodological tool to understand what takes place when a heterogeneous group of people with diverse ethnic, national, religious, and regional backgrounds come together in the political architecture of an international airport. Within the airport frame, expressive behavior is constituted by a different set of expectations and rules than by which normal life outside the frame proceeds. What are the specifics of the international airport as a performance frame? Augé (1995, 102) differentiates between non-places and anthropological places. Non-places create "solitary contractuality," whereas anthropological places create organically social spheres. Non-places involve people passing without meeting and people coexisting in each other's vicinity without living together (Augé 1999, 110; Crang 2002, 571). At the psychological level, the airport, as a non-place, is taken to refer to a regressive and infantilized experience (Crang 2002, 573). The lack of social features may be taken to imply that these spaces are flat and empty in their meaning other than those having to do with delocalization and fragmentation.

The airport is often treated in terms of people being in limbo. However, I argue that airports differ from non-places like commuter trains, subway stations, supermarkets, elevators, waiting halls, and hotel lobbies. The international airport frame and the experiences in it provide one of the constitutive elements of contemporary empire building, which is defined by the so-called war on terror. In a certain sense, the aviopolis is a place of global order, rather than a non-place.

In the frame theory, the related concept of "flow" denotes the ability of the performance to capture attention. As stated, flow refers to the "cognitive state attained when total engagement with an activity is achieved" (Beeman 1993, 374). Inside the airport frame, the ways in which people become engrossed in the "airport performance" vary: for example, the prototypical figure of an international businessman proceeds through the airport without much cognitive or emotional engagement, whereas the figure of a terrorist is deeply engrossed in the airport performance when he nervously proceeds through the surveillance. The emphasis here is on the politico-psychological flows through which the didactic meaning of the world order is passed on to the differentially ranked populations of the world.

The omnipresent system of signs, codes, and instructions defines the airport experience. They exist everywhere, for example, in the form of tickets, machine-readable passports, boarding passes, visa applications, in-flight forms, and luggage tags. Checks, instructions, prohibitions, and warnings from the monotonous "watch your step" and "unattended bags will be destroyed" to threats of fines and imprisonment provide the context in which people chat, stare, rest, eat, drink, work online, fidget, shop, worry, wonder, call, and so on. The highly coded frame provides a type of operating system, a modus operandi, to manage the flow, the passage through the aviopolis. Its apparent function is to facilitate, differentiate, control, and regulate. However, its pedagogic function is to instruct and prescribe about the "natural" or "apolitical" character of the contemporary imperial order. The governance of the flow manages to show itself as a self-evident system, rather than a highly political tool for teaching the "proper" shape of order.

It is important to realize that the international airport provides a generic and standardized form of architecture. The physical airport architecture has a clear international pattern (e.g., Edwards 1998, 117).[2] However, standardization and conventionalization are also crucial parts of the airport's political architecture (e.g., Crang 2002, 571). As a standardized stock type, the international airport offers a setting for the coming together of an aggregation of people, a model for the world body. The aviopolis is a place where different codes of contact collide and, to a degree, become reconciled. Through offering a common frame, an airport reduces the complexity of codes. However, one should recognize that "the coming together" at the airport modulates and differentiates people's movements, rather than mediates between them. The flows inside the airport frame have different consequences for all its participants: for example, some are stopped, while others are allowed to bypass long lines. This type of airport drama is different from frames where understandings are fused and mediated: "These enclaves of the global elite are places where people do not cross cultural boundaries or experience alterity in interaction. Far from being spaces of mixture or openness, these are heavily hierarchical spaces" (Crang 2002, 572). Thus, airport performance may be regarded as differential in its nature; it is meant to show a degree of difference between figures and to teach according acknowledgment that such differential experience and treatment is inherently acceptable and even natural. The centrality of modulation refers to the recognition of meaningful and value-laden disjunctions between different "types" of people.

Although the public performances at the international airport are overwhelmingly scheduled, regular, well-rehearsed activities that take place according to recognizable patterns, the main focus in the airport frame is deviance. Deviance provides the political emotionality at the airport as the eye is fixed to detect the rogue. From this perspective, interactions in the airport frame can be regarded as "morality plays" (Ericson 1998, 84). Morality plays picture things in a way that is culturally significant: What are the prominent ways of portraying persons of authority and those who are exceptionally deviant? Who are the villains and heroes of the airport play? It is argued that the airport frame stages events in the cloaks of the global, cosmopolitan, and, most importantly, hegemonic or imperial. It puts relevant actors into their respective positions and gives them roles and backgrounds. The metaphors of a terrorist or customs officer, the tropes of the border, sniffer dogs, or duty-free shopping and other political figures of language present at the airport provide the color palette for the visualizing of the contemporary world order. A healthy state of affairs is visualized as smoothness. An unhealthy danger is visualized as chaos, where the rogue has been able to penetrate the checks between the levels in the "proper" hierarchy. People welcome the healthy state and fear any signs of transgression. The air is humorless. Everybody knows that one cannot joke about bombs or terrorists.

One important political emotion that people feel at the airport is different types of world-order compassion. The state of the world order is felt at the airport. Different related sentiments emerge.

My argument is that the narratives of the "American empire" can be used to gain further insights into the airport morality plays. This means that the imperial morality plays give content to what is meant by the world-order pedagogy present in the airport frame and flows. It is important to note that the contemporary notions of U.S. hegemony[3] may be said to be based on different forms of declinist normative images (e.g., Aysha 2003, 429). One major theme of recent hegemony writing has been that of regression, of decline and fall. Arguments of decline have been widely disseminated (e.g., Kennedy 1987; Kupchan 2002; Todd 2003; Diamond 2004).[3] In part, this declinist emphasis is to be expected. It is generic because hegemony has to do with the dynamics of decline and fall. Decline and fall provide a prescription for the use of the concept of empire (Starn 1975, 3). This means that part of the declinist narratives consists of the hegemony/empire being a diagnosis with a powerful prognostic inference. Although the notion of empire is a signifier of great power and vast resources, it also augurs eventual doom and makes its contemporaneous observers acutely sensitive toward the symptoms of decline. It can be argued that the U.S. morality plays, focused on the belief that tomorrow will be theirs, are complemented by speculations of imperial doom and gloom and of the U.S. empire as an "enterprise gradually fading" (Laqueur 1993, 388).

In a more specific sense, it can be argued that the declinist imagery provides the dramatic tension necessary to sustain the flow of imperial morality plays at airports. This can be exemplified by the cat-and-mouse type of narrative of terrorists running loose and the eleventh-hour type of narrative of a shoe bomber being stopped by a vigilant flight attendant. The general flow is energized by declinist visions of mass destruction and increasingly vulnerable homeland security. The striking contrasts and dramatic tensions are managed and maintained with the help of these narratives. The result is that the legitimacy of the wide-ranging measures taken in the war on terror is passed on.

The visual signs on the aviopolis's skin, or exterior, become important. When one arrives at an international airport, the eye equipped with Western standards scans around to see signs of decay. The shoddy state of the airport, the age of its equipment, the cleanliness of its corridors, the stench of its waiting area, and the neatness of the authorities' uniforms turn into emotional signifiers. They either reassure or repulse. The visuality of the airport tells a story of the position of the location in the international order of things and about the state of the hierarchy itself. Such experiences arouse political emotions of inferiority and superiority. They translate into an identity experience. One feels one's position in the hierarchy, while also constructing a schema of that hierarchy. In certain cases, these identity plays lead to worry. For example, when visiting a Western airport, bad visual cues can lead to a sense of deteriorating world order: "The West is not what it used to be." This political emotion consists of feelings for the world order and of world-order nostalgia.

Declinist feelings often concentrate on the signs of decaying public virtue and disrespect of the public creed. In this respect, the deviance is read as a sign of norms, values, and institutions falling into disrespect. The morality plays of the airport frame concentrate on pointing out proper behavior and the dangers of deviance. Dangerous deviance is embodied in the forms of the drug smuggler, the illegal immigrant, the abuser of asylum policies, and, in particular, the form of the international terrorist. The regular nature of the airport and the smoothness of the passage across the global space signify the power of the prescribed rules of imperial wholesomeness and revivalism as opposed to declinist prognosis. In this way, any single traveler who successfully and smoothly passes through great distances can be said to indicate the strength of the underlying imperial values and its core civil religion. In the same way, the drug dealer who is caught at arrival by a sniffer dog provides a public demonstration of the effective existence of the global normative structure.

Imperial Hub-and-Spoke and Declinism

In order to better understand the imperial morality plays and the dramatic flows contained in the frame of the international aviopolis, the wider political architecture of its spaces needs to be explored. On the regional scale, the airport is integrated into a wider transport network, most notably through rail connections. The different means of national transport are increasingly fully integrated. On a more global scale, the system of smaller and larger airports provides the wider political architecture. The creation of the hub-and-spoke network was one of the biggest developments in the airline industry during the 1970s and 1980s (Bhadra and Hechtman 2004, 28). Hubs refer to major airports with many connections radiating from them, whereas a spoke is a place with only a few connections. The hub is used by a major airline as the base of its operations. The hub-and-spoke network is based on the idea that it makes more economic sense to fly planes from one major airport to smaller ones than to try to connect all airports to each other: "The reasons for the prominence of hubs is simple: by combining passengers at a common connecting point, carriers can offer more service to more cities at much less cost . . ." (Butler and Huston 1999, 52).

Who feels at home in an international hub? And who feels out of place? The airport provides a setting for the expression of the underlying values of being a member of the global community. One way of answering the questions concerning who is at home in the global space is to look at various airport rankings. The 2003 International Air Transport Association's (IATA) Global Airport Monitor Survey included 51 hubs—25 in Europe, 9 in the Asia Pacific, 14 in the Americas, and 3 in Africa. The purpose of the survey was to measure customer satisfaction and the level of customer service at the "top performing airports," based on tens of thousands of interviews. The measures included ground transportation to/from the airport, the ease of finding one's way through the airport, and restaurants/eating facilities. On IATA's list, the top places for overall passenger satisfaction went to the Asia Pacific airports. The top three are in Dubai, Singapore, and Hong Kong. The IATA list can be compared to the Airports Council International's (ACI's) measures of passenger traffic, cargo volume, and aircraft movement in major airports. Measured in passenger traffic (in 2003), the world's top hubs were Atlanta, Chicago, London, Tokyo, Los Angeles, Dallas, Frankfurt, Paris, Amsterdam, and Denver. As expected and seen from these surveys, globality as defined by feeling at home is very unevenly distributed on the map.

If one examines more closely the airports included in the IATA survey, the hierarchical network structure becomes even more evident. For example, the performance evaluation concerning the world's "major airports" lists airports from the "Americas." The 14 airports from the Americas were Bermuda International, Cincinnati/Northern Kentucky, Detroit Metropolitan, Washington Dulles, Los Angeles International, Miami International, Minneapolis/St. Paul, San Diego, Seattle Tacoma, San Jose Juan Santa Maria, Halifax, Montreal Dorval, Vancouver, and Toronto. The list does not include airports from the Latin American countries. Actually, the list includes airports only from the United States, Canada, South Africa, Australia, the so-called Asian economic miracles, and Europe. In several respects, the imagery contained in the global airport network resembles various known visions of the so-called new world order led by the hyper-power, the United States. Another famous depiction of world order comes to mind: The famous map—listing the "hub civilizations," the relations between them, and the "spoke civilizations" (e.g., Africa and Latin America)—produced by Samuel Huntington (1993, 25) bears a close family resemblance to the way in which the aviopolis is arranged. This map of clashing civilizations to a degree then becomes the object of power replication and the political pedagogy of the space. The traveler is meant to construct this hierarchical hub-and-spoke system as the world's body and internalize its modus operandi when constructing himself within it.

The list of the world's busiest airports reveals that the imperial imagery may provide a more relevant clue to why and for what purpose the political architecture of the aviopolis exists. Besides bearing a resemblance to the Huntingtonian map, the global hub-and-spoke system can be compared to the other modern imperial visions. Lieven (1999, 163) draws a relevant dichotomy between minimalist and extensive visions of empire: On the one hand, there are modern maritime and network centered empires, and, on the other hand, more ancient alternatives exist that are composed of "huge, multi-ethnic polities, governed by . . . centralized bureaucracies and absolute monarchs."[4]

The more or less explicit lesson from past experiences seems to be that a modern world power should rely on a network of nodes and linkages rather than on extensive and direct occupation of territory (e.g., Modelski 1983, 1; Thompson and Zuk 1986, 249). Territorial occupation is considered a dangerous trap for a world power, which, instead, should rely on a system of military bases that guard important global connections: "And as territorial responsibilities proliferate, there is an increased need for land-based armies (and their associated expenses) first to conquer the new territories, then to defend them against rivals, and, inevitably, to suppress/ police subsequent tendencies toward revolt, unrest and disintegration" (Thompson and Zuk 1986, 250).

The hub-and-spoke system allows for the creation of a global communal core without extensive and direct territorial contact and, thus, without the dangers of a "territorial trap." It may be said that the network-based imperial hierarchy is knit together by the air travel system. Air travel can create a physical region out of a network covering tens of thousands of kilometers. It manages to create an economically vibrant and political power hub of the world "whilst simultaneously separating and bypassing other, 'irrelevant', people and places" (Dodge and Kitchin 2004, 211). Thus, much stress is placed on an efficient and flexible, yet also hierarchical and differential network structure.

Individuals experiencing the stop-and-go flow through the aviopolis sense the more extensive world body of which they become a part. The existence of a network of imperial imagery can be linked to the consistency of travel between the nodes. It can be suggested that the secure and safe nature of travel along the global arteries provides the fundamental prescription for the world order. The hegemonic network conveys a sense of extensive geographical existence spreading across local boundaries. The continuous existence of the world order requires advanced knowledge and skills connected with maintaining long-distance links and with consistent travel along these global arteries. In other words, the continuing existence of the present power hierarchy requires the related knowhow and consistency. The state of this knowhow may be readily evaluated at international crossroads. Smooth travel along such passages signifies a healthy, stable, and predictable world order. Delays, cancellations, and long waits translate into one's disempowered position in the hierarchy or to the bad shape of the whole hierarchy.

Kaplan (1993), in his declinist essay, "The Coming Anarchy," reads signs of things to come from changes in the global and local transportation network. Kaplan senses the decline while traveling through the aviopolis and observing the state of affairs from an airplane. The Kaplanian world atlas is composed of "cities and suburbs in an environment that has been mastered". A large number of the similes and metaphors that Kaplan employs refer to places where people meet and come across each other. These are the knots which he uses to predict the alarming future, the spread of "criminal anarchy." He looks into the state of airports, roads, schools, police stations, and bridges in the Third World. These crossroads are at the same time sites of gradual demise and the last strongholds against the spread of the criminal anarchy which threatens to spread to the First World. In this sense, the modus operandi of Kaplan's political cartography refers to the cordon sanitaire type of thinking (Dalby 1996, 472).[5] Kaplan's declinist imagery is composed of intersections and connecting lines of communication, which are at the same time channels of contagion of the disease of failing civil religion.

Thus, in Kaplan's markedly conservative declinism, the world atlas is being replaced by a system of nodes and connecting lines. The international mosaic of clearly demarcated and bordered states is being replaced by a map consisting of passages leading from one island of political order to another. The connector connotes a sense of travel and of space that needs to be crossed while traveling. Not surprisingly, Kaplan's imagery resembles Samuel Huntington's famous map of civilizational conflict, which is also comprised of nodes and links; the system of connectors, which stand for a type of influence, conveys the idea of cultural separation between the nodes, or civilizations. For practical purposes, the more antagonistic the relationship, the longer the connector between the nodes. The length of the connector seems to reflect the uncertainty of the relationship and, thus, gives a sense of unsafe and difficult travel/contact between the distant nodes.

The bleakness of the Kaplanian and Huntingtonian visions refers to the decaying and dangerous connectors which make the long-distance world order increasingly more difficult to maintain. In this submergence type of declinist imagery, there are two intertwined reasons for the decaying staying power of modern empires. On the one hand, the maintenance of technological skills becomes threatened by a lack of adherence to proper rules and procedures. On the other, the task in hand becomes increasingly complex when more and more places and people become knitted into the global fabric. People are simply overwhelmed by their connectedness.

Thus, it can be suggested that the morality plays at global crossroads take two corresponding forms. First, they are celebrations of rule following and consistency. This is when people at the airport demonstrate faithful adherence to procedures, signs, orders, and types. The state of modernity becomes evaluated in the orderliness of the movements across the global space. The orderliness of people's movements at the airport embodies the existence of a global knowhow and the prescriptive force of global norms. A clear airport sign system and smooth flows of people signify the health of the underlying political order and reassure the traveler of its power against the declinist imagery. Random and arbitrary flows translate into experiences of injustice. One's movements in the intestines of the world order are signifiers of its possible convulsions. This reading of the emotionality of the airport corresponds with the neoclassical vorticity model. The kinetics of movements constructs the mood one has about the world and its futurity.

In the sense of rule following and consistency, the aviopolis signifies linkage and connection. One may argue that inside the hub-and-spoke network, the morality and pedagogic plays concentrate on the skills of being in contact. On the other hand, the homage of major international centers of contact to the airport itself becomes important. In this respect, the airport turns into a place of reverence. It may be said that inside its structure and through movements across it, the local, regional, and imperial power and legitimacy are measured, acknowledged, and affirmed. One concrete measure is the condition of the airport itself, which is seen as a signifier of the place where it exists. The airports at the imperial centers are expected to be more state-of-the-art than the airports at the periphery. This is the measuring rod of power.

At Western airports located in the hegemonic heartland, the iconic departures board should indicate smooth flows. The expectation is that the flow of "right" people, businessmen and tourists, should also be efficient and the facilities the latest and most sophisticated.[6]

However, an additional anticipation is that the notion of security should be very visible. The global body is expected to be on guard. The stops need not be entirely negative in this regard. The lines through security checks, when people take their shoes and belts off and put their liquid goods into plastic bags, can lead to feelings of a secure order. This is especially true of the U.S. airports in the core of the empire. However, an intricate balance exists between legitimate security delays and one's expectations of smoothness of travel. The general rule seems to be that while the international "road warriors" experience relatively smooth rides, the flow of some other people is hampered and that of still others even stopped altogether to signify an undiluted imperial character.

Second, the morality plays are meant to demonstrate that the core imperial element is not going to be submerged and diluted. The membranes separating different people are inherently semipermeable. The declinist sense of submergence takes on an explicitly hierarchical and differential form. They point out the different places for different people. The stage is set for the argument that when it comes to the citizenship of the world, not everybody is treated as equal. This is taken for granted. At the airport, people feel this to be the legitimate starting point. They are compliant to differences in treatment. The specific content of the submergence plays includes long lines at the immigration counters under the sign "Others" as compared to "U.S. Citizens Only". The efficient and secure reduction of people into a hierarchy of types is considered imperative even at the cost of efficiency and smoothness.

For Kaplan, suspended and delayed flight connections provide the central metaphors for attempts to stop the spread of anarchy and decay. The following quote is illuminating: "Returning from West Africa last fall was an illustrating ordeal. After leaving Adibjan, my Air Afrique flight landed in Dakar, Senegal, where all passengers had to disembark in order to go through another security check, this one demanded by U.S. authorities before they would permit the flight to set out for New York. Once we were in New York, despite the midnight hour, immigration officials at Kennedy Airport held up disembarkation by conducting quick interrogations of the aircraft's passengers—this was in addition to all the normal immigration and customs procedures. It was apparent that drug smuggling, disease, and other factors had contributed to the toughest security procedures I have ever encountered when returning from overseas" (Kaplan 1993, 478). The disturbed and torturous flight connection illustrates the problems of the global space, yet, in the Kaplanian imagery, it also points to the fact that the West is protecting itself against being submerged by the coming wave of criminal anarchy. This protection is justified and legitimate according to him, although he senses trouble in the future.

International airports, as the places for contemporary international borders, provide the scene for the imperial morality plays of submergence. This is because, in declinist imagery, the danger of submergence is often associated with the alarming influx of immigrants. Huntington (1998, 304) singles out immigration as the source of potential decay in a political community. Flows of migrants dilute and overwhelm the proper moral order of the West. Of particular concern are those immigrants "from other civilizations who reject assimilation and continue to adhere to and propagate the values, customs, and cultures of their home societies." It seems that Huntington equates global civil religion with Western greed.

What make this source of decay even more potent are the modern forms of communication. Previously, once immigrants crossed regional and continental divides, they largely lost contact with their native landscape. According to Huntington (1997, 38), contemporary forms of contact do not cut immigrants' umbilical cords in the same way. Links and contacts remain, turning people coming from different civilizations into bridgeheads of decay and erosion. They are sources of dangerous connectedness between incompatible civilizations and, therefore, turn into something akin to a lethal contagious disease. Huntington refers to the "contagion model" when he evokes the psychiatric metaphor. He sees decaying countries suffering migratory flows as schizophrenic (Huntington 1998, 306). This disease results from allowing foreign elements into domestic environments and even cherishing this in the name of diversity. For Huntington, this is a sign of submergence because it creates promiscuous mixtures of different civilizations and countries composed of people who are incompatible. The hierarchy is threatened by leakage between its levels, which should be cordoned off.

Airports, Stop-and-Go Movement, and Memory

People are on the move in the contemporary world.[7] This chapter has focused on the political pedagogy inherent in the airport experience, which ties together individual movement and the dynamics of world order. The relationship between this public performance and personal airport experience needs to be expanded in order to understand how people sense political fundamentals through their experiences. It is claimed that the airport relates to a larger political context by offering a shared place for remembering and memorizing. The intimate relationship between memory, thought, and movement is central to understanding the memory-creating and memory-shaping effects of the international airport. The argument is that the physical motion of a private person through the various places of an airport corresponds to movement in a shared memory of the world order. This correspondence produces not only specific memories, but, more importantly, an acknowledgment of a particular method of recognizing substance, worth, and legitimacy. This acknowledgment of a method of ordering cannot be achieved without a degree of emotional engrossment. The declinist morality plays provide the necessary dramaturgy that integrates the psychological flow, the creation of memory, the movement through an airport, and the acknowledgment of a hierarchical ordering method into one pedagogic performance.

Instead of merely referring to a passive storage capacity, memory can be understood as an active faculty that is inherently intertwined with action and motion (Carruthers 1990, 130). It is significant that in the Western art-of-memory tradition, public speech is based on the ability to remember and to relate extempore the content of memory to a particular situation at hand. In this tradition, different parts of the speech are placed into a carefully constructed imaginary locus. From a historical perspective, the models of proper loci included valued buildings, for example, temples, public buildings, or churches.[8] The speaker places the "items" inherent in his speech into this normatively sanctioned imaginary locus. The locus, then, contains rooms which "stores" different parts of the speech in them. In order to recollect, one has to move his mind in the imaginary locus. Thus, the act of public speaking becomes a counterpart to the mind's imaginary movement in the place of memory. The movement of the speech corresponds to the mind's movement in the imaginary locus. Generalizing from this culturally influential tradition, coherent public behavior corresponds to smooth movement in the imaginary space where the collective inventory of "proper" memories is stored. From this perspective, it is possible to examine the content of the airport and the political mnemonics contained therein.

In the traditional art-of-memory practice, the models for the imaginary memory locus had to have a clear and consistent architecture. It was thought that the details of the structure facilitated memory through being clearly patterned, but also through containing a remarkable quality. In this spirit, influential classical scholars from Cicero to Aquinas stressed the use of "striking images" to remember the parts of the imaginary locus where precise memories were stored, that is, the rooms. It was generally held that these parts/rooms should be characteristically extraordinary and outstanding to be emotionally unforgettable. The striking images put into these template places were meant to facilitate remembering by being unforgettable. In this respect, the proper memory holds strange, extraordinary, and odd images inside a clearly patterned architecture.

The airport architecture assists remembering and memorizing by containing an overall consistent form, together with striking parts. In this regard, the airport is a vehicle of memory and understanding. It can be argued that the wandering of the eye and the corresponding movement of the mind while a person walks through an airport is not a passive reflection, but a tool in the production of socially sanctioned, virtuous, and prudent understanding. In this way, the art-of-memory tradition can be used to discern the normative content of an airport. Airports can be thought of as repositories of global memory and public ethos.

The movement-memory link becomes consequential. It is relevant that the smoothness of the movement in the physical airport space and in the corresponding imaginary locus indicates one's position in the global space. It can be argued that the smoothness of movement is related to one's capacity as an author of/in public functions. It also relates to what one remembers at the airport. The lower one's position in the global hierarchy, the more difficult one's movement should be and the less world-order memory is revealed. The airport contains normatively sanctioned memories—valued memories from the perspective of moving in the imperial hierarchal networks.

Besides concentrating on the movement in the overall airport locus, the particular places of the airport are noteworthy. The places of the airport locus—for example, check-in, security control, departure hall, customs, and passport control—have unforgettable images attached to them. These images serve the function of pointing out the bad, odd, and deviant in global life. It can be suggested that these striking images become meaningful in the overall political architecture. This means that imperial morality plays provide the overall form for the striking images.

From a more general perspective, the specific places where people collect their airport memories comprise trams, shuttle buses, check-in halls, departure lounges, airport shopping malls, walkways, airport buses, lounges, gates, flights, security checks, baggage reclaim areas, passport controls, and customs. Although most people collect memories from only a rather straightforward passage through the airport, almost all are well aware of the existence of other places inside the airport locus—the immigration offices, interrogation rooms, and airport detention places. The "rooms" of the airport are suspenseful repositories of instructive memories. People stopped at the check-in, immigration or security-check counters recollect meanings about their position, about the relative position of others, and about the common global framework defined by the differential positions.

The morality play of submergence provides an unforgettable context for the striking images of 9/11. Many remember the image caught from the surveillance video at Dulles International Airport on September 11, 2001, which showed a terrorist passing through. The whole video shows five of the day's terrorists going through the security check. Three of them are exposed to additional scrutiny by handheld metal detectors, but are allowed eventually to continue on their fateful mission. The images were striking enough to make the front pages of major newspapers around the world when the Congressional report on 9/11 was released in July 2004. The report states: "Nawaf al Hazmi set off the alarms for both the first and second metal detectors and was then hand-wanded before being passed. In addition, his over-the-shoulder carry-on bag was swiped by an explosive trace detector and then passed. The video footage indicates that he was carrying an unidentified item in his back pocket, clipped to its rim" (*The 9/11 Report* 2004, 7). The striking images of 9/11 stand for surprise, but also for lack of alertness: "[The hijackers] defeated all the security layers that America's civil aviation security system then had in place to prevent a hijacking" (*The 9/11 Report* 2004, 7). These security layers correspond to the differences between the hierarchical levels in the level of world-order imagery. From the perspective of submergence and associated political emotions, the ease with which the hijackers cleared the checkpoints contains a lesson regarding the consequences of lax boundaries and failed hierarchies.

The collective images of 9/11 provide the most important contemporary memory template related to air traffic and airports. For example, Carolyn Ellis (2002), in an article on the meaning of 9/11, recounts from an ethnographic perspective her personal experiences in flight and at the airport on the morning of that fateful day. She starts by recalling the state of normalcy in which her flight began. The captain had said that ". . . we'll have you at the gate early. The skies are clear and it should be a smooth flight." The fact that the plane was on schedule had a reassuring effect. However, from small signs, she started to perceive that something out of the ordinary was taking place: "I am almost finished with the *USA Today* when suddenly the three flight attendants march decidedly and briskly in step to the front of the plane, enter the cockpit, and close the door." After this, Carolyn's body got into alert mode. She was in a heightened state of tension, looking around for potential signs of trouble. The captain stated what was taking place and that the plane, together with all in-air planes, would land at the nearest airport.

The anxiety and nervousness, together with the extraordinary images of the day, provided a locus for understanding and recollecting what 9/11 meant. The interrupted flights crashing into buildings became signifiers of memory and meaning. Much of this locus found its embodiment in airports, air traffic, and airplanes. Ellis (2002, 377) continues by stating that what took place had a strong effect on her memory. The impact was frame-breaking in that what she previously took for granted, like "walking through an airport," was no longer a certainty.

The fact that the movements through an airport were affected signified and represented a shaken world order. It translated into a very emotional walk, into a politically meaningful walk. The disturbed movements across the airport offered another locus for constructing the emerging meaning of 9/11. Ellis continues her personal story at the airport by recounting the difficulties of placing a call, the impossibility of collecting luggage, the people gathered around the TV screens, the long lines at the car rental area, and the relief of finally getting a car. The interruptions to her supposedly and normally continuous flow, together with the associated striking emotional experiences, contextualized the events for her and for many others.

The smoothness with which people proceed through the global arteries and across hierarchical layers is no minor matter from the perspective of imperial pedagogy. The notion of a stop-and-go movement allows a tool for the fuller appreciation of the airport experience. There are places where everybody has to stop and places where only some are stopped. It can be argued that stops are places with content. From places such as passport control, customs, and check-in counters, travelers collect content for their memory that can be later recollected in accounts of airport experiences. It can be further claimed that the "stops" signify the presence of a higher authority, while the "gos" indicate a sense that one is authorized, imbued with authority.

More importantly, it may be suggested that the properties of a stop-and-go intertwine the individual airport experience with the overall flow of the world order. The overall flows can be distinguished in terms of pace, viscosity, consistency, and degree of confinement (Urry 2000, 32). The crucial link between the private and the public is provided by the hypothesis that the airport's political architecture provides the context in which the larger flows of the world's political architecture can be experienced, acknowledged, and memorized. In a sense, a person realizes his own identity and place in the prevailing world order through the pace of the walk through an airport. This acknowledgment of one's own identity involves the recognition of a particular form of world order which fits the identity. The consistency of the walk through the airport further raises the level of acknowledgment as does the degree to which airport walk-throughs are confined, clear, or easy. From this perspective, the following description of an airport experience is inherently connected with tales of the American empire's gradual decline: "Meals, overcrowding, abusive passengers, cramped seating, poor cabin service, and the sheer boredom of being stranded in air terminals for inhumanely long waits are also on the growing lists of laments from consumers. . . . Flying is now a scene in which progressively more people express outrage at overcrowding, frequent delays, bumping, poor service, and lousy meals" (Gottdiener 2001, 2, 4). The link between this spreading culture of inconvenience and the declinists' visions of world politics exemplifies the pedagogic function of international airport hubs: troubled and anomic movement through an airport indicates sparse worldwide political networks, nondynamic political space, and a future which lacks consistency.

To sum up, an airport can be said to comprise a place where one goes to collect a sense of identity. A vital ingredient of the airport experience is that one goes there to see who one is in the worldwide who's who. This collection of one's identity is inherently connected with recollection, or with the airport's ability to provide unforgettable images. Complementing the recollection of identity is the learning and memorizing of the interrelated framework in which the individual identities fit.

Intertwined Bodily Kinetics

The international airport may be regarded as a place where global thoughts and memories are made. Much of this is based on the imagery of the airport as an inventory of types. Along with "legitimate" types of people, such as businessmen, tourists, immigrants, natives, and Westerners, the international airport also holds stereotypical figures of terrorists, suspect Arabs, Third Worlders, people of different ethnicities, people of color, and illegal immigrants. The politically meaningful distinctions between the many types of people are fine and nuanced. An airport provides a particularly well-suited place to study the present-day hierarchical world-order imagery. The experienced eye, which has been politically conditioned through frequent airport experiences, quickly looks around for the airport types. This eye does not belong only to the border or security guard. It belongs potentially to any person placed in the intensity of intermeshing with people at an airport. Placed in the airport, a person recognizes the types and remembers his own respective position among them. To walk across the airport frame is to simultaneously learn and remember the global context of the international airport.

The airport experience has an ontological quality to it which connects airport behavior with the production of identities. Airports have become the loci of reassurance and security against the submergence of identities and disruptions in vital flows. They signify the sovereignty and security of the imagined worldwide political community. The smoothness of one's entry and exit represents one's position in the political community. In this way, the whole community is present in the halls of international entry and exit. The way one moves across these spaces represents one's status and identity. The trip through an international airport reassures people of their belonging to the world; however, there are people whose identities are shaken and whose sense of coziness is taken away. The experience sets up an image around which people can deposit not only their anxieties, but also themselves (Daniels et al. 2001, 386). It seems that the question of "how real the security threats actually are" is not as significant as the perceived need to secure the continued existence of the imaginary landscape in which "cosmopolitan," "global," and "imperial" people belong.

It can be said that the economy of satisfaction constitutes one layer of the wider economy of anxiety in the airport frame. Another important layer is constituted by suspicion. The sources of the economy of suspicion are connected to how one behaves in the political architecture of the airport and who one is turned into. This means that there is a behavioral—how one behaves—and prejudicial—what is one's type—component to the economy of suspicion. The evaluation of these components derives from how the current imperial form of world order is pictured. The changes in the world order toward a more hierarchical form, as symbolized by 9/11, have had an enormous influence on what takes place at an airport. From this perspective, the selective and highly skewed distribution of anxiety, satisfaction, and suspicion across various people are tightly connected with the airport hub's pedagogic mission. This political architecture of the airport performance is meant to teach people of the basic importance of the United States–led war on terror. The striking reminders placed throughout the airport frame are meant to drive home the fact that survival is at stake and that the need to survive makes it necessary and legitimate to be on the lookout for certain types of people. At an airport, the public world-order interests converge with the private traveler's interests in a way that often goes understated when the airport is treated in terms of a non-space. The modern airport hub highlights knowledge and skills that are thought to be fundamental for a life in the contemporary world order.

The complexity of the international airport poses a direct challenge to its normative function as a socially pedagogic crossroads and memory locus. Irrespective of the specific reasons for getting lost, being delayed, deported, arrested, or killed, hindrances at the aviopolis signal problems in what it stands for, that is, in the normatively sanctioned form of global space. However, when interpreted against the background of declinist imagery, a small number of problems at the imperial airport provide the necessary dramatic tension for the morality plays. The occasional inconsistency and an element of submergence work only to underscore the pedagogy of the aviopolis. From this perspective, declinist drama is needed so that the didactic meaning won't be lost in monotony. It is at the tense moments, when the individual at the airport is being reminded successfully of the value of the sanctioned world order, that the decline and fall is transmuted into memories of Western revival and triumph.

6

Political Compassions under Pandemic Spectacles

> Once again, nature has presented us with a daunting challenge: the possibility of an influenza pandemic. . . . Together we will confront this emerging threat and together, as Americans, we will be prepared to protect our families, our communities, this great nation, and our world.
>
> *President George W. Bush, November 2005*

World-order compassions that take place under pandemic threats provide an additional way to understand the various implications of the vorticity model. Similar to the increasing worry over global warming, (re)emerging pandemic threats lead to communal sentiments, which perceive in them a common enemy to the human polity as well as a hierarchical vision of that polity. Pandemics also directly bind individual bodies with the hegemonic body, thereby leading to what may be considered politico-somatic links. I will review here how the changing global hierarchy—the post-9/11 wars in Afghanistan and, more particularly, in Iraq—were reflected in the politico-somatics of the severe acute respiratory syndrome (SARS) and avian influenza. In order to realize the admittedly ambitious aims of this chapter, I will contextualize the present pandemic sentiments in a long history of encounters with lethal epidemic diseases. The main idea is that "dis-ease" at the level of the individual somatic body may be seen as a part of a larger movement in the global political hierarchy.

This chapter reviews different historically and culturally conditioned roles and positions available to actors in pandemic dramas. Although it concentrates on the contemporary pandemic scene, the aim is to examine also precursor epidemic scares such as bovine spongiform encephalopathy (BSE, or mad cow disease), tuberculosis and Spanish flu, going back all the way to the plague. The politics of pandemics can be better appreciated though the concepts of legitimacy and pedagogy plays that have been developed in the last two chapters. International actors use pandemics to further their own visions of world order. This means that pandemics are turned into demonstrations, theaters of proof of the value of the hegemonic order. Lethal epidemic diseases occur all the time without pushing their way up into global awareness—for example, HIV/AIDS and malaria. At the same time, the alarm and panic over these short-term human and animal epidemics have often reached spectacular proportions even though the actual human health consequences have been less than dramatic. The aim is to review specific cases to determine what situations in international politics are predisposed to the politicization of diseases and what types of diseases are especially prone to this.

Contemporary Visions

In his *New York Times* book review published on November 27, 2005, Matt Steinglass examines Mike Davis's book, *The Monster at Our Door: The Global Threat of Avian Flu*. The debate that ensues highlights the discourse dynamics of recent epidemic scares. Mike Davis's argument is that humanity is going to face a catastrophic encounter with a pandemic influenza if it does not stop sleepwalking. His rhetoric or, more clearly, pedagogic strategy is to alarm though powerful descriptors given to the emerging viruses: These "monsters at our door" are "extraordinary shape-shifters" capable of "ultra-fast evolutionary adaptation." He explicates the "root" causes for the coming into being of such threats: the profit-focused pharmaceutical industry and the breakdown of the leadership in world health, together with social changes in the globalizing world (e.g., Third World urbanization). He sees that these twofold factors pose an extraordinary strain on "human solidarity." On the other hand, environmental changes, such as global warming, are going to cause an upheaval in the nature–humanity relationship. In his review, Steinglass considers these often-mentioned points valuable, but considers the main argument rhetorical. In other words, it is not the description it claims to be, but an advocacy piece meant to hype up the book and to foster a particular way of thinking about global health: "[People like Davis] are wielding apocalyptic anxiety as a tool toward a greater end: the construction of a global system of influenza surveillance and vaccine research and delivery to protect mankind wherever the next pandemic does, inevitably, break out." If the review is of value, what may be considered "pandemic-speak" is closely related to the earlier genre of health propaganda, which serves multiple purposes under the shadow of pandemic anxiety.

Davis argues for the importance of "human solidarity," or together-minded compassion for each other. This way of defining human polity reminds one of the classical formulations of politics as a human space for deliberation over the conditions of just and happy life. Rhetoric, as part of political deliberation, is based on the existence and on the (re)discovery of the area of together-mindedness in order to allow for further communal persuasion. From this perspective, the politics of pandemic-speak tries to continuously rediscover the persuasive element that allows human polity to maintain its immunity from environmental hazards. The political pedagogy of pandemic-speak is there to advise and warn against intra-communal disorder—for example, greedy pharmaceutical companies—and to remind people of the continual threat posed by nature.

However, pandemic-speak is not value-neutral. It interacts with the other political worries of the time—with terrorism and globalization in the present era. It inevitably contains a particular vision of human solidarity, namely, of the particular shape of the political order. I will examine how historical cases have demonstrated the world-order–pandemic nexus as well as how the various actors of the present pandemic scares establish their visions of human solidarity. The avian flu scare is the focus of this chapter, although the approach is general. The role of the different stakeholders needs to be mapped out vis-à-vis each other in any comprehensive study of pandemic emergencies (Padmawati and Nichter 2008, 32). What types of political arguments are involved in their global health rhetoric? What are the roles available for the customary actors of international relations? What types of co-optive and collaborative patterns have materialized during the recent avian flu scare? How do the grand movements in world politics interact with pandemics?

Contemporary Pandemic Frame

Although the transmission of avian flu to humans takes place almost exclusively through domesticated species, much of the global attention is curiously fixated on the disease in wild birds (e.g., Jennings and Read 2006, 21). This highlights one of the most persistent themes or thresholds of recent pandemic scares—humanity's relationship with nature, or the nature/humanity boundary.

In his tellingly titled book, *Landscapes of Fear*, geographer Yi-Fu Tuan expresses a crucial aspect of lethal epidemic diseases when he states that "sickness forcefully directs a people's attention to the world's hostility." The association between sicknesses and hostilities is the key point. It can be interpreted in two ways. First, epidemics direct the attention to the hostility between nature and humanity. Many of the recent health scares translate into "crossing of the species barrier" dramas. The common theme is that a border that should not have been violated has been transgressed with the result that nature has turned hostile to human ways. Recent examples of these "crossing of the species barrier" dramas include avian flu, BSE, and HIV/AIDS. The narratives of the origin of HIV/AIDS offer a case in point. It was reported early in the 1980s that the pandemic originated from Africa, where it jumped from chimpanzees to human beings (e.g., Fauci 1999). This story was revisited in Keele et al.'s (2006) study, which localized the epicenter of the transmission to southern Cameroon and to the decade of the 1930s. BSE provides another clear example of the anxieties associated with the species barrier (e.g., Mahy and Brown 2000, 33).

In these boundary dramas, societal human factors are also considered. Many diseases are connected with the pathologies of globalization. Although nature is seen as hostile, it changes at the societal level and allows lethal epidemic diseases to emerge. The spread of Ebola in 1996 in what was then Zaire was blamed on new infrastructure development in Africa and the anxiety it caused was explained by the possibility that the global hub-and-spoke system of air travel could spread the deadly Ebola virus all around the world in a matter of hours. Many (re)emerging diseases are also associated with environmental degradation and global warming. They are seen as signs of failures by the globalizing world community and of nature fighting back at "unnatural" human ways.

Second, the idea resonates with hostility within humanity—the multidimensional fractions that run across humanity become acute when epidemics receive their communal interpretation. The political boundaries of states and nationalities in particular provide ready-made signifiers. The existing patterns of political hostility offer a means of translating epidemic diseases into culturally understandable roles. The records of both BSE and SARS offer evidence of this. Before spring 1996, BSE was considered to be a managed disease. It was thought to be confined to animals and largely to the United Kingdom (UK). The crises of 1996 turned the disease into a "British disease," embodying the UK government's independent-minded Europe policy and rapid de-regularization during the Thatcher years. SARS was regarded as a novel disease threat and perceived as an especially dangerous and difficult to contain problem. However, its meaning was partly synchronized with the existing patterns in world politics. The patterns of blame reflected existing political animosities: in Canada and Taiwan, news reports blamed Hong Kong; Japan blamed Taiwan; Taiwan blamed China; the Chinese press blamed people from the Guangzhou province; and the Western press placed the blame on China. In many places, the disease was perceived to be associated with China or with people of ethnic Chinese origin. To a degree, the images of China as secretive, closed, incompetent, and corrupt contributed to this association. China is still an outsider in the international community and seen as a country with limited transparency, partial reform, and uneven development.

It may be argued that pandemics are produced through patterns of collaboration between a diversity of actors representing different relevant background themes. This interaction is part of wider world politics in a way that exposes pandemic-related international interaction to the world's political vorticity. The contained emotionality, or the more general background mood, varies with changing epochs. Consequently, pandemics, as embodiments of "dis-eases," are reflective of the underlying form and state of the prevailing political community and the motions in its power hierarchy. In this sense, the specific forms that diseases take are revealing of the underlying political dynamic. Figuratively speaking, they provide an X-ray of their embeddings (Herdt 1992, 8).

Thus, it may be argued that different political environments develop different politicized pandemics. For example, Ebola's emergence in the bipolar world of 1976 raised few concerns, whereas its post–cold war era reemergence in Zaire in 1996 led to worldwide attention and fear. The BSE crisis of 1996 stemmed from the underlying anxieties felt over the enlargement and deepening integration in Europe and the SARS of 2003 had a lot to do with the growing pains of the United States–led world order. It took shape in the anxious environment leading to war with Iraq. This war was based on the premise of Iraq's alleged weapons of mass destruction, which included biological disease agents. Susan Sontag's (2001) notion of epidemic diseases as always ideally comprehensible entities in their own time is illuminating. They fit their political power surroundings and their alarming nature takes shape in contrast with the prevailing sensibilities.

Diseases seem to exist, flourish, and die in bio-political environments, where they adapt to local memories, practices, and power hierarchies. In the case of pandemics, this environment is global. For example, the international community's responses to avian flu were commonly based on the practical logic developed based on existing stereotypes, media representations, government information campaigns, and popular rumors (Padmawati and Nichter 2008, 31). However, in most studies on lethal epidemic diseases, this political aspect is missing or only implicitly recognized.

It has often been suggested that communities have socially adaptive responses to familiar diseases—recurring diseases have led to the development of social practices with political implications. In other words, studies indicate an adaptive wisdom that stems from the local memories of past epidemics. This cultural resource is considered as a knowledge base which can be put into operation when an outbreak hits (Zhang and Pan 2008, 19). Studies attach much value to these communal coping mechanisms, although they are seen as very different from the responses of the modern international community. The communal responses are often deemed even to be rational. However, the qualitative difference does not change the fact that even the responses of the international community are based on collective memories and practices.

However, what is often left unrecognized is that embedded in these practices are power hierarchies, which, consequently, are reproduced in any communal crisis such as a pandemic emergency. Recurrence, in a certain sense, supports existing hierarchies and governance practices. The case of newly emerging epidemics is different. Ungar (1998, 37) states that hot crises "are startling, as presumed in-vulnerabilities appear to be challenged." The air is thick with fear and the issues involved are on everybody's lips. These epidemics embody and encapsulate the fears of the moment and are reflections of changing power hierarchies. The key question then becomes: What are the relevant features of the contemporary epoch? What are its invulnerabilities caused by motions of political power? The power structure of world politics has been hegemonic, unipolar. As in most cases of hegemonic world order, the major focus is on deviance. The existing Western hegemonic mood detects motions from the margins in the form of "rogues" of different kinds—for example, terrorists, rogue states, illegal migrants, and mutable disease agents. The drama of world politics is often animated by different visions of possible decline and regression. The ways in which pandemic scares are enabled reflect these themes.

Contemporary Perceptions of Risk and Precursor Diseases

It is possible to treat the recent heath-related scares in terms of Beck's influential idea of a risk society. According to Beck (e.g., 1999), postmodern societies are increasingly risk aware. The failures in risk management and in economies of risks give rise to much societal anxiety. The fear of failure provides stimuli for vast governance measures with corresponding control and surveillance policies. However, this view can be contrasted with the hypothesis that epidemics have always been at the center of political communities' self-understanding in a rather stable way. Lindenbaum (2001, 377), who provides an overview of this debate, states that diseases can be used as indicators of underlying communal beliefs. A serious epidemic disease illuminates social patterns and political relations between and within various communities. Beck's categorical statements can be countered with the historical perspective that reveals the huge importance placed on diseases throughout human history. The failing governance technologies have remained much the same, although material technologies have developed and expanded to the scope of human control. The context-dependent manifestations of this important historical continuum can shed light on the postmodern fuzz made about mad cows and feverish birds. Rather than being categorical, the difference is in degree. The emergence of an increasingly intensive global community is matched by the reemergence of the communal awareness of epidemic diseases and the collective rituals to deal with them. This awareness was missing during much of the twentieth century, when most epidemics seemed to have been eradicated or been in the process of being vanquished. Beck's notion of risk itself may be read as a contemporary cultural expression of what epidemics mean for the new globalized community and what its specific variety of collective self-understanding is. These expressions can be quite easily placed in the long cultural history of epidemic diseases and of the political effect they cause.

To better appreciate contemporary disease imagination, a review of some specific epidemics is useful. The influenza pandemic, perhaps more than any other, is seen as human influenced and technologically induced. In the case of the Spanish flu, the mass mobilization of armies, together with new transportation technologies, provided a breeding ground for the first influenza pandemic. In studies of general influenza, the disease is often connected with the coming into being of the global transportation infrastructure. For example, David Patterson (1986, 10) states that "not until the 1889-1890 pandemic, when railroads and steamships were available to transport man and virus, can we document a truly worldwide pandemic." Earlier influenza outbreaks were more localized and the global seasonal pattern harder to discern. Contemporary research connects influenza pandemics with technological changes: The threshold with nature is defined by expanding communal infrastructure and their interlinked nature.

The recent conceptual history of diseases reinforces the link between the various technologies of the global space and human diseases. The source of major health risks are increasingly seen as stemming from specific technologies: "In a primitive society, the major hazards are those posed by nature. In complex modern society, the acts of individuals or corporate bodies may also involve serious hazards to other members of society" (Phillips et al. 2000, 2). The sense of exposure to the global space leads to increasing vulnerability. The anxieties over the emergence of the global political body are met at the individual level: "anxiety about bird flu gets translated into anxiety about the Christmas turkey" (Corcoran and Peillon 2006, 140). This link is induced by the mechanization and "technologization" of everyday life (work-, domestic, and public places). People's dependence on technology—for example, industrial food production—leads to worst-case scenarios of dependence-related failures. This sentiment reinforces disease-related awareness and puts such phenomena as bioterrorism, drug resistance, and pandemics stemming from global warming to the forefront of popular imagination. Such themes connected with technology as cloning, industrial food production, medical trials, pollution, genetic engineering, and toxicity elicit anxious sentiments. It is not surprising that this imagination often identifies the likely source of "the coming plague" as originating from hybrids between modernity (technology, industry) and nature.

The recent scare over avian flu was an event in a long sequence of pandemic spectacles. This sequence contains the relevant memories and modes of representation which render contemporary events meaningful in a particular way. Out of the recent pandemic scares, SARS, the reemerging tuberculosis and BSE appear the most relevant. They also provide three different aspects of the avian flu discourse: tuberculosis provides the background frame for flu-like pandemics, SARS provides for an exceptional sense of emergency, and the BSE discourse enables the hybrid connection between animals, food production, and politics.

Tuberculosis

In 1882, Robert Koch singled out the organism, *Mycobacterium tuberculosis*, which caused tuberculosis. The pattern of contagion though human contact was also described. The prevention plans included the separation of infected people, sometimes by force. These new measures blended with older ways—the old miasmatic idea, for example, suggested cures such as being exposed to fresh air. The disease also influenced social habits ranging from a frowned upon spitting to the romanticization of the disease (e.g., Sontag 1990, 143). The early twentieth century witnessed large-scale health programs against the disease that often took the form of a "war on consumption." By the late 1940s, antibiotics led to the belief that tuberculosis had been defeated. However, as attention decreased, the programs and drug development, which were highly dependent on continuing political commitment, suffered. The recent resurgence of tuberculosis in the United States and other industrialized countries has taken place among certain communities and "risk groups." In 1993, the World Health Organization (WHO) declared tuberculosis "a global health emergency."

Severe Acute Respiratory Syndrome

SARS was first discovered in February 2003. The ensuing pandemic lasted about 8 months. During the epidemic, there were about 8000 known cases of SARS, with around 800 deaths globally. The death rate of SARS was estimated at 15 percent (19 percent of the SARS cases occurred in health-care workers). SARS is believed to be a strain of the Corona virus, which is linked to the common cold. Symptoms include a high temperature and a dry cough. More severe respiratory symptoms follow within 10 days and many patients develop pneumonia. There is no vaccine, but antibiotics and antiviral drugs have helped some patients. The disease is difficult to transmit and is passed by close contact with an infected person. Transmission may result by being around when an infected person coughs. Hong Kong announced early on that 80 percent of the SARS cases could be tracked to a doctor in the Guangdong region of China. China reported the disease a full 4 months after discovering it—by that point, 305 had fallen ill and 5 had died.

In the pandemic discourse, the state is often seen as an obstacle in the way of effective public health action. States are seen as secretive, nontransparent, and deceptive (e.g., Slack 1991, 119). SARS challenged China in several ways (e.g., Freedman, 2004). The control of the outbreak in such a populous and rapidly urbanizing state posed significant dilemmas. For China, legitimacy management at the political front was a significant problem. The apparent secrecy and denial led to the widespread perception that China, with its "alien" political system, was the root cause of the epidemic. The Chinese government was perceived to be opaque in its handling of the disease and was accused of being "excessive" several times during the outbreak.

The government in China was seen as trying to cover up the severity of the epidemic. For example, on April 18, *Time* magazine reported that health officials in Beijing tried to cover up the scale of the city's SARS infections by driving around dozens of patients in ambulances and moving others to hotels during hospital inspection visits by WHO officials. The secrecy of any government is seen as having many detrimental effects. It allows for the further spread of the disease and delays the ability of the world to prepare and research possible vaccines for the illness. Secrecy can also encourage media-fed hysteria. Many felt that the disease was sudden and quick-spreading when, in fact, it had been spreading for a full 4 months. This perception furthered the sense of urgency and increased anxiety in the average citizen. It made it appear as though one could get the disease just walking down the street. The perceived Chinese secrecy during the SARS outbreak prompted a large political backlash, with many countries calling for political reforms in China. In some ways, SARS turned into a tool for transformational diplomacy.

A specific pattern of blame is, thus, one of the memories of SARS. It is still seen as an Asian, and specifically Chinese, disease. It is noteworthy how SARS created or reinforced several antagonist roles. China was blamed by governments and the WHO became the protagonist of the drama. SARS also reminded one of the dangers of globalization and interconnectedness. Chinese minorities all around the world were treated with suspicion. On the other hand, SARS quickly became stereotyped as a disease caused by globalization and international travel, and not one of "immorality" like HIV/AIDS. It was a seen as a wake-up call to realize that international travel brings us closer to each other and this, in turn, allows for the introduction of "foreign" diseases in a manner unheard of earlier.

Bovine Spongiform Encephalopathy

The sick, jerking, stumbling cows of the UK came to define European politics during the spring of 1996. Before that, BSE was considered a contained disease. It was contained in specific animals and largely to the UK. The British Secretary of Health's announcement, on March 20, 1996, of the finding of a new Creutzfeldt–Jakob disease (CJD) variant that was able to cross the species boundary, initiated the sudden crisis. The announcement raised the strong possibility of a link between the new variant in humans and BSE-contaminated meat. Such meat had been eaten by millions and millions of British at home and through fast-food chains.

One way to approach the crisis and appreciate its legacy is to examine the novelty or the rogue nature of BSE. The origin of the sense of "madness" during the crisis is indicative of the complex nature of the health scare. First of all, the association of the disease with prions, which were a new type of disease agents, reinforced the mystery surrounding the disease (Yam 2001, 12). Shimkus (1998, 82) refers to the situation under the title, "Mad Cows, Strange Science." In this way, the "madness" of BSE was often associated with the uncertain science and with the unclear methods of testing for the disease. Second, the madness was also associated with the unrestrained and "deregulated" nature of the various actors involved. Two players receive particular attention in the literature: the food industry and the UK government. The food production industry, it was thought, wanted only to make money and to cut costs. Shaoul (1997, 182) concluded that the inner logic of the food industry, driven by financial interests, was a public health problem. Much blame was placed on industrial food-processing methods and intensive farming practices based on the maximizing of profit, instead of a respect for "natural" ways of doing things (Barker and Ridley 1996, 242; Hildebrandt et al. 2002, 77).

An additional aspect of the formative BSE experience was that the madness also signified the panic and hysteria caused by the disease. The theme of the health scare offered an additional element for the understanding of mad cows. The health scare was seen as a fundamentally irrational process that could, under certain circumstances, overwhelm rational behavior. Jasanoff (1997, 221) studied the cultural antecedents of the BSE scare. He points out the tendency of European culture to overreact or to act irrationally in panic. The different quarantines and bans put in place by the

European Commission and its various member states were seen as driven by panic and fear, rather than rational decision making. Finucane (2002, 31) emphasizes the role of cultural perceptions of risk in connection with food-related illnesses. The situation in Europe was one of advancing integration and enlargement of the communal boundaries. At this political level, the context of BSE was very fluid and unstable, which may have promoted the notion of mad cow disease "madness" (Aaltola 1999, 127). The culturally charged meanings led to nationalistic reactions and stereotypes, which were further fed by the sensationalistic press (Giesecke 2000, 588).

When BSE became identified with the UK and its previous policies, the European Union was able to look legitimate and decisive. Partly, this "success" stemmed from the historically conditioned perception that states are secretive when it comes to their public-heath problems. It can be argued that, for the EC, the substance of valorous decisions centered on making the disease geographically and conceptually analogous with the UK and its past "rogue" policies. In other words, the policies aimed at controlling BSE consisted almost exclusively of measures imposed on and required of the UK. The containment of the BSE crisis consisted of checking the UK as the source of the outbreak. Two factors were usually emphasized here: the majority of the BSE cases occurred in the UK and the information concerning the link between BSE and CJD was made public there, too. Thus, the BSE problem was localized into a British problem. The control of the disease and its effects required clear concessions from the UK, regardless of whether these measures would have any real effect on the causative agents. The dynamics of the BSE situation profiled national authorities as corrupt and, therefore, incapable of taking care of their own people. The general message told a story of the supranational power of the European Union's institutions as the last guarantor of people's physical security and explicated national authorities as the problem.

An important legacy of BSE was that it reinforced one perceived illegitimate form of pandemic collaboration. Too close marriage-like relations between the government and industry are seen as deducting from the focus of common interest. During the BSE crisis, the previous deregulation of the food industry was deemed irresponsible. Deregulation, a lax administrative culture, and the excessively close interests of government and industry were held directly responsible for the dangerous situation (Kleinert 1998, 584).

Different Pandemic Dramas

To better appreciate these relatively contemporary epidemic-related crises, the historical mythology dealing with such crises needs to be probed. As the mythology and history of plagues become manifest when the physical diseases agents are given cultural interpretations, some common patterns emerge. They are often treated as omens, puzzles, warnings, retributions, and teachings. Throughout history, they have inevitably turned into signifiers of moral transgressions, with a political message about the necessity of restoring legitimate communal boundaries and hierarchy. In the sense of the global community, they translate into reestablishing structure and firmness in the face of fluidity.

More often than not, plague dramas have highlighted the existence of horizontal boundaries such as political borders between nations. These boundaries can be reestablished though the drama of potential or real quarantines, cordons sanitaires, and embargoes. The vertical boundaries of a hierarchical political order are more perceptual. Plague dramas usually caused upheavals in these hierarchies. Or, they led to drastic measures on such boundaries. Different sorts of "foreigners" and other disempowered groups were treated harshly. This meant, for example, the persecution of minorities—for example, during the European outbreaks, Jews were routinely subjected to genocides. The plague epidemics in the Middle Ages commonly reinforced the gender and moral boundaries by leading to the burning of young women as witches. They reinforced the existing politico-religious order by activities such as almsgiving and church building. In the contemporary, increasingly delocalized global community, the re-acknowledgment of the hierarchical world order is where the emphasis is in the pandemic plays. Many Asian countries and minorities are treated with suspicion when it comes to flu-like epidemics and Africa has been stigmatized for its heavy HIV/AIDS prevalence rates. The diseases influencing the marginal areas are easily translated into the most threatening ones. The hierarchy threatened by the rising Chinese political clout and Asian economies is reestablished in the SARS and avian flu plays. The threat stemming from "below" is ultimately managed by Western institutions, states, and expertise.

Global health plays are dramatic. They restage the "real" drama of human struggles and point to the fragility of human existence. The drama associated with an acute pandemic shows itself in communal reactions. From a historical perspective, this drama usually involves fits of what may be called civil religious righteousness. People look for security in their perceived communal strength and traditional perceptions of communality. What come about are outbursts of customs, family values, nationalism, and ethnicity. The essential elements connected with one's sense of belonging to a group are highlighted and strongly expressed.

The other side of these outbursts, which bring out the essential elements, is that they repulse the unessential as harmful and suspect. People are marginalized and stigmatized. As stated, in plague-ridden Europe, the normal communal responses to plague included the building of churches, giving of alms, pilgrimages, burning of witches (mainly young women), and the killing of Jews and other "foreign" groups. Large segments of the population were forced into the roles of "plague spreaders" or "well poisoners." The act of fleeing has always been a vital part of the communal reactions to epidemics. Interpreted as a metaphor, "fleeing" sums up the common communal reaction to epidemics—people flee away from diseased sites or isolate or quarantine themselves from the people associated with the disease. This background illuminates a central role in the pandemic plays—that of the antagonisms inside the human political order.

In the plague dramas, the deviant figure has a history that needs to be taken into account. This gives further substance to the "rogue" that has been defined in the earlier chapters. At the mythic level of the community, the slaying of the disease-spreading "monsters" was often performed by saintly figures—for example, saints, communal or ancestral spirits, and personifications of piety in general. It would appear that diseases as physical maladies were inseparable from their moral and political implications. The transgressions behind outbreaks of epidemics were first and foremost moral in nature. Because moral transgressions translated easily into the language of violated borders, epidemic diseases have had powerful political consequences between different communities and polities of people.

As compared to the rogue figure, the protagonists of the "plague plays" are commonly conceived of as problem solvers. Mythology often connected plagues with problem-solving and border-restoring activities. This meant that disease as a physical, yet also always moral, question was so framed as to require the exercise of judgment in discovering its meaning and in devising an appropriate response to it. The coming of the Christian Middle Ages manifested a marked change in the way diseases were portrayed. The deviant figure embodying the disease turned into a dragon. The monster that lurked at the edge of the polity, ready to kill its inhabitants, was often embodied by a hybrid half-reptile, half-bird creature. This dragon emitted foul yet fiery breath. The deadliness of dragon breath was related to the then common notion that diseases were caused by bad air, "mal-air," or miasma. The dragon as the embodied transgression burned the community down and polluted its atmosphere. The struggle with the dragon—for example, the famous hagiography of Saint George slaying the dragon—led to it being either slain or driven back to where it came from, usually caves. In the caves, there was always damp and stagnant air. The driving of the beastly disease away (i.e., purifying the communal atmosphere) required physical acts of courage and sacrifice. The disease emergency called for fearless dragon slayers. But more than anything else, the elimination of the disease was connected with critical moral judgment.

Different plagues were taken to be manifestations of communal immorality and evil. The sense of broken, transgressed boundaries is still very much present in the iconography of contemporary epidemic emergencies. SARS and avian flu have often been treated as fevers caused by a globalizing world, which contains dangerous transgressions, porous boundaries, and hybridity. In the case of avian flu, much of the anxiety stems from long-distance routes of bird migration and from the fact that industrial food production connects the Western consumption of poultry with distant poultry farms. The morality play of avian flu is animated by a sense of rapid global spread, somatic connections to distant lands through food, nature turning into a threat, and localities exposed without the ability to protect themselves. It is in relation to these anxieties that the avian flu legitimacy plays are actualized.

Legitimacy Plays

Epidemic-related legitimacy plays contain a strong moralist note. They are used to reaffirm or reinvent a sense of civil religion and ideology (Lindenbaum 2001, 264; Rosenberg 1992, 279) and as signifiers of communal values and beliefs (e.g., Turner 1957, 107). Legitimacy plays involve a fight by the protagonist—often presuming the guise of all humanity—against bad elements of a perceived hostile nature. These elements are seldom the viruses, bacteria, or other agents of disease. Rather, the disease and disease-causing agents become easily associated with some minority community or other perceived to be a hostile political entity. These two extreme types define a continuum along which there exists a whole variety of other types: for example, emigrants, tourists, drug addicts, air travelers, truck drivers, prostitutes, homosexuals, food production industries, greedy politicians, and so on. These types find their historical equivalents in the more aged, collective memories about polluters, untouchables, plague spreaders, and well poisoners. The protagonists of the morality plays include such stock figures as watchful doctors, alert health surveillance institutions, efficient national, international and transnational health agencies, and politicians "who did their job."

Legitimacy dramas pass a communal verdict: A judgment is passed about the moral status of those involved. These dramas put the limelight on actors' values and their ability to make the correct choices. The main question becomes how well actors choose in the course of the events. The vital question is how their choices reflect progressive or regressive moral health. In connection with lethal epidemic diseases, the underlying moral health may be interpreted in a retroactive or proactive context. Retroactive legitimacy plays set the stage for spectacles in which events are at a critical stage. From that moment onward, there is a strong sense that events can continue either negatively/regressively or positively/progressively. In their contemporary form, these morality plays are set in "hot spots," where epidemics are being contained by people wearing masks and protective gear.

The proactive legitimacy plays manifest themselves in spectacular acts of being on guard, sounding alarm and surveillance. In these plays, the sense of legitimacy derives from the ability to maintain a certain sense of safety and the absence of outbreaks or hot spots. It can be argued that one major way of doing morally virtuous labor in contemporary times is through sweating over health-related concerns. The perspiration in connection with the feverish agitation of the globalizing world provides the setting for the staging of the epidemic-related morality plays. These morality plays contain a stern moral lesson about the disastrous consequences of laxness and lack of vigilance. In this respect, the morality plays are not so much focused on the teaching of correct behavior and the virtues and values of a well-functioning—healthy—global order and governance.

In the context of legitimacy plays, it is possible to examine pandemic scares as moral panics. There are various types of moral panic. A common dichotomy exists between elite-induced and spontaneous grassroots types of crises (Goode and Ben-Yehuda 1994, 97). These crises give different roles to different actors. For example, spontaneous crises can lead to the elite reassurance of the status quo and of a sense of invulnerability. The opposite may also occur when the general population is not engrossed by a sense of panic and ignores the alarm signals coming from different elite groups. This type of failure might indicate in-group problems within the elite. Thus, it seems that the situation is often a mixed one: different in-groups compete over the sense of crisis and reflect the opinions of their respective audiences at the grassroots level. In many ways, the emergence of an epidemic frame indicates who is who at the elite and grassroots level. Epidemics embody different strains and motions in these hierarchical orders.

There is the initial sense of alarm over a threat from within or without the community. However, the sense of surprise is crucial for the emergence of an engrossing disease frame. This unexpectedness may be due to the temporal or conceptual nature of the initial happening. The timing of the event may be surprising. For example, something that is already known reemerges. This was the case in the outbreak of the bubonic plague in Surat, in India, in 1994. Large-scale bubonic plague epidemics were thought to be things of the past. The outbreak or the leaking of information about it caused significant embarrassment to India and harmed India's external image. Conceptually unexpected happenings demand attention because of their novel or unconventional nature. For example, it may be suggested that HIV/AIDS reinvented the meaning of epidemic disease in the twentieth century or that BSE with its mysterious nature—for example, prions—was salient because of its originality. What is temporally and conceptually unexpected is dependent on the specific community and relative to the community's self-identity. This means that the community's memory is more important than its history when one evaluates what is surprising in sense of timing and in the sense of nature.

When the perception of acute epidemic disease intertwines with the polity's production of security—whether it is local, national, regional, or global—the situation becomes tense, charged, and dramatic. The heightened sense of looming disaster thickens the air and sets the engrossing frame. The frame has to do with what is at stake, what is taking place, and what the past precedents are. Besides the frame, the performers become vital parts of the epidemic-related political dramas. The performers are those who are expected to do something, who do something, and whose actions are judged. The spectators are everyone whose health is perceived to be under threat and who is seen as evaluating the various performers. Often, the media comes to represent the spectators and their judgments.

History of Political Epidemic Plays

Plagues and borders are conceptually and historically intertwined closely. Because of this tight connection, international relations often provide the scene for plague plays. When one considers the potential collaborative forms that epidemics can take in politics, it is useful to first review the specific history of human reactions to epidemics that cross political boundaries (Aaltola 1999, 127). Although much of the interplay between lethal epidemics and the realm of states' interaction is contingent upon specific circumstances, some general, recurring, and conventional themes and shapes can be detected:

1. *Instability.* Disease can strike some individual statesperson, causing power vacuums, internal squabbling, periods of indecision, and increasing uncertainty.
2. *Imbalance.* The uneven distribution of the burden of disease among states can cause shifts in the prevailing balance of power.
3. *Signifier.* Epidemics are evidence of the bad shape of governance in some states, which can be read as a sign of weakness.
4. *Propaganda.* Lethal epidemic diseases can offer effective propaganda tools in eroding perceptions about the enemy.
5. *Co-option.* A state can use the outbreak of some lethal infectious disease as an excuse for politically motivated actions such as a military maneuver or economic sanctions.
6. *Scare.* Epidemics cause panic and drastic reactions, which can cause economic hardships (e.g., in the shape of market failures and loss of tourism).

From the perspective of this book, I will bypass the political plays that revolve around decision-makers' illnesses (e.g., Karlen 1984, 16; L'Etang 1970, 1; Park 1986, 12; Robins 1981, 154).

Imbalance or the Asymmetrical Effect of Lethal Epidemic Diseases

The capacity of diseases to afflict some states disproportionately constitutes an important way in which epidemics react with international relations (Robins 1981, 76). This aspect also ties directly into the vorticity model because it refers to upheavals in the world political hierarchy. In a general sense, asymmetries can be used to discern who is who in the world map of power. In more specific cases, asymmetry affects the outcomes of specific turns of events. The brutal fate of Napoleon's Grande Armée provides a case in point of the lopsided and decisive effects of lethal epidemics. In the moribund Russian expedition of 1812, the typhus epidemic destroyed most of Napoleon's half a million men. The Russians, largely untouched by the disease, only had to complete the annihilation (Marshall-Cornwall 1967, 1; Robins 1981, 77).

Similarly, the asymmetrical effects of epidemics manifested themselves in the tragic outcome of the contact between the Spaniards and the Native Americans: "The lopsided impact of infectious disease upon Amerindian populations therefore offered a key to understanding the ease of the Spanish conquest of America—not only militarily, but culturally as well" (McNeill 1977, 2).

The historian of the Peloponnesian War, Thucydides, who was himself afflicted by plague, gives a valuable and dramatic account of the consequences of asymmetry in the distribution of epidemic disease. Although plague was not the only factor which brought about the eventual demise of Athens, it did deprive Athens of much of its war-waging capability against its formidable enemy.

A more recent example is that of the very uneven HIV/AIDS burden. The developing countries, especially in southern Africa, face a relative disadvantage as compared to the developed north. Thus, sharp asymmetries in the distribution of disease can result in and have resulted in dramatic changes in the distribution of capabilities.

Moreover, the uneven distribution turns easily into disempowering stereotypes. As is evident from Thucydides's account, the uneven way in which the pestilence struck aroused the imagination of many and charged the epidemic with persuasive analogies to other relevant themes of the day. Many of these ancient and biblical conceptual connections carried through until the Middle Ages. During the Middle Ages and the early modern period, one of the most puzzling and mysterious features of the plague that cried out for an explanation was that it struck in some places and killed most of the people living there, while other places were completely spared. The pattern of its spread attracted culturally meaningful explanations. It caused emotional storms that swept over much of the populations in both the affected and the spared places. In many stereotypical explanations, the irregular and asymmetrical pattern of the plague epidemic correlated with the relative righteousness of various nations, localities, and individuals.

As the medieval system was replaced by the state system around the time of Westphalia, the nature of epidemics as an international political phenomenon lost much of its religious charge and became instead part of the mythology and political religion surrounding the state itself. The "innate" tendency of states to derive legitimacy from a certain sense of physical and moral superiority with respect to other states led to the common belief that other states or groups of states were more prone to the horrors of epidemics. Every time an epidemic struck somewhere else, the state's legitimacy as a secure, privileged, inimitable, and exemplary entity, predestined and chosen for sovereignty, was reinforced.

For example, during the early 1830s, this sense of national self-confidence and pride was particularly conspicuous in the French attitudes toward the advancing cholera epidemic. Apparently inspired by a sense of national pride, one French citizen proclaimed that cholera could not conquer France because "in no other country of (the) globe have civilization, industry, and commerce achieved a higher degree of perfection and in no country but England are the rules of hygiene more faithfully observed" (Larrey 1831, 28). In the end, the high degree of "civilization" that the French and the English attributed to themselves did not spare them from the cholera epidemic. However, it did, for a moment, allow some French people to regard themselves as a first-class nation at least in comparison to such "corrupted" and "disorderly" countries as India or Turkey (Delaporte 1986, 16). As the religious explanations of pestilence were gradually complemented and supplemented by beliefs and attitudes that had to do with administrative and scientific actions, the underlying coupling between concepts such as decay or decline and disease-related notions such as death, suffering, and fear remained in place. The legitimacy and viability of a state became dependent on its ability to avoid outbreaks of lethal epidemics, with the result that the asymmetrical distribution of diseases—the ability to keep in check a disease that was rampant elsewhere—was considered to selectively reinforce the legitimacy of states.

Signifier of Decline

Public health is, thus, not only important in the eyes of one's own citizens, but it also provides an invaluable instrument in proving the political community's worth as full and respected entities. The vital political power dimension of public health translates into attempts to prove one's ability to abide by the international standards of public health. In international proclamations concerning public health measures, states make use of practices associated with diligence, dutifulness, and readiness. Thomas Hobbes famously justified the existence of states in terms of them making people's lives less short, nasty, and brutish. The ability to provide external security is the most common reading of this. States provide for people's right to belong to a certain bordered territory. However, states have historically borne the pressure to provide for their citizens in other senses as well. Their legitimacy depends on their ability to provide economic well-being, property rights, rule of law, religion, and culture. However, it can be claimed that one of the foremost ways in which states can fulfill these constitutive functions is by contributing to the health of the population.

Starting from the quarantine regulations in fourteenth-century Italy, states have tried to stop the spread of epidemics. The pattern of spread gradually turned into a signifier of the worth of the inherent political rule. Securing borders against the plague tuned into one of the fundamental elements of state security before the eradication of major epidemic diseases in the late nineteenth century. One notable fact concurs with the border – epidemic – security nexus: the maturing of the European state system and the coming into being of state borders in the seventeenth and eighteenth centuries was also the time when plague disappeared. These two processes may be seen as having reinforced each other. Against this nexus and historical background, a rampant lethal epidemic disease is easily read as a state failure. Under such conditions, the imagery and anticipation turn into those of decline. An important constituent of a state or political community in general (e.g., empire) is the ever-present possibility that it may decline and even fall. The motions associated with epidemics lead into the political sentiment of decline. Diseases are among the most important triggers of the aged proscriptive stock narrative of decline in linking individual bodies directly to the state body.

In the declinist framing of epidemic diseases, the epidemic becomes only one symptom of a more acute and dangerous "political dis-ease" and the distortions in the underlying politico-religious order. In modern literature, the term "state failure" or "failing state" discourse can be associated with the inheritance of declinist thinking. When the state cannot fulfill its basic modern function of providing for the health of its citizens, the stigma of failure comes to be associated with it. This type of marginalization is in evidence when one reviews the way in which current news concerning sub-Saharan Africa is framed. The frame and the fact that the prevalence of HIV/AIDS is very high in these regions cannot be without consequences when it comes to the flows of structural power. Much labor, human security, financial investments, and production capacity are lost because the life expectancy in some states of southern Africa has fallen below 40 years. In many cases, those people whose lives are "short, nasty, and brutish" are from certain areas and groups inside the state. The dynamics of the spread cannot be without consequences for the political hierarchy and for the maintenance of the limits of the order. From a perspective, the state-ness is not distributed evenly throughout the territory. When this condition cannot be kept at the margins, hidden from the view of the outside world and, in many cases, from national self-awareness, serious image and prestige problems may result.

To reiterate, in the absence of any objective measure of a state's relative capabilities, the persuasive analogies and connotations associated with a serious outbreak of an infectious disease can cause serious harm to a state's international standing. When bubonic plague hit Surat in 1994, concern over the international repercussions led initially to attempts to hide the problem and, once that had become impossible, to downplay the seriousness of the outbreak. The Indian government has tried persistently to rid itself of the image that Western countries often associate with postcolonial, developing countries—that they are uncivilized, weak, chaotic, and second-rate states inherently unable to take care of their own citizens. This Western view translates into India's lack of political and economic influence, which is unfitting to the world's most populous democracy. What made the outbreak of bubonic plague an even more embarrassing and conspicuous sign of incapability was the fact that the knowledge of how it spreads and how it can be cured and eradicated has been there for a full century. In political power games, an outbreak of this type was "a euphemism to embarrass a less developed country in the hopes of making the more developed look better and safer" (Lin 1995, 2913).

The fear that a disease can be seen as a symbol of a state that is in ruin, with the corresponding political and economic consequences, led the Gabonese government to try and hide an outbreak of Ebola in 1996 and to confiscate blood samples from international health workers (Troy 1996, 22). A further example of attempts to conceal an epidemic disease is provided by Thailand's efforts to conceal an outbreak of cholera in 1997 by calling it a case of "severe diarrhea." This tendency to hide diseases in an attempt to avoid international embarrassment, which could potentially harm the state's political and economic interests, can be witnessed all over the world. As the UK's failed attempts to hide the BSE demonstrated, states are rarely totally open about the outbreak of a potentially serious epidemic disease. They have too much to lose in terms of respect, legitimacy, and status.

Propaganda

As forcefully as they impose themselves on communities, diseases have always called for explanation. During the centuries of plague, the pestilence was a divine punishment for sin and moral corruption. Not surprisingly, for a short moment when the plague epidemic struck, the city-states and other localities became citadels of righteousness. However, as time passed by and as people grew more accustomed to plague and to the fact that it killed both the righteous and the corrupt in equal numbers, regardless of their moral merits, the divine origin of plague had to give way to more mundane explanations. The various ways in which the people of the time viewed plague outbreaks were closely interwoven with the existing political conditions. In other words, what was politically expedient also became a tool in controlling the societal effects of plague. As previously argued, plague spreaders and well poisoners became people's enemies, and people's enemies, whether domestic or foreign, were easily presented as plague spreaders and well poisoners. These foreign elements and states, which were already viewed in negative terms, were not hard to come by for purposes of apportioning blame.

As the state system became increasingly stabilized, the range of potential plague spreaders expanded accordingly to include the state's external enemies. The effects of the plague at the individual level were intertwined with broader societal and international considerations. The experiences at various levels were connected through parallel metaphorical dynamics that mingled plague with evil and enemies, instead of conceptually differentiating between them. The ontology of enmity offers an easy to understand template for disease causation and vice versa. Because the analogy between plague and sinful life brought shame upon the proud citizens of city-states, it was relatively easy to claim that plague originated from foreign and evil elements. This logic was reinforced by an uncomplicated deduction—that it was clearly in the interests of the enemy states to use the epidemic of plague to cause devastation and disorder to their rival. What the enemy states could not accomplish through honest economic and political competition, they now achieved through the vicious act of spreading plague. Thus, it was not difficult through governmental persuasion to convince patriotic citizens that the misfortune in the form of disease was not due to their own failures and practices of bad governance, but caused somehow by the enemy's immorality and trickery. In the same way, a serious epidemic outbreak in an enemy state was treated as further evidence of the enemy's politico-religious badness and the perversity of its constitutive element. Thus, it may be suggested that there exists a natural tendency to project emerging epidemic diseases onto existing patterns of hostility. The way in which both SARS and avian flu have been associated with China provides some support for this hypothesis.

The stock narrative of an epidemic, thus, contains a well-established narrative dynamic that easily leads to the attribution of death and destruction to foreign sources and political adversaries. This tendency has been particularly pronounced during periods of heightened interstate conflict and world-order tensions. Not surprisingly, the spread of HIV/AIDS in the early 1980s was soon adopted for politically advantageous purposes. The Soviet authorities insisted that HIV was the outcome of a U.S. military experiment that had gone terribly wrong (Nelkin and Gilman 1991, 39). The purpose was to point out that the United States was a vicious and underhanded super-power that should not be trusted. Furthermore, for the Soviet Union, the HIV/AIDS epidemic offered an opportunity to point out that it was free from HIV/AIDS, that it had no "degenerated" and "corrupted" homosexual elements. However, HIV/AIDS never became a very potent propaganda weapon because it could be further attributed to undesirable internal elements such as homosexuals, prostitutes, and drug users. In other words, many people in the West connected the disease with the "unnatural" ways of the gay community, rather than with the general "corruptness" of Western societies. It was effectively used by the U.S. neoconservative movement in the beginning of the 1980s to promote its own message about family values and the need for religious revival in the United States. During the cold war, the HIV/AIDS epidemic did make some international relations appearances, not because of its deadliness, but because of the age-old political reactivity and charge contained in stock memories of lethal epidemics.

The propaganda and public diplomacy values of epidemic diseases were demonstrated in the case of the Spanish flu. The discourse about any pandemic influenza often refers to the 1918 Spanish flu as a benchmark outbreak. It came from the United States across the Atlantic Ocean before turning into a significant outbreak. Influenza started spreading among the British forces in Spain, thus the name. "Within a few cycles of infection, it was apparent that the disease had become more virulent, with a tenfold increase in the death rate amongst cases" (Nicholson et al. 2007, 102). This more virulent virus spread throughout the world. The death rate was about 10 times higher than in a generic influenza pandemic. The disease hit people in the 20–40 years' age group. This made it especially deadly among the soldiers and greatly complicated the war efforts. The co-option between the war and the pandemic became clear in the health propaganda of the time. For example, it was commonplace that the images used in poster campaigns linked fighting the disease with fighting the war.

Health propaganda that tried to tackle tuberculosis in the first half of the twentieth century offers another important precursor example.

Tuberculosis can be seen as providing much of the background for the contemporary influenza imagination. From this perspective, it is relevant that many of the health propaganda posters from the beginning of the twentieth century connected the national struggle with tuberculosis with national defense. The protective barriers of the national border and the human body were equated. The iconography was militaristic.

The strong tendency to equate fighting a disease with the language of war and military security is still evident in contemporary language. For example, the frantic struggle to contain SARS in 2003 was associated with wider national security prerogatives. The U.S. documents on SARS often highlight the close connection between naturally occurring and intentionally inflicted outbreaks of diseases. The foremost connection is that the measures against naturally occurring outbreaks are conceptualized also as important practice grounds for fighting bioterrorism. The combined dynamics is captured in the term "health security." The documents conceive of "new health threats" stemming from "(re)emerging diseases and biological warfare agents." From the U.S. perspective, the SARS-related outlook was part of a larger vision to the world: the presidential directive, *Biodefense for the 21st Century*, "provides a comprehensive framework for our nation's biodefense. [It] builds on past accomplishments, specifies roles and responsibilities, and integrates the programs and efforts of various communities—national security, medical, public health, intelligence, diplomatic, agricultural and law enforcement—into a sustained and focused national effort against biological weapons threats." The probable result of the integrated approach is that the occurrence of natural epidemic disease heightens the urgency of security concerns and recontextualizes the epidemic in question in quasi-security language.

Diseases as Pretense or Diversion

Diseases do not appear in the domestic and international realms as distinct entities void of any reactivity with already existing political conceptions. In other words, decision makers speak about diseases in a language that is laden with analogies and connotations, which are meaningful from the perspective of the state as an entity with a history, identity, and role. Diseases are linked up with the most common international relations concepts of strategy, deception, and secrecy and, on the other hand, with the idea of the enemy. By assigning the role of plague spreaders, well poisoners, and conspirators to some external enemy, such as Catholics, Protestants, or other states, or to conspicuous internal groups such as Jews, women (witches), and other "enemies of the state," a state could both divert people's anxiety and frustrations away from its own actions and also justify its actions against these perceived enemies. It was not extraordinary then that, during the epidemic, the hospitals set up to accommodate the patients were full of political enemies; nor is it extraordinary in modern times for politically unwanted elements to find themselves in quarantine or isolation of one form or another for reasons of public hygiene. The manipulation and trickery have not been confined to the abuse of internal enemy images—they have been extended to the level of international interaction, too.

The management of epidemics can be an act put on deliberately to divert attention or to legitimize actions that would have been unjustifiable otherwise. States' declarations of intention are often deceptive and misleading. Throughout the history of states' interaction with epidemics, it has been very difficult to distinguish between their genuine efforts to minimize the health implications of epidemics and their opportunistic attempts to minimize or gain political benefits from an outbreak. States have been well placed to take advantage of the mystery surrounding such diseases as plague in the seventeenth century, cholera in the nineteenth century, and BSE, SARS, and avian flu in the twentieth century. Moreover, the character of this manipulation is entirely dependent on one's position in international interaction. The truth value of different points of view is notoriously difficult to ascertain. However, mere appearances and suspicions are enormously compelling reasons for taking conventionally appropriate actions in international relations, which means that propaganda and prestige are of immense importance and have to be taken into account in managing epidemics.

International relations have witnessed some attempts to use epidemics as a pretense for military or strategic gain. States have used regulations whose original purpose was to stop the spread of epidemics by containment in order to "reap political benefit" (Delaporte 1986, 142). For instance, the French restoration government used epidemics as an excuse to declare a cordon sanitaire against Spain, which was in the middle of a revolution at the time. The French monarchy feared that the revolution might spread to France and, therefore, an army was deployed along the border under the pretext of the cordon sanitaire (Bertier de Sauvigny 1966, 191). The U.S. government considered the term blockade to be too offensive during the 1962 Cuban missile crisis (White 1996, 142). So, instead, the Americans officially imposed a quarantine, which carried at least some sense of international legitimacy. The long co-evolution between states and epidemics has fixed and ritualized some compelling analogies, which carry with them a sense of legitimacy that cannot be totally dismissed even when abused.

Ever since the beginning of the modern state system, it was important for a state's viability that its vital economic interests be taken into account when decisions were made concerning action against epidemics. In other words, various economic and political considerations emerged as strong arguments for and against the use of drastic quarantine and cordon sanitaire measures. It was not long after the introduction of quarantine measures that state authorities started to use these quarantines to advance the interests of their own trade and industry. There was a great temptation to make favorable exemptions from the quarantine regulations. The resulting political situation was highly complex and intricate, as the interests of the affected parties were often conflicting and irreconcilable. The disagreements over the most effective and reasonable policies extended beyond mere domestic considerations into international relations, which meant that miscalculations could have potentially serious repercussions. Thus, the internationally shared disease-related language provided ways of legitimizing otherwise politically impossible decisions, which were primarily motivated by economic and political self-interest, ruthless ambition, and power politics.

As the BSE–CJD crisis demonstrated, the imposition of disease-related restrictive regulations against a certain state will almost certainly lead to accusations that the real motives behind these actions are economic and political. The economic vitality of a state and, consequently, its relative capabilities depend very much on the level of economic and political content among the relevant domestic actors. Not surprisingly then, the well-being of most vital parts of the economy, such as agriculture, tourism, and foreign trade, is a very important determinant of a state's policies. In many respects, the German ban on U.S. pork products in 1880 offers an example of the relative ease with which real health concerns are intertwined with economic protectionism and political interests: "The German ban has proved the most interesting animal product ban of the era because it was clearly argued on sanitary grounds, but was consistently tinged with a very different motive, namely, the protection of domestic livestock producers in particular and economic nationalism in general" (Hoy and Nuget 1989, 199). The health scare was based on the discovery that meat infected with *Trichinella spiralis* could kill humans. Regardless of the "true" motives of the ban, it is clear that the dispute had much to do with protectionism, not only because the American side believed so, but also because the ban benefited Germany's own pork industry (Snyder 1961, 4). The ban was lifted in 1891 after the adoption of satisfactory meat inspection laws by the U.S. Congress. Although the ban on U.S. pork and the lifting of the ban were grounded in reasonable public health arguments, the episode as a whole clearly illustrates how legitimate health concerns are intimately connected with the concept of national interest. It also offers an often used precursor template. In contemporary world politics, there are numerous import bans of food products that are justified as health measures, although their ground is clearly political.

Scares and Panics

One the most common narrative paths of the recent epidemic-related reactions has been the predictable market reactions. For example, when a mad cow or sick chicken is found, the consumer reactions almost automatically lead to havoc in the related markets. The markets panic and the economy suffers when there are sharp changes in consumption patterns or the establishment of trade barriers between states. In the globalizing world, this reaction is one of the most common communal reactions to the anxiety provoked by diseases.

Food provides a major channel for the anxieties and related market problems caused by disease epidemics. Another important way of projecting pandemic fears is through the worry over air travel. One of the foremost aspects of global fevers such as SARS and avian flu has been the connectedness with the global infrastructure. SARS in particular was connected to the backbone of global culture, the hub-and-spoke structure of international air travel. There is a close relationship between air travel and microbial traffic (Ali and Keil 2006, 30; Naylor 2003, 10). SARS created problems for the aviation industry because the rapid spread of the condition was associated with intercontinental flight connections. The markets speculated that the industry most under pressure from SARS were airlines. The spread of the foot-and-mouth disease in the UK caused heavy additional costs for the airlines. The feverish pace of global interconnections is based mostly on the hub-and-spoke system initiated by the topology of international airports. It is perhaps not surprising that the industry most under pressure during pandemics is the aviation industry. While the aviation industry represents the crossing of political and continental boundaries, the food production industry brings with it the perception of crossing the nature versus humanity barrier. Whatever the underlying narratives, the fact remains that in today's international political economy, market reactions provide a key gauge for lethal epidemic diseases.

In the case of avian flu, the collaborative pattern that was significant for the different actors' perceived legitimacy was the one between institutions and industry. Among the most distinct role differentiation among the pandemic crisis actors is the one between pharmaceutical traders and public health protectors (e.g., Abbot 2005, 317). Big pharmaceutical companies' investment-related arguments have to fit into the general humanitarian frame. Their role highlights the common interest-related importance of having strong property rights protections: patents need to be protected and price controls resisted. These policies, so the argument goes, will benefit the poor as well because the industry can undertake expansive drug development. However, the public health advocates argue that the common benefit has to allow room for governments to break patents so that the poor also will have access to life-saving innovations. Health is seen as a priority over the protection of intellectual property rights. Both stands have their lobbyists and supporters. Among the states, intellectual property rights are promoted by the U.S. and other Western governments, whereas the public health advocates find supporters among developing countries such as Brazil and South Africa.

It is important to point out that these viewpoints influence collaborative arrangements. For example, when industrial accidents are perceived to be more likely and devastating, the relationship that community groups have with industrial groups is influenced negatively. The situation leads to new patterns of conflict and coalition. Loyalties shift to reflect the underlying perceptions of liabilities and blame. This collaborative dynamic delegitimizes close cooperation between industry and state. Any perception of this can lead to assignment of blame for the disease, its hiding and failures to control it to these collaborative relationships. This type of blame dynamics took place during the initial 1996 BSE crisis. Blame was put on the industrial food production industry. Furthermore, the governmental regulators were deemed to have been too intimate with the industry. The crisis delegitimized such linkages and new policies were implemented to prevent similar ones happening in the future.

The perceived illegitimacy of collaboration with industrial interests emerged during the avian flu scare, too, in the form of two antiviral drugs called Tamiflu and Relenza, both of which enjoy patent protection. This means that the patent holders have the ability to limit the manufacture of their respective drugs to their own company or contractors. At the current pace of production, it would take Roche 10 years to meet the world demand for Tamiflu stockpiles. The United States currently has stockpiles for less than 1 percent of the American population, while the WHO recommends stockpiles for 40 percent of the population. The unequal distribution of vital medicine is clear. Only about 30 countries are purchasing large quantities of the two drugs. This means that most developing countries will have no access to vaccines and antiviral drugs. This perceived injustice led to the decision of the Indonesian government to stop providing WHO with samples from the country.

Pedagogic and Proof Plays

Another feature always present in the politics of lethal epidemic diseases is the idea of teaching, of political pedagogy. Health education is a pervasive characteristic of most, if not all, human societies. Didactic plays are rooted in this deep cultural resource. Didactic plays refer to spectacles that start by dialectical definition, which is then amplified and dramatized by narrative and rhetoric in order to teach people global health issues and advise those with less experience. Pandemic-related didactic dramas come in two forms: introductory didactic plays and advanced didactic plays. The didactic aspect subordinates the unfolding spectacle to the exigencies of the pedagogic purpose of the political variant of a particular pandemic threat. This characteristic varies from direct "preaching" of the facts of by now politicized pandemics to refraining from explicit moralizing and trusting the reader to draw his own lessons from the outcome of the story. The work teaches the facts and figures, but also an advanced moral attitude (prudence). Information is directed to the less initiated and the more nuanced deeper story to those more deeply immersed. These two levels are subordinated in that the teaching of the facts and figures is based on a framework that also teaches right consciousness and attitudes toward the globalizing world.

The overall dynamic actualizes in pandemic spectacles. Latour's (1988) idea of "theater of proof" can offer a history of the medicine-related way of looking into these performances, in which the various actors take on their roles and form different types of collaborative relationships. These relationships may range from strict, authoritative ones to those based on flat network patterns. The key is to demonstrate legitimacy in meeting the challenges posed by the rogue elements of a pandemic.

It is fitting that the theater of proof draws from a famous medical demonstration—the famous 1882 experiment through which Pasteur revealed the effectiveness of vaccination. The experiment lasted for several days and was the focus of intensive attention by the French media. Twenty-five sheep were vaccinated against anthrax and another 25, which were not vaccinated, were painted with red marks. The success of the demonstration was vividly visible to the onlookers, who witnessed the death of all the animals who were not vaccinated, but were visibly marked. This experiment was widely talked about and gave medical research an air of certainty. It offered clear-cut revelatory knowledge about the power of the new health science. Pasteur managed to make the underlying, difficult-to-comprehend hidden reality visible and controllable. Such experiments were conducted around the world. At the level of popular imagination, these laboratory experiments, once transferred into the field, turned into modernity's testing grounds, into theaters of proof. At stake was the legitimacy of modern medicine and the state that had produced it. It also propelled into the foreground a new collaborative arrangement between the heath-science and political authorities. It helped to produce a legitimate system of governance.

What qualities are inherent in the pandemic theater of proof? Latour's idea is that the scientific theater of proof is powerful because of its seeming objective clarity. In this sense, Latour's theater of proof refers to "a physical space where the objects of science are said to be freed from rhetorical distortions, faulty vision, and the inadequacies of the 'lesser' senses" (Crawford 1996, 67). In the same way, the universalizing ethos of the pandemic spectacle contains a tendency to see it not as a social setting only. The humanity vis-à-vis inhumanity confrontation turns into a direct test of modernity's power to govern the rogue qualities of nature.

In this type of setting, the representative of health is a figure that observes the external reality directly. This position is provided to it by the seemingly "true" and "authentic" foundations of Western civilization. These ultimately political foundations are at stake in the emergence of a pandemic. The staging of the theater of proof is meant to produce an acknowledgment that there is a technology of life which has a precise nature, definitions, and protocols. The field of a pandemic contains the visible signs of this technology. Medical personnel in white protective suits, masked doctors, helicopters hovering about, field hospitals, and military presence have been constant features of post–cold war epidemic performances. Another fairly constant and highly visible feature has been the culling and burning of animal carcasses. One of the most unforgettable scenes of BSE, SARS, and avian flu was the piles of killed animals. These visible demonstrations are needed because the pandemic scare is turned into a moment that renders transparent the underlying truths concerning who promotes heath and who does not. For example, the images of SARS in 2003 provided a drama that demonstrated the goodness of organizations such as WHO and held China as suspect when it came to its trustworthiness in an increasingly interconnected world. This demonstrative pattern revealed at a single glance to the average spectator the media representations of SARS spreading in Hong Kong, the presence of the threat, and what was done about it. The theater of proof conveys power and ideology in these seemingly nonpolitical acknowledgments. This pedagogic aspect makes it evident that what is done in the name of disease control and eradication is inherently beyond doubt. It recreates a particular way of defining humanity with an inherent underlying hierarchy. Pandemics are refined into governance exercises that are thought to be beyond politics. Those elements that are feared will hamper the demonstrations are turned into examples of negative politics or into direct enemies colluding with the rogue qualities and hostility of nature.

Modern health propaganda has highlighted the general human interest as its main motivating factor. Because of this apparent humanity, the political agenda of health policies often go unrecognized. However, even a cursory look into the avian flu debate reveals that different actors have their own at least partly incompatible goals. For example, on the surface, the sharing of epidemiological data and samples with the WHO seems the self-evident, right thing to do. It is in accord with the common wisdom that such sharing benefits the whole of humanity and human polity. WHO has a 50-year-old system for sharing influenza virus samples. Countries donate samples to the WHO so that manufacturers relying on the data can maintain the effectiveness of the vaccines. This system had to be renegotiated in early 2007, when Indonesia refused to send samples to the WHO. Indonesia's concern was that it did not stand to gain from the system and that the real beneficiaries were the Western governments in terms of vaccine supplies and the pharmaceutical companies in terms of profits. The vaccines developed from the samples were too expensive for the developing countries, while the Western countries were emptying the markets. Another important reason for the Indonesian decision was its willingness to negotiate with specific drug companies. Indonesia wanted to give its samples directly to a specific pharmaceutical company, bypassing the WHO system. This arrangement would have guaranteed Indonesia more direct benefits in terms of supplies and shared profits. In the end, the crisis was resolved by granting Indonesia the "final say" when it came to the commercialization of drugs developed based on Indonesian data. The Indonesian government's actions offered a rare glimpse into the deeply political nature of the Western pandemic spectacles and into the underlying hierarchical definition of human polity.

The controversy over sharing data illuminates the politics of health: alternative visions, different agendas, co-optive purposes, and clashing interests. It differentiates among actors and defines the way in which they collaborate. Even the modern expert-driven functionalist health governance recognizes some legitimate forms for politics. "Heath-production politics" offer insights into the contemporary ways of defining politics and governance.

In health governance, a positive form of politics is often seen as providing for the functioning of effective apolitical public health. Such positive politics allocates adequate resources and institutions (Siddiqi 1995, 170). Public health involves a more mundane, yet equally necessary, role for politics: institutions and programs have to be established and allocated adequate resources. One has to choose the personnel to work in the functional field, provide funding for the building of offices and laboratories, finance large-scale inspection programs, and so on. As long as the justifications and reasons are based on common interest, this supportive role of politics is not seen as harmful even when it results in disagreements, as long as they do not result in the paralysis of expertise. Perceived harmless disagreement includes "competition" of states over the right to host health institutions, for example. There is also the politics of expert debates over the most effective policies. Experts can argue over the best course of action in maintaining public health. Scientific debates, disagreements, and compromises in the field of expertise are not seen in themselves as political in any negative sense of the word.

When reading public health literature, it soon becomes apparent that the line between positive politics and negative politics is crossed when politics does not enable the functional field, but co-opts it for other purposes. General opinion seems to be that such co-option leads to less effective health policies and that it reflects badly on the perceived legitimacy of global health policies. However, it should be noted that careful co-option relies at least seemingly on effective and legitimate global health. This type of co-option leads to a horizontal, "partnership" kind of collaboration between those professing the modern global health perspective and those with other agendas. This partnership tends to reaffirm and reestablish the underlying rhetorical persuasiveness of the public health perspective while serving additional goals. Besides this, it is possible to conceptualize two other forms of collaboration between political and public health actors. Co-option may be based on a hierarchical situation, where global health is directly subordinated to other goals, such as a strong vision of national security. Health becomes defined as one front in the wider struggle toward a preferred goal. For example, the U.S. HIV/AIDS-related PEPFAR programs—part of "transformational diplomacy"—explicitly aim at preventing state failures and spread of terrorism through effective health programs. The third co-optive collaborative arrangement involves actors who purposefully resign from the modern public health paradigm. For example, the Indonesian refusal to share samples might be seen as a direct challenge to expert-based health governance. An alternative co-optive form of collaboration is the apparent lack of transparency of some of the actors. China was accused of this during the 2003 SARS and later avian flu scares. This type of co-option leads almost invariably to negative prestige and lowering of international status. This co-optive pattern is seen as directly hindering public health efforts, and, as such, it becomes directly associated with the causation of disease. It is handled as a deviant and rogue element.

An example of apparent supportive co-option is the recent regime development stemming from the avian flu—the formation of the International Partnership on Avian and Pandemic Influenza. According to the U.S. Department of State, the partnership aims to elevate the avian flu issue on national agendas, coordinate efforts among donor and affected nations, mobilize and leverage resources, increase transparency in disease reporting and the quality of surveillance, and build local capacity to identify, contain, and respond to an influenza pandemic. On the U.S. side, participation in the partnership is coordinated by the Department of State, which established the Avian Influenza Action Group in March 2006. This group is worked in collaboration by the Departments of Health and Human Services, Agriculture, Homeland Security and Defense, and the U.S. Agency for International Development and other such agencies. The process led to an unbinding declaration ("global partnership initiative"). Among other things, this text states that "enhanced global cooperation on avian and pandemic influenza will provide a template for global cooperation to address other types of health emergencies." These other emergencies refer to biological warfare. The co-option between nation security and international public health is thus clear here. On the surface of it, this co-option is not perceived as negative. It is seen as beneficial to both parties.

The apoliticization of governance action in pandemic emergencies is among the most important places to look for the ways in which politics and power hierarchies matter in contemporary humanitarianism. All the actors talk on behalf of humanity. The failure and success in this process are relative. Some actors co-opt better than others. This circulation of legitimacy provides different opportunities for co-option. The actors close to the top of the Western hierarchy—that is, Western governments, international actors, and multinational businesses—have a long co-optive tradition. To answer these questions, it may be suggested that diseases manifest themselves in engaging and engrossing public plays of legitimacy and experimentation with various instruments of international legitimacy.

Further Elements of the Pandemic Theatre

The "coming plague" narratives provide an additional aspect of the imagined scene for pandemic performances. There exists a growing strand of literature that reinforces the idea that several historical turning points have come about when a serious epidemic disease has afflicted a population (e.g., Diamond 2004). The impact of lethal epidemic diseases is described in terms of a catastrophic blow against populations that exist in a confined geographical space—for example, the collapse of the Mayan culture or the ability of the Spaniards to conquer the Americas. Epidemics manifest themselves in geographical confines by affecting mortality, population density and distribution, and behavioral patterns. In this general line of research, it is fairly common to examine how often unrecognized human behavioral patterns—for example, the relationship between humans and domestic animals—affected the emergence, spread, and distribution of diseases.

The metaphor of "population" has, in recent pandemic research literature, been complemented by the concept of civilization. Especially in the research dealing with the first contact between the European and Amerindian civilizations, there is a tendency to treat the impact in terms of disease exchange between civilizations. The hypotheses about syphilis and smallpox as vital factors in civilizational contact are widely used and deemed probable. Often, these arguments are made in order to obtain some contemporary relevance. They contain the message of a possible coming plague that might threaten the Western populations. The theories about past inter-civilizational encounters are made to matter and cause alarm in the present context.

Much of this influential interdisciplinary discourse uses population-based ideas of human behavior. This discourse can be further illuminated by contrasting it with other notions of politics. For example, a wider look into political theory should reveal that human behavioral cohesion is not due only to geographical barriers, but mainly to the existence of multidimensional political boundaries. This basic realization is often bypassed by the slogan that "political borders are porous to diseases." In this respect, there seems to be a "human animal" metaphor inherent in the popular concept of a population. The apparent bypassing of the Aristotelian notion of humans as political animals living in polities, instead of populations, is in itself a political practice. It refers to the desire to treat epidemics as apolitical threats. The terms chosen are meant to achieve certain objectives. For instance, they make politics disappear. Politics is made to cease at the populational or civilizational level. The population metaphor contains a sense of geographically and naturally contained entities. Civilization is used to evoke a sense of the widest possible human polity, humanity, which lacks "politics" in the sense of there being conflict over the interests or purposes of human polity. The dual movement toward human population and humanity finds its most natural home in contemporary humanitarian thought.

At the level of metaphorical political bodies, the sufferer in the pandemic plays is imagined as an individual and humanity. The individual as the body in pain is the topos of modern humanitarian compassion. The individualization of the sufferer points to an important watershed in the history of the sufferer construction. The modern sufferer is often a contextless figure existing in the heavily temporalized situation of the health emergency. The figure represents all humanity through being human at the mercy of the outside elements of inhumanity—that is, birds spreading avian flu or cows turning into BSE-polluted hamburgers. This "zooming in" to the individual level allows for the construction of the epicenter of suffering, where the voiceless sufferer communicates only through the visual language of hospital patients or health-care workers wearing protective gear. The complexity—for example, the historicity of various groups of people, their self-understanding, and the variance of the importance placed on collective suffering—recedes to the background and the patient as an expression of humanity's pain crops up. For example, a person dying of Ebola in Zaire starts to embody fear and danger. His individual qualities are lost if they are not regarded as vital for the cultural explanation of "what is happening." The distant sufferer in some faraway location, with distinct and shared memories, beliefs, and myths about what has happened, why, and for what end, is cleansed when the figure is refined into Westernized form, into a generic representation of what, how, and where things might go wrong (e.g., Malkki 1996, 380).

For a distant sufferer to become a member of the general human polity, it has to be denied membership of other seemingly narrower political communities. The only exception is when such sufferers are closely associated with the rogue. For example, the skin color of the Ebola sufferers might be used to evoke negative sentiments connected with Africa: people "there" are close to nature and might, therefore, allow a portal for "rogue" nature to hit the main trunk of humanity.

The theories of the origin of HIV/AIDS contain these sentiments. The largely mythological point of origin story argues that decades ago, somewhere in Africa, there was a close encounter between an infected monkey and a human being, which led to the crossing of the species barrier. The sexual orientation of people living with HIV/AIDS provides a vital icon for the popular depictions of the syndrome. It matters also in the visual production of the disease and in the embodiment of fear. The Ebola stories share the same "Africa, where infected monkeys come into close contact with men" sentiment. The avian flu stories treat Asians in the same way. A person from the "populous" continent is turned into a person whose fever is due to close contact with domestic and wild birds. The visual rhetoric of pandemics uses some individual qualities of the infected people to translate the pandemic into a culturally readable form.

The perceived apolitical conditions inherent in the humanitarian imagery of human polity are comparable to those produced by the related notion of developmentalism (Ferguson 1990, 16). The term "antipolitics machine" refers to the "development" industries' application of technical solutions to such political problems as conflict, poverty, suffering, and hunger. The machine—that is, the developmentalist discourse, repertoire of established "solutions," and the infrastructures/networks of actors involved—renders the politics of the distant others into a series of rational/technical problem-solving exercises. Although this production of subjects is itself a political act, it is political in a specific sense of the word: it is politically privileged by its appearance of being apolitical. Ronald Barthes's (1984, 145) concept of "depoliticized speech" sheds further light on the humanitarian antipolitics machine. The practice of depoliticized speech is based on mythologizing political actions and turning them into something that is self-evident, required, and essential. The sufferer is produced as an ahistorical and universal humanitarian subject in the apolitical governance language of international agencies (Malkki 1996, 378). However, such speech only hides the deep political power significance of this manner of constructing the body in pain. The rendering of humanitarianism into a realm where ethics, not politics, matters enables specific types of humanitarian action and its co-option by actors in whose interest it is to turn the distant place into an apolitical object of Western intervention (e.g., Minh Ha 2004, 269).

Pandemic diseases become apoliticized in a particular way through the legitimacy, pedagogic, and proof plays. Firstly, the scare becomes localized. Diseases are identified with a particular area and, often, with particular people—"racialized", gendered, sexualized, and "ethnicized." In both the avian flu and SARS episodes, the people whose diseases were considered alarming were found in Asia. These people are in the foreground of Western media because of outsourcing and fast economic growth. Both print and TV used repetitive images such as Asian citizens in masks and animals in the southern Chinese "wet markets." Another important aspect of pandemics is their tendency to temporalize the situation. Time becomes increasingly salient. There is a rush to find a cure or solution, to track and isolate the carriers. The tempo of the globalizing world easily finds its correspondence in the disease imagery. It is often the case that conclusive scientific proof cannot be achieved without time-consuming research. This situation often leads to immediate actions based on worst-case scenarios. Often, the worst-case imagery blends with stereotypical and popular beliefs.

The avian flu episode encapsulated many of the aforementioned features. The scare made governments all over the world spend billions in planning for a potential influenza pandemic—buying medicines, running disaster drills, and developing strategies for tighter border controls. These actions are seemingly apolitical because they take place inside the humanitarian, pro-humanity frame. They are perceived as necessary and unavoidable. Many of the planned or implemented policies concentrated on different isolation procedures. Isolation is aimed at separating individuals with the infectious illness in their homes, in hospitals, or in designated facilities. Quarantines bring about separation and restriction of movement, that is, of a group of people, who, while not yet ill, have potentially been exposed to an infectious agent. The isolation plans often referred to different forms of social distancing (e.g., within the workplace, social distancing measures could take the form of placing moratoriums on hand-shaking, substituting teleconferences for face-to-face meetings, staggering breaks, and posting infection control guidelines). Places of assembly, such as churches, schools, and theaters, were closed. At the level of the national and international borders, the plans included drastic modifications in movement patterns—restricting movements at the border, instituting reductions in the transportation sector, and applying cordon sanitaire procedures.

At the moment, the apolitical machine of avian flu works through two major programs. At the international level, avian flu has led to two cooperative initiatives: the United States–initiated International Partnership on Avian and Pandemic Influenza and the Global Preparedness Plan led by the WHO. The United States–initiated partnership is meant to improve international surveillance, transparency, timeliness, and response capabilities. President Bush, addressing the UN General Assembly in September 2005, said: "As we strengthen our commitment to fighting malaria and AIDS, we must also remain on the offensive against new threats to public health such as the avian influenza. If left unchallenged, this virus could become the first pandemic of the twenty-first century. We must not allow that to happen. Today I am announcing a new International Partnership on Avian and Pandemic Influenza. The Partnership requires countries that face an outbreak to immediately share information and provide samples to the World Health Organization. By requiring transparency, we can respond more rapidly to dangerous outbreaks and stop them in time" (available on http://italy.usembassy.gov/viewer/article.asp?article=/file2005_09/alia/a5091309.htm). The partnership's apparent emphasis is on transparency. Transparency means international access and wide collaboration with the international community. It requires countries facing an outbreak to immediately share information and provide samples to the WHO. The WHO plan assists WHO member states and those responsible for public health and medical and emergency preparedness to respond to pandemic influenza-related threats. It is meant to assess risks and come up with preparedness plans that can then be recommended to the member states.

The policies reinforce political boundaries. Most clearly, they reinforce the unequal distribution of influence in world affairs. U.S. dominance is clear as is its co-optive relationship with the private and public international health actors. Various isolation and transparency measures complement and reinforce the hierarchical distribution of power.

It can be argued that the global political space is in flux, constantly shifting and changing. The primary concern is over the consequences of earlier national, ethnic, and religious boundaries being rapidly transgressed. The conventional borders, which have been the foundation of the world view, trust, and loyalty, are becoming porous and weak. New processes such as global warming and the war on terror are capturing the imagination. The declinist sentiments, anxieties, and concerns over the nature, purpose, and consequences of events provide much of the dynamics for the prevailing pandemic frame. It is in this frame that pandemics such as the avian flu actualize as a global concern that embodies much of the myriad background anxieties. Besides anxieties, the episodic pandemic dramas provide a staging ground for demonstrations of legitimacy, effectiveness, and power. The episodes turn into highly readable plays that transform and can be used to influence the background frame. These captivating plays are used as a momentary criterion or standard for the morality and legitimacy of the various political actors. Failures translate into a deficiency in fulfilling the perceived obligations that are essential for membership and the consequent rights of the increasingly global community.

The avian flu episode may be read as a reminder of the world's networked nature. The apparent necessity to secure the global network is judged to demand increased coordination and harmonization or preparedness, prevention, response, and containment activities. The pandemic was perceived as a global danger that manifested itself at the local level. This connection enables global "acts of responsibility" at the local level. In a way, the disease came with a message that demands further governance or integration between localities. It demanded reimagining political organization.

Pandemic actions have become an integral part of the humanitarian frame. Compassion is felt toward the human polity and, implicitly, for the order within. People feel for the fate of humanity through the pandemic plays. This feeling is political in that it regards the present civilization as worth feeling for. It also connects the imagery of human suffering with the fate of the civilization. The resulting politico-somatics is an important part of neoclassical vorticity. The deepening and enlarging spread of the grand movement has found its way to human bodies. The post-9/11 movement in the world order is arousing emotionality—anxiety, fear, and compassion. These sentiments are essential ingredients when the human polity faces threats in the form of pandemic diseases.

7

Beyond Humanitarian Compassion

> Though our brother is on the rack, as long as we ourselves are at our ease, our senses will never inform us of what he suffers. They never did, and never can, carry us beyond our own person, and it is by the imagination only that we can form any conception of what are his sensations. . . . It is the impressions of our own senses only, not those of his, which our imaginations copy. By the imagination, we place ourselves in his situation.
>
> *Adam Smith, The Theory of Moral Sentiments*

Ludwig Wittgenstein saw knowledge in terms of acknowledgment and recognition of authorities and Michel Foucault suggested that at the end, all knowledge is associated with forms of cruelty. In spite of the superficial nature of this combination of thoughts, when it comes to humanitarianism, they become mutually coherent: Acts of violence lead to recognition of compassionate knowledge. The tradition of humanitarianism acknowledges various forms of violence in terms ranging from recognizable humanitarian crises to humanitarian military interventions.

Humanitarianism poses ethical dilemmas and expresses cultural beliefs, but it also offers ways for establishing the communicability of humanity. Humanitarianism offers a major way of imagining long-distance human contact. In this chapter, I will chart this multifaceted and paradoxical contact from the perspective of imaginative memory. The ability of getting into the minds of the distant others has often been pictured as an act involving seeing the plight of others in their terms and through their eyes. It is suggested that this "revelatory" connection is based largely on the imaginer's own inter-subjective memory images, on the memories of past moments of humanitarianism. I will clarify the theme of humanitarian memory by placing it in the tradition of artificial memory and of combining memory images (i.e., combinatorics). I will review some recent cases of political mobilization of compassion from the mnemonic perspective. The aim is to chart the limits of humanitarian types of knowledge, or what is recognized as humanitarian and requiring humanitarian action.

The strong role played by the perceived power of imagination in the history of humanitarianism justifies the examination of its role in the modern constructions of the passion for compassion. What is a global mobilization of empathy? What are the various ingredients of its construction? It is evident that bursts of humanitarianism may have wide consequences in world politics. Cases such as Bosnia, Somalia, and Kosovo provide proof that humanitarianism can be the basis of argumentation for international action. The politicization of suffering may refer to the mobilization of empathy at the grassroots level. In most cases, these mobilizations are routed through the transnational community and their impetus provides a visible agency to the various NGOs. Acts such as urgent appeals for generosity, spontaneous donations, collection of eyewitness accounts, views from the ground, and testimonies of inhumanity are constituents of this type of mobilization. Under certain conditions, these mobilizations may include a more or less prominent international aspect. Governments and their organs are propelled into action in political movements of solidarity. In some cases, the solidarity is not limited to international emergency aid, coordination of donations, or intergovernmental meetings, but proceeds along the path of a humanitarian intervention and humanitarian war. My aim is to chart the factors that influence how human suffering becomes an issue in world politics and how world order takes the form of humanitarianism. In other words, what are the preconditions for this type of politicization?

The instinctive connection between signs of mass suffering and humanitarian reaction is rare. The more synthetic, political aspects of humanitarianism are examined here: the nuanced iconographies, sophisticated "figuralities," and intricate patterns of authority that mobilize humanitarian actions. Moreover, this contrived humanitarianism has a strong relationship with the configurations of world order. Humanitarian actions target those at the peripheries and margins. They identify who is who and by what means the different levels of the power hierarchy interact and communicate.

It may be argued that the politics of global indifference comprises a culturally crafted tradition, which is closely linked with that of humanitarianism. The "images of the heart" are based on skilled use of "codes and conventions" that manage the different outcomes of the action – inaction dialectic. When images manage to create alarm and a spreading sense that something must be done, they do so because they remind one of the powerful images of past humanitarian crises. It is suggested that the art of humanitarianism consists of combining the right humanitarian memory images with current images. The same political skill is involved in the creation of sanitized and "pretty" images of mass suffering that will not react with the old images in ways that will mobilize people for action. In the hybrid concept of humanitarian war, both these aspects of political skill come into play simultaneously. This combinatory synergy clearly reveals the hyperbolic stakes involved, and identifies the protagonist for humanity, the suffering victims, the witnessing audience, and tells them apart from the barbaric antagonists. While illuminating roles and responsibilities, humanitarian wars acknowledge patterns of power.

What is the place of humanitarianism in the international relations thought process? Humanitarianism may be considered as an institution developed for a particular purpose in international society. It is connected with imagination, communication, and identification. In the history of humanitarian thought, the feeling of compassion is often based on the logic of mirroring. This refers to the ability to identify with others and their plight—this identification takes place in the imagination. This thematic may be formulated in terms of contemporary international relations thought. In constructivist international relations literature, which looks for answers in inter-subjective processes, identity is often considered an equation consisting of ego and alter ego (e.g., Wendt 1992, 392). This means that the acknowledged sense of sameness contrasts with the sense of difference and one's desire to identify with something is paralleled by turning away from something else (e.g., Katzenstein 1996, 109). The idea is that the stark contrast inherent in this dual movement provides an actor with the spark of its own identity. In an important respect, this identity equation contains an ethical theory concerning the relationship between the two dichotomous components: Identity is a statement concerning the relationship of the one over the other—for example, superiority, inferiority, integration, segregation, antipathy, and, most importantly, empathy—and brings forward the various justifications and statements of moral worth of the ego over the alter ego. The common stock constructivist framework is often strengthened with a more fully developed understanding of the dialectic playfulness. Further appreciation may be brought about through the inclusion of the general imaginative aspect into the plays of identity. The memory, in particular, as an aspect of the imagination, plays a crucial part in these tense plays of attraction and repulsion.[1]

The Visual Rhetoric of Sanctity

In a legitimate humanitarian intervention, it is often the case that humanity itself is imagined as being challenged to intervene. Its existence and values are being called to test. An important part of these pedagogic and ethical dramas is the collectively felt sense of immediate human tragedy. It is hypothesized that the precondition for the emergence of this tense sense is an acknowledged connection of the present circumstances to past instances that are similarly revelatory in nature. This connection highlights the role that acts of combination play in humanitarianism. They bring forth a particular view to the victims, envision them as sufferers of a specific type of mass violence (e.g., indiscriminate killing, deportation, genocide, and ethnic cleansing), and identify them as a bonded group of people being violated by another identifiable group. The scene of decomposition is set for the distant Western viewer: Sudden political regression violently and acutely affects a geographically, religiously, or ethnically distant group of people. This view has an epistemological dimension. This "knowledge" exists in two forms. On the one hand, it refers to the antiepistemology process—that is, covered and erased knowledge—that transpires where the groups are engaged in a violent relationship. The parties of the mass violence engage in the undoing of any certain knowledge that might have been previously shared. Elaine Scarry (1985, 7) uses the term "radical epistemological doubt" to describe these processes in which violence goes hand in hand with nonacknowledgments of former knowledge and the accompanying unraveling of knowledge/power relationships. On the other hand, there evolves a revealing relationship between this violent locus and its distant spectators.

The knowledge inherent in strong bursts of humanitarianism is felt rather than cognized. This type of lived epistemology may be compared to the kratophanic experience. The situation, which carries with it a sense of awe-inspiring power, is tense, dramatic, and open-ended. The coexistence of contradictory forces—that is, the victims of violence, the protagonists of humanity, and its antagonists—is further reinforced by the anxiety over hidden intentions and undiscovered identities. The spectator is tantalized "by the probability of the improbable" (Gaines 2002, 784). Kratophany describes humanitarian drama at its most critical moments when the "images of heart," values of humanity, and bad elements are suddenly brought forth. Spectators are drawn apprehensively to the repulsive violence through their sense of compassion. Whereas kratophantic knowledge refers to sudden manifestations of contradictory forces, the related awareness of hierophany conveys a sense of extraordinariness that contrasts sharply with the more mundane praxis. The spectators suddenly become aware that what is taking place is extraordinary and carries a sense of "something higher." Hierophany also reveals who are the actors with the power to do something under extraordinary circumstances, and what is the "map" of world order at a more "metaphysical" level.

Revelatory-political epistemology emphasizes the role of sudden experiences and engrossing spectacles. It also highlights the existence of preexisting and well-rehearsed communal means for the production and consumption of such experiences. Hahn (1997, 1079) uses the phrase "visual rhetoric of sanctity" in reference to the rhetoric that condenses the significant past and the imaged sacred essence present within the particularities of a given space. This act of combining images creates a charged frame where the experience is one of revelation. The rehearsed nature of the humanitarian frame—or, the visual rhetoric of humanitarianism—points to the importance of remembering and memory in the connection of creating a sense of humanity under threat. Humanitarian spectacles may be appreciated in terms of key memory images. The intervention in Bosnia provides an example of a humanitarian spectacle. The publishing of images portraying starved men behind barbed wire in 1992 restaged suddenly what was taking place in Bosnia in terms of humanitarian memory. These famous photographs, which combined holocaust iconography with the events in a disintegrating Yugoslavia, caused an immediate outrage and, in the course of a single day, seemed to shift the opinion of many Western governments in a drastically more interventionist direction. Judging from this type of anecdotal evidence, memory images may play an essential role in humanitarianism. The moment of revelation is constituted in terms of past cues. The various sedimented key images left by past instances of humanitarianism can be innovatively recombined to produce new instances of empathy relevant to international politics.

The Beginnings of Synthetic Humanitarianism

The general epistemological position of this work has been based on appreciation of the imaginative memory's role in the creation of prudent brute facts.[2] This starting point leads to the examination of humanitarianism as a phenomenon connected with acts of memory. It is significant that imaginative acts of identification have occupied a central role in the history of humanitarianism. According to the Enlightenment era thinkers, it was through imagination that a person was thought to be able to enter into the shoes of another. With the help of this imaginary placement, the feelings of a sufferer could be understood. However, a significant watershed remained. Was this act of compassion due to selfishness or altruism?

When one places oneself in the place of a sufferer, then the compassion might arise from one's own interest: "What is happening to the other person might happen to me one day, therefore, I have to help." This type of humanitarianism is based on recognition of mutual self-interest (Slim 2001, 325). On the other hand, the imaginative act may allow one to better appreciate another person's suffering. The basis of compassion may be the better understanding of another's situation, instead of the "what if this were to happen to me" type of thinking. Thus, imagination was thought of in terms of a faculty that allows one to form a bond with others and, moreover, to communicate with their plight.

The communicative channel that opened between spectators and sufferers has often been thought of in terms of the outward signs of suffering. Instead of having a symbolic social status, this communication was imagined in more instinctive, iconic terms. Compassion was more of a natural reflex than a conscious decision: "The doctrine of irresistible compassion as found in the eighteenth century was probably not more than a hundred years old. It grew up with and was one of the motivating forces behind humanitarianism, and it contributed to the spread of humanitarianism by establishing an image or an idea of human nature that made humanitarian feelings insistently 'natural'" (Fiering 1976, 196). This natural humanitarian instinct competed with the expressions of more cynical writers. Their emphasis was on the morbid nature of animal passions and on the calculative tendencies in human nature. In contrast to these writers, moralist thinkers such as Adam Smith stressed passions as a means of imaginative communication. These thinkers drew from the likes of Thomas Moore, who perceived that outward signs of oppression, such as tears, sighs, or weeping, strike a chord with human inner senses and appeal to compassion.

On the other hand, the tendency to equate compassion with relatively naturally occurring emotional communication contrasted with the more artificial emphasis. Besides the tendency to naturalize humanitarian communication, the nineteenth century conceived of human compassion in emergent, synthetic, and artificial terms. Commiseration was given a communal status, whereby it stood for a modern, enlightened, and sophisticated humanity. To reiterate, the increasingly influential progressive model of humanity saw compassion as an artificial or emergent property. According to this important strand of humanitarianism, "it . . . is a historical stage in the education of the emotions" (Fiering 1976, 212). Humanitarianism entailed an innovation of a new prototypical person, who was capable of transmitting and receiving commiseration.

Humanitarianism thus turned into a skill consisting of sharpening and refining the naturally occurring ability of identifying with the situation of others. Compassion was seen as involving active stimulation and requiring sources of inspiration. Furthermore, the iconic humanitarianism began to interact with a more communally significant, symbolic, and ritualistic humanitarianism. Artfully performed humanitarian actions turned into social signifiers and conveyers of legitimacy at the international level as well.

Contemporary Setting: Humanitarian War

Kofi Annan, on September 20, 1999, told the UN General Assembly that "[m]assive and systematic violations of human rights—wherever they may take place—should not be allowed to stand." After the end of the Cold War, the United States's role in the world was reinvented. The "ends" and "means" underwent major developments and innovations. These changes led to the emergence of the contemporary history of "humanitarian war." The beginning of this combination of concepts may be traced back to the war in Bosnia. The images of the skeletal figures behind barbed wire, which crystallized the perception of ethnic cleansing and massacres, aroused a strong sense that immediate relief should be delivered and that military means could be a major component of the rescue. There were calls for action—for a humanitarian militarism.

The next important stage in the evolution of the hybrid concept was Somalia in 1993. The events there showed the limits of the practical applicability of the concept and, thereby, caused rethinking of the confines of the practice. The development and further sophistication of humanitarian war was greatly induced by the 1994 massacre of 600,000 Rwandans. After the Rwandan failure, the more conservatively inclined thinkers brought in the themes of the United States's moral mission and stopping the spreading contagion of anarchy in the form of failed states. The sense of duty was seen comparable to resisting the perceived tide of the "evil empire" during the cold war. It was in the shadow of Rwanda that those with a more liberal ideology started to shed their instinctive resistance to military operations. The iconic meaning of U.S. military intervention as "imperialism" started to be less clear-cut.

Further images of out-of-control dictators ruling by barbarous means were added to the gallery of figures following the 1995 massacre of Srebenica: Milosevic and the leaders of the Bosnian Serbs. The new developments during the 1999 Kosovo War amplified the repositioning of American relatedness to the rest of the world in terms of humanitarian war.[3] However, the hybrid concept was also a signifier of a larger framework. The concept blended the just war tradition, international humanitarian law, and universalistic ethics with the United States's role and mission in the increasingly hegemonic world.[4] The synthesis of the 1990s redefined the evil empire in terms of genocide actors, enemies of freedom, and threats to the international community. It is possible to see the extension of this line of thinking in the post-9/11 humanitarian wars. However, the innovations and extensions in preventive warfare intermingled with the humanitarian aspect, and in the cases of Afghanistan and Iraq, overshadowed it (e.g., Coady 2002, 7).[5] This newer hybrid emphasizes the use of "sanitary" means of violence against enemies in the efforts to protect civilians from human rights violations. However, the language of humanitarianism is still present in preventive war rhetoric.

The discourse of national interest has become more difficult to tell apart from the more universalistic language of humanity. Perhaps, this is not surprising. There are some historical precedents for the coincidence of hegemonic interests and moral interests. A hierarchical world order tends to find its legitimacy in its role as the protagonist for humanity. Under these conditions, world disorder is often defined in terms of the mass suffering—imagined to be caused by warlords and bandits who do not have any "viable" moral claim of their own—that exists at the margins of the "civilized" world (Hobsbawm 1969). The calls for compassion for the distant other in combination with an overwhelming military force establish a powerful tool. It may be used to show a humanitarian image and to control the margins of world order. Another important feature of a humanitarian war is that it specifies the enemies of humanity. What follows are bush wars against largely unstructured and socially less sophisticated distant enemies. The enemy has traditionally been faceless. It has been defined only through the quality and quantity of violence that the imperial state has used against it (Hobsbawn 1969, 14). More recent times have brought the quality and quantity inflicted by the "marginal elements" into the equation. The images of such violence, in combination with the more imperial use of force, turn distant and obscure places into examples of power and identify the destructive evilness of the enemies of humanity.

Artificial Memories and Agent Images

One way of approaching synthetic humanitarianism is to contrast it with the tradition of artificial memory. This connection is meant to illuminate the use of images and their combinations in producing engrossing sentiments. What is memory as an artificial cultural tradition and as an imaginative device? The art of memory was developed as an artificial tool for the perfecting of natural memory by authors such as Cicero,

Quintilian, and the anonymous author of *Ad Herennium*. Already, the classical method of memory was based on "generating visions or fantasies (phantasmatae)" in the locus of the mind (Enders 1999, 52). It was presumed that the utility of the memory relied on a vivid imagination, whereby things could be remembered and reproduced. Without the vivid imagination, things could not be remembered and that which cannot be remembered is not part of the inter-subjective reality—that is, it cannot be brought before the inner eye of the audience by direct reference or indirect allusion. The art of memory was first and foremost a tradition connected with the act of public speech-giving, a performance that was more or less political in nature. The idea was that any powerful, impromptu, extemporaneous speaker derives these qualities from a well-constructed mental "container," where the schema of the speech is present, "written" on an orderly memory locus with the help of striking memory images and phantasms. It was generally thought that these parts of the artificial memory work together to produce dynamic movement. The crux of the art was agency extempore, which works for the speaker and helps to establish a general persuasive element among the participants of the communicative act.

Different from the concepts of cultural or collective memory, which highlight relatively stable and durable structures, the art of memory tradition was founded on the capacity of changing situations to produce added value and to dramatize and animate things in manageable ways. With the art of memory, things can be brought into illuminating relationships that "stick" in the mind. This organizing and orienting work performed by the memory apparatus gives it practical meaning and justifies its use despite its artificialness. Mary Carruthers (2000, 17), in her well-argued mapping of Christian and, in particular, the monastic art of memory, states that memory is best understood as an imaginative apparatus, or as a "machine of thought." The work done with this machine is connected with the ability to produce meaningful thought sequences—speech acts—in communicative and dialogical situations. It should be noted that this machine is an active part of its larger environment. It helps its users to orient themselves vis-à-vis particular embeddings. Memory becomes a device that works to orient one's agency in a particular way. Therefore, the process of refining one's memory through artificial means amounts to perfecting the actor's ability to orient. Memory provides a way of seeing the environment in a particular way by illuminating the persuasive element in any particular communicative situation. In an important way, the machine of thought gives the capacity of serendipitous ad-hoc-ness to its user, which allows an actor to use contingency, arbitrary happenings, surprises, and even errors in an advantageous manner. Thus, the power of the machine of thought may be measured in its ability to orient an actor to see possibilities in chancy situations.

The artificial sharpening of memory has two major traditions. The purely dialectic and imageless Ramist memory technology was developed mainly by Pierre de la Ramée (1515–72), who was a Huguenot and became a martyr of the Saint Bartholomew's Day massacre.[6] His Ramist memory systems were championed by the Protestants, especially in England (Yates 1966, 130). Ramism developed the idea of the orderly memory locus toward dialectic logic. This logic starts from a general viewpoint and branches out toward particulars by drawing dualistic distinctions like a tree of knowledge or branches of science. The general disciplines of knowledge are ever further subdivided into more specific topics. The "knowledge tree" of reality branches out from abstract to practical in the form of ever-expanding dichotomies. From the sixteenth century onward, the dialectic logic was pictured in the form of classificatory and encyclopedic maps, which were thought to be helpful in gaining insights into the inherent order in the apparent heterogeneity of the creation.[7] The underlying teaching was that there was a fundamental logic behind the diversity and the utility of memory consisted of the ability to systematically order this complexity (White 2005, 133). What made Ramism appealing to Protestant and scientific thought was that it was based on the application of strict form, rather than images. This resonated well with the iconoclastic trends of the time. The movement against religious idols managed to wipe away images, not only from physical sacred spaces, but also from constructs of a more personal and communal metal type.[8]

What were these mental images—"idols" or "demons"—resisted by the Ramist dialectic logic? The Ramist memory system competed with a more image-centered Brunoen memory technology (Yates 1966).[9] Giordano Bruno (1548-1600), a martyr for a different cause, drew from the church fathers, Thomas Aquinas and Albertus Magnus, in his emphasis of powerful and mind-arousing images. They had been very influential in their strong, yet qualified, support for such memory images.[10] It is important to note that images were held in suspect. For Magnus and Aquinas, the noble cause of getting into the Civitas Dei ("City of God") made the use of artificial and sometimes monstrous memory images more legitimate. For the likes of Bruno and Leibniz, the more image-based systems of memory provided ways to form new innovative insights into nature and human affairs.

The skill of making things stick in common memory—and thus to remain part of momentary reality—had to do with active animation and dramatization. It is important to note that the images of memory were not only striking—for example, monstrous, strange, arbitrary, or violent—but also active. The anonymous author of *Ad Herennium* said that phantasms should be striking: "We ought, then, to set up images of a kind that can adhere longest in memory" (*Ad Herennium*, 3, 37). Besides striking, the images had to be active: "And we shall do so if we establish likeness as striking as possible; if we set up images that are not many or vague, but doing something (agents)." In this tradition of stressing activity and action, the images were called agent images, imagined agents.[11]

The idea of agent images had a lasting impact. In modern times, the evidence of agent images and their creative combinations are present in diverse fields such as marketing and political communication. For example, Sharrad (1995, 100), in his study of post-colonialist memory, refers to the phantasms by studying the writer Wilson Harris: Harris views images as "agents of the imagination which remind us or the protagonist of different aspects of experience." The agencies of the images are like reapplicable "masks," which (re)define that what they remind us of. A properly made agent becomes a type of automaton which "lives" and does its work within the memory. Agent images are active agents due to their ability to orient and inspire. An agent image may be considered a powerful memory aid that can inspire or captivate the imagination and move an actor to action.

Deweyan and Wittgensteinian Combinatorics

Before proceeding to further examine humanitarian imagination, I have to point out an important development that took place in the art of memory tradition in the seventeenth and eighteenth centuries, which took it toward the art of combining and innovating. It appears that the relatively fragile nature of natural memory was the impetus for the devising of both types of artificial memory schemata. In this sense, art of memory techniques try to consolidate memory. However, in the case of image-based memory, the consolidation is of a specific type. It tries to tap into the serendipitous consequences of this fallibility: "[t]he very fallibility of memory involves us in mutual reconstructions beyond solipsistic enclosures" (Sharrad 1995, 106). The aim is not to eliminate error, but to play with combinations that naturally result from it. It is possible to exploit paradoxical inversions and complex complementarities in ways that make memory an active tool, instead of a passive repository.

The artificial devices of memory developed in this direction after early modern times. The idea seems to have been to move toward designs for memory loci that could utilize randomness for advantageous and innovative purposes. This may be compared to the way the double-helix structure of DNA allows cells to tap into random mutations for the purposes of adaptation and evolution. Many of what can be by now called memory technologies were based on schemas of concentric wheels.[12] These wheels, which could be spun relatively to each other, provided a new dynamic development in the construction of an orderly memory locus. The symbols contained on these imaginary wheels functioned as memory images (Rossi 2000, 177). By spinning the wheels mentally, various innovative combinations of the symbolic images were possible. The combinations brought up complex thoughts that were meant to open novel ways of thinking about something and the corresponding innovative rhetoric. Thus, the Brunoean art of memory developed into models that saw memory as an innovative technique. The philosophy of this technology was based on the added value that expanded and novel perspectives can bring into social situations.

The motives for revolving the mental wheels ranged from mere curiosity, willingness to explore different possible combinations, and analysis of the complexity of reality to the more practical aims of remembering and innovating in relation to changing situations that demanded flexibility and ingenuity.[13] With the coming of a dynamic combinatory locus with active agent images, the emphasis of memory technology changed to the direction of innovation and generation. It turned more into the theater of life, into a dramatic device meant to capture and use the lively, fickle, and imaginative aspect of existence (Yates 1966, 312). One such later schema was the nineteenth-century idea of serendipity, which has a connection with the theater of life tradition. The common element was that these later schemata of combinatorics emphasized the innovative features of explorative human thought. The ability to see connections between seemingly disconnected concepts or ideas was thought of as an educative game of awareness that allowed its player to expand his mental horizons.[14]

The combinatorics moved further away from mere cognitive framing of memory in a more formative direction. This type of thinking can be seen in many twentieth-century writers. For example, the general spirit of combinatorics finds affinity with Eric Voegelin, who regarded political concepts as "evocations." Voegelin's use of the term refers to the formative rather than descriptive nature of political concepts. They call up something new and assist in meaning making at the same time that they attempt an objective account of political reality. These two functions of political concepts enable each other: "Above all: the political idea is only to a limited extent descriptive of any reality; its primary function is not a cognitive, but a formative one. The political idea is not an instrument of description of a political unit, but an instrument of its creation" (Voegelin 1997, 226). The combinatorics, as a tool in the service of evocations, is one way to understand the influence that artificial memory technologies had on more contemporary thought.

Agent images and their combinations call up orienting and inspiring tools that examine novel sides of reality. To further explore this thematic and take it toward humanitarianism, John Dewey's thoughts on art offer a relevant bridgehead. More specifically, Dewey's ideas concerning art as experience may be read from the perspective of combinatorics. This bridge will further explicate the role of agent images in contemporary discourse and, especially, in contemporary practices of conveying humanitarian sentiments. In his *Art as Experience*, Dewey (1980, 7) wants to deglorify art from the high pedestal on which it has been placed and reposition it in the stream of everyday life and as a part of the "significant life of an organized community." According to Dewey, art punctuates and accents the "emotions and ideas that are associated with the chief institutions of social life." In this way, Dewey intends to recover "the continuity of esthetic experience with normal processes of living" (1980, 10). Through this move, Dewey also redefines the term "art." Art was part of everybody's life and, as a practice, in everyone's possession. The importance of this repositioning is practical: through everyday art, anybody can beautify, refine, and expand their everyday experience.

The Deweyan practice of art is a means to an end: the end is just and fair democracy. Art contains a general transformative tendency besides establishing a shared persuasive element for a community of people. The transformative element, for Dewey, is one of recombination. It extends existing connections between good and evil, acts as a catalyst in thinking beyond the taken for granted, offers new insights, and broadens the potential for new meanings (Goldblatt 2006, 17). Deweyan art highlighted the ability of artistic details to refine people's thinking and open their minds to new and alternative connections. Dewey (1980, 131) quotes approvingly from Albert Barnes: "There are in our minds in solution a vast number of emotional attitudes, feelings ready to be re-excited when the proper stimulus arrives, and more than anything else, it is these forms, this residue of experience, which . . . constitute the artist's capital. What is called the magic of the artist resides in his ability to transfer these values from one field of experience to another, to attach them to the objects of our common life, and by his imaginative insight make these objects poignant and momentous."

Dewey seems to suggest a refined memory—a residue of experience—that can be used in the "magical" reattachment of feeling, value, and meaning to a new circumstance in ordinary life. The excitable memory cues provide a vehicle for rendering new events "poignant and momentous." This transformative and democratic magic of "everyman as an artist" appears to fit well into the scheme of things in combinatorics. Dewey's (1980, 122) notion that the magic of art provides "knowledge of something else" seems to find its place in the tradition of innovative memory in which memories are not only about the past, but a vehicle for "remembering" something anew. Thus, it is possible to find justification for the Deweyan version of combinatorics. This type of combinatorics refers to the possibility of transformative remembering of the possibilities of richer and more democratic lives with the help of art.

From the perspective of combinatorics, the act of seeing new connections allows for the recognition of knowledge of the what-if type. The ability of this type of knowledge to convey certainty derives from the intensity of the accompanying experience. When the intensity reaches a high point, the term "revelatory" seems appropriate. These moments when hitherto unattained possibilities are "acknowledged" contain a guiding tendency whereby people act "in deference to" what they have acknowledged (Dewey 1958, 144). The poignant and momentous revelatory moments carry with them a particular sense of certainty about what is taking place. The sense of reality can be seen as a function of being engrossed with events in particular way. Interpreted in this way, the sense of reality becomes a quality attached to circumstances; certain ways of being engrossed with events produce a sense that the situation is especially real and true. It is significant that the developer of frame analysis, Erving Goffman (1974, 2), locates himself in the tradition of Dewey and ultimately William James, and follows James's modus operandi expressed in the question, "Under what circumstances do we think things are real?" The emergent moment may reveal something as real. For example, the revelatory moments of humanitarianism may carry a strong certainty that an international crisis needs to be interpreted in one way. In this way, the pictures of starving Bosnian men behind a barbed wire triggered in 1992 the real urgency of doing something to stop the horrors in Bosnia. The engrossing images carried with them a profound message about the meaning of the times and what should be done. The murky multiethnic conflict was illuminated as a relatively clear-cut example of evil. It was also given a clear reference point in the prevailing collection of agent images.

Furthermore, the connection to James points to the noncognitive emphasis in pragmatist thought. It is possible to contextualize Dewey's ideas about extending and transforming meaning with Jamesian emphasis that religious-like experiences have a fundamental role in the way meaning and certainty are apprehended. James highlights the role of noncognitively gained preconceptual revelation over empirically verified objectivity. He seems to suggest that the broad aspect of experience is fueled by noncognitively gained disclosures (James 1985, 352). This suggests that the grounding of everyday experience is not intellectual and conceptual, but noncognitive, emotional, and religious-like (e.g., James 1985, 397). This resonates well with the notion of Ludwig Wittgenstein—who was a close reader of James and influenced by Dewey's philosophy of education—that knowledge is based on acknowledgment (Wittgenstein 1972, 378). For Wittgenstein, to know was often connected with the recognition of authorities (Wittgenstein 1972, 493). The important point here is that this acknowledgment is not based on occasions of reasoned choice, but on moments of believing, learning, experiencing, growing up, inheriting, and accepting. This type of knowledge requires constant reminding and reminders. For Wittgenstein, these reminding "pictures" are best understood in their practical function. They should not be given a more foundational character because they are artificial aids of rather limited and specific use (e.g., Wittgenstein 1968, 89).

Wittgenstein's emphasis of reminders provides one further element to the more contemporary art of combinatorics. More precisely, his later philosophy may be used to shed some light upon the degrees of freedom in combinatorics. Discernible wholes of language, in the Wittgensteinian sense of language games,[15] do not come together in some strictly formal way (Wittgenstein 1968, 108). Wittgenstein uses the term "family resemblance" to bring forth the elusive and indeterminate character involved in language use (Wittgenstein 1968, 23, 67). However, Wittgenstein continuously points out another possibility (e.g., Wittgenstein 1968, 426-8) that language games can and often do "conjure up" fairly determinate senses that go beyond mere family resemblance. To reiterate, on one hand, language offers a highly desirable way of showing—demonstrating and teaching—how things can be and, on the other, an imprisoning way of conveying how things must be. In the first sense, the means of a language game can be used to bind things together whereby the game brings up patterns of similarity and dissimilarity: "The language games are rather set up as objects of comparison which are meant to throw light on the facts of our language by way not only of similarities, but also of dissimilarities" (Wittgenstein 1968, 130). Besides this character of language games, they have a more dogmatic use as well, which can "hold us captive" (Wittgenstein 1968, 115). The "picture" invoked by a language game holds the language game users captive and they cannot "get outside of it, for it lay in our language and language seemed to repeat it to us inexorably" (Wittgenstein 1968, 105). Reminding, in this Wittgensteinian sense, refers to the activity of offering objects of comparison meant to awaken those captivated by determinate ideas of knowledge and authority. This understanding of combinatorics offers a way to "unfreeze" the consolidated memory systems. This Wittgensteinian continuum between "showing how things can be" and "demonstrating how they must be" offers a clue to the political use of image combinations that comprise modern ideas of humanitarian war.

Humanitarian Combinatorics

In her 1994 article about the violent breakup of Yugoslavia, Bette Denich introduces the topic by remembering a play. In the early 1980s, a play called *The Pigeon Cave* surfaced among Yugoslavia's Serb population. The play restaged the massacre of the Serbs, Jews, and the Roma by the Croatian state during World War II. The play had been banned under Tito's rule, when most reminders of ethnic conflicts were erased from the national memory. However, such reminders were not permanently rubbed out: "The banned performance of *The Pigeon Cave* was but a forerunner for events that became frequent and widely publicized during the late 1980s, when nationalism burst from its hiding places and swept people by hundreds of thousands into mass movements, then elections, then into confrontations that escalated, with astonishing speed, to civil war" and eventually to Western humanitarian intervention (Denich 1994, 367). In the article, the memory sediments of this escalating sequence are connected to David Apter's (1985, 269) notion of disjunctive moments. This concept refers to a moment when images, myths, and memories are reshuffled and combined into innovative new complexes that bind theory, ideology, and myth. These moments are similar to the Goffmanian frame breaks in their ability to disturb and suspend the ordinary flow of events.[16] *The Pigeon Cave* contained a reminder of such a revolutionary time. It told a contemporary story in terms of old images and, thereby, recombined what was happening with old meanings. Furthermore, the process of reshuffling of images went beyond the local mobilizations of nationalist sentiments. The Yugoslav wars eventually produced the mobilization of international humanitarian sentiments.

It seems that the act of combinatorics—that is, spinning the sediment growth rings of memory—may produce powerful and politically contagious ignitions. The revelatory moments of acknowledgment are contagious—they are easily socially shared. The pictures from Bosnia spread around the global media in August 1992. Their source was the footage shot by the British ITN film crew in Bosnia.[17] Pictured in them were clearly emaciated and barely clothed men staring at the camera from behind barbed wire, with desperation in their eyes. These images were clearly special because in just one day, they circled the world's media. In their immediate aftermath, President George W. Bush changed his hands-off policy. After an emergency session of his cabinet,

Prime Minister John Major announced that British troops would be sent to Bosnia. The pressure authorizing UN involvement grew significantly. The economic sanctions against Serbia were tightened. The willingness to recognize the republics of Slovenia, Croatia, and Bosnia grew. The images seemed to offer an iconic and clarifying interpretation of the situation in the Balkans. The following outcry heightened the sense that something must be done in the name of the international community and humanity. The images turned into something poignant and momentous. They offered new objects of comparison, unlocked new similarities, and revealed new underlying knowledge. Their acknowledgment contained the impetus for political mobilization and propelled action. The photographs unleashed an agent image that stimulated behavior and led to the humanitarian intervention and bombing of Serb targets.

The newspaper photographs of the starving Bosnian men triggered a strong link between the events taking place and earlier iconography. Accordingly, the seeming meaning of the photographs turned into real images in comparison with the iconology of the Holocaust. It can be hypothesized that this connection in memory extended the meaning of Bosnia and made it stand out in a new way. The agent image was remembered anew and recognized/reactivated in Bosnia. The "camps" in Bosnia quickly turned into death camps—even the term "concentration camps" was often used—in the media and the people running the camps—the Serbians in Bosnia and in Serbia—came to stand for the perpetrators of mass death.

The immediacy and acuteness of a crisis seems to contribute to the engrossment of agent images. The way in which the photographs and other visual evidence of the Holocaust penetrated the collective memory at the end of World War II offers support for this hypothesis. The photographs of starving men, women, and children behind barbed wire and of mass graves and bulldozers doing the burial rites haunt the memory of humanitarianism. However, much is left unsaid in the iconography of this most monumental crime against humanity. This elliptic nature of images works to accentuate the horror. It also points to the complicity of the seemingly unaware masses. This compounds the agency of the iconography. It compels reflexivity and never-again type of activities.

Humanitarian images are many and politically relevant mobilizations very rare. The combinatorics involving holocaust imagery does not always result in successful re-remembering. For example, People for the Ethical Treatment of Animals's (PETA's) 2003 animal rights campaign backfired because it compared images of slaughterhouses to concentration camps (Delevie and Ingham 2004, 67). This controversy points out the limits of image combinations. The acts of remembering the Holocaust demand certain kinds of rites that elevate it to the position of the sacred in the Western civil religion. The usability of its images must recognize this essential quality for the combinations to be successful. A combination where treatment of animals is made comparable to the treatment of the Holocaust victims seems to violate the sacred and does not effectively contain the successful experience of extended meaning. Another example is provided by gross violations of people's gender and sexual rights. The visual rhetoric portraying the plight of innocent girls, who are drawn into prostitution before being mature enough to know vice from virtue, provides a case in point (Taylor 2003, 242). Although this theme figures in the humanitarian memory, it does not lead to such mobilizations of power in international relations as the images of the fleeing Kosovo Albanians in 1999. The images of forced commercial sex workers as young as 5-7 years in the brothels of Cambodia do not cause armed humanitarian interventions, although these are signifiers of massive human suffering and, due to the rampant HIV/AIDS epidemic, mass death.

Evidently, just certain types of catastrophes can be turned into skillful images. There exists a genre of art that fits this definition. Scherpe (1983, 98) calls this genre the "aesthetics of resistance," which resists "the mass-destruction of human life." From the perspective of this essay, such images turn into agent images that perform their work and stage revelatory, or "poignant and momentous," spectacles. They orient innovative remembering and invite the person to recombine his immediate understanding to fit with a combination of agent images. Goldblatt (2006, 31) invokes the examples of two such artistic images, Gericault's *Raft of Medusa* and Picasso's *Guernica*. These images, which were also referred to by Scherpe, "demand response" to the question, "How do we deal with others in and out of terror-filled and possibly life-threatening situations?" It seems likely that the empathy felt for the victims transmits an ethical theory that predisposes one to justifications of helping actions in situations of mass destruction, where these agent images are reproduced and recombined in memory.

The power of images has led to such poignant and momentous experiences since the beginning of modern humanitarianism in the British and French Enlightenment periods. One of the first signposts of such art was Gericault's *Raft of the Medusa*. The painting fits well with the traditional genre of crisis at sea. This symbolism is wide, for it allows one to represent anything from personal, societal, to state crises (e.g., Landow 1982, 56).[18] However, it contains a sense of acute and desperate need for help. The agent image is tense and emotionally charged. Time is scarce and the situation is temporalized. The ancient theme of crisis on the high seas implies distance. The castaways are in dire need of help, but they are remote and far away. Sinking and being engulfed and submerged combines with the theme of being cast adrift. The means of rescue are hampered by an unsupported existence, which lacks connection to the trunk of humanity. The distance implied is not necessarily physical, but also social and emotional. Often the images convey a sense of injustice and of dangerous masses unjustly threatening small, yet pious, minorities. The raging sea is a signifier of disproportionate and illegitimate violence by the many toward the few. The agent image compels immediate action.

The painting's title partly explains its intended meaning. An ancient Greek myth has Perseus decapitating Medusa and offering her head as a prize to save his mother, Danae, from an unpleasant marriage. Medusa was a hybrid creature; her deformed head was covered with snakes instead of hair. The mere sight of her could turn one into stone because through Medusa's vision, one could see one's fate all the way to eventual death. Turning into stone was a sign of standing face to face with one's own death. This agent image of humanitarianism contains an element of the "if nothing is done, this might happen to you" type of thinking. The painting suggests the fear paralysis that results when its viewer identifies himself with the fate of the people on the raft. It suggests a direct link between the immediate suffering taking place on the raft and the eventual suffering of the viewer. Action is required to stop this fate. This action is to stop people anywhere suffering horrible injustice, or the wrath of Medusa. The message is one of co-suffering, compassion, and empathy. It is a message of the immediate danger of doing nothing. This paralysis is a symptom of the pathological condition of inhumanity, just as is depicted in the painting.

Besides the Holocaust images, the post–World War II international community and the accompanying civil religion have often highlighted the notion of the mass deaths produced by war crimes against civilian populations. One of the most memorable agent images of this genre is Picasso's *Guernica*. The painting depicts the atrocities committed by Franco's regime against the village of Basque on April 27, 1937. The atrocity itself was mostly a cold test of new technologies of air power by the German war machine. The photographs from the massacre spread to the world media and caused an immediate reaction. May Day demonstrations around Europe became public protests against the mass murder. Picasso's later painting is a remaining key to this sense of humanitarian outrage. The iconic value of the black-and-white painting allows for the easy reproduction of the "outcry against inhumanity" sentiments ingrained in it and re-remembering something new in the light of it.

An important humanitarian image is that of a medical doctor who works tirelessly for the benefit of humanity. This image may be combined with images of foreign policy action. The presence of these pestilences turns into telltale signifiers of weak or failed political communities. From this perspective, it is significant that President Bush refers explicitly to the biblical story of Lazarus in a speech on Africa and AIDS (April 29, 2003). Bush uses the allegory to point out how U.S. initiatives can bring people back from certain death. His explicit reference was to the new HIV/AIDS policies of the United States, which offer hope to the otherwise doomed people of Africa: "There are only two possible responses to suffering on this scale. We can turn our eyes away in resignation and despair, or we can take decisive, historic action to turn the tide against this disease and give hope of life to millions who need our help now. The United States of America chooses the path of action and the path of hope." In the same speech, Bush draws an explicit connection between the high political agenda and HIV/AIDS: "We believe that everyone has a right to liberty, including the people of Afghanistan and Iraq. We believe that everyone has a right to life, including the children in the cities and villages of Africa and the Caribbean" (available on http://www.state.gov/g/oes/rls/rm/2003/20064.htm). The Lazarus effect refers to the United States's ability to set people free from the plight of oppression, irrespective of whether the oppression results from authoritarian regimes or deadly epidemics. Thus, what becomes of importance is the ability of the United States to set the scene, whereby people of different cultures understand what is taking place. This act of combinatorics has been omnipresent in the recent iconography of U.S. foreign policy. In his "mission accomplished speech" of May 1, 2003, Bush presents the essence of the U.S. mission in Iraq as follows: "In the words of the prophet Isaiah, 'To the captives, *come out*— and to those in darkness, *be free*.'" The combination blends the humanitarian images of cure with the traditional Christian imagery of freeing the captives.[19]

In remembering the importance of freeing captive nations in the U.S. foreign policy, on July 13, 2001, Bush stated: "In 1959, the Congress promulgated a Joint Resolution authorizing and requesting the President to declare the third week of July as Captive Nations Week and to continue this annual statement until such time as freedom and independence shall have been achieved for all the captive nations of the world." Next year, the proclamation for the Captive Nations Week had gathered added impetus in the post-9/11 atmosphere. Bush likened the foundations of the United States to work for freedom—setting captives free—around the world: "The United States is proud to stand on the side of the brave people everywhere who seek the same freedoms upon which our Nation was founded. Each year . . . we reaffirm our determination to work for freedom around the globe." The theme of bound people in captive nations finds its cultural background in the notions of binding and loosening.

The ancient times witnessed a strong preoccupation with the imagery of slavery and imprisonment, which were tightly related to binding. It is not surprising, therefore, that these themes were adopted both by Christian thought and by pagan undercurrents and were, thus, passed on to modern times. The agent images proceed toward the loosening of the righteous from the bonds brought to bear by the illegitimate forces. These unfixing spectacles in the contemporary setting involve people rising up from their bound and "frozen" existence to find a new life of liberty, democracy, and justice: "Recently, the world saw [freedom prevail] in Afghanistan, where people took to the street to celebrate the fall of their Taliban oppressors" (President Bush, July 17, 2002). In the case of Afghanistan, this message of unfixing—people streaming out into the open streets to celebrate—was reinforced by images of caves where the captors were hiding. Unfixing, or liberation, refers to a process in which people are made to recognize the proper way of being part of foreign policy spectacles. The miraculous war of liberation involved reciprocity. The war efforts of the United States are sought to be matched by acts of gratitude by the "liberated" people. It means that the new political parties in these states are expected to respect U.S. interests and wishes in order to be considered legitimate. This image of healing and liberation is reminiscent of Philippe Pinel's description of a psychiatrist: "[The aim of the treatment] was to in a way overpower and tame the alienated, by bringing him into a close relationship with someone who, by his mere physical and moral qualities, inescapably holds him in his grip" (Vandermeerch 1990, 75).

Another important and related humanitarian memory image is that of the antislavery movement. The political movement against slavery and the slave trade dates back to late eighteenth-century Britain. This movement, primarily organized by the Quakers, demanded the end of British involvement in the slave trade. The movement quickly grew to include most sectors of British society. The political mobilization led to state action, when so-called free towns were established in Africa. The British navy also started to intercept ships on the high seas to stop the trade. The drawings, poetry, and writings of William Blake were especially important for the movement, which led to the Slavery Abolition Act 1833. Erdman (1952, 244), who later called Blake a "prophet against empire," stresses human cruelty and the victim's dignity as the two most important aspects of these images: "Blake's engravings, with a force of expression absent from the others, emphasize the dignity of Negro men and women stoical under cruel torture: the wise, reproachful look of the 'Negro Hung Alive by the Ribs to a Gallows', who lived three days unmurmuring and who upbraided a flogged comrade for crying."[20]

The combination of the three humanitarian—"medical," "unbinding," and "abolitionist"—agent images served the purposes of the British Empire during the nineteenth century. The slave-owning areas were not located in Britain, which was on the brink of industrialization, and the industrial movement took the growing empire away from cheap slave labor, while some of its rivals were still dependent on it: "By mid-century, the success of the antislavery movement, the impact of the great Victorian explorers and the merger of racist and evolutionary doctrines in the social sciences had combined to give the British public a widely shared view of Africa that demanded imperialization on moral, religious and scientific grounds" (Brantlinger 1985, 167–8). The agent image of healing and medicine was particularly important in this process whereby people became convinced that imperial policies were nonpolitical and essentially humanitarian. Health and freedom from diseases has proven to be a powerful reminder of the legitimate interest of those able to produce them: ". . . the idea of indigenous peoples benefiting from the colonizer's medicine contributed to the ideological formulations that supported assimilative Canadian Indian policy in the period before 1950. Ostensibly removed from the realm of land and politics, colonization viewed through the lens of salutary medical aid was made seen essentially humanitarian" (Mary-Ellen Kelm 1998, 101). Ronald Barthes's term "depolititicized speech," which Brantlinger (1985, 168) takes to mean a "discourse which treats its subject as universally accepted, scientifically established, and therefore no longer open to criticism by political or theoretical opposition," describes well the political power of medicine and public health. From the sense of more Deweyan–Wittgensteinian combinatorics, such a closed system or cognitive scheme tyrannizes the political imagination. These combinatory "do good," "cure the sick," and "feed the poor" images are effective in hiding the close relationship between humanitarianism and the hierarchical world order (e.g., Zoya and Leung 2004, 269).

The Changes of Going Beyond

The stage is set for a perspective on collective memory, which highlights the sedimented nature of reminders. These rings of memory consist of engrossing depositories of powerful images. The sense of overall clarity of what is currently taking place may often be heuristic. The sense of "knowing what is currently happening" may be achieved through the planting of suggestive agent images here and there. The heuristic sense of overall clarity refers to knowledge that is not formal and conventional in nature. This type of clarity is elusive and resistant to exact formulation. Ludwig Wittgenstein (1968, 89) links this type of vague knowledge with the notion of reminding. For Wittgenstein, reminders point to "[s]ome-thing that we know when no one asks us, but no longer know when we are supposed to give an account of it . . ." Suggestive reminders dissemi-nated here and there lead to a sense of fragmentary evidence. The logic is simple: the skillfully scattered reminders lead to a sense that there is something underlying, deep, and meaningful in the events before our eyes. The reminders turn into fragments of this underlying essential quality. The element of similarity is detected in fragmentary evidence, whereby the reminders are turned into examples of the correspondence by the mind which is engrossed by them. The similarity easily turns into something that contains a sense of sacredness. Against this sense, the fragments are set alive. At this level of the sacred, the reminders illumi-nate what is at stake and what seems imminent in the future through their revelatory capacity. These momentary signs are powerful and persuasive sources of temporary knowhow and meanings.

The reminders refer to important emotional content and deeply held values, and to past instances when these values have revealed themselves. In many cases, the reminders are associated with a larger sedimented gallery of images, the concentric wheels of combinatorics. Reminders work as triggers to illuminate dramatic associations. For example, in the middle of the rap-idly moving events leading to the fall of Baghdad in April 2003, the story of the U.S. prisoner of war Jessica Lynch offered a poignant reminder of what the war was. The largely fabricated story about "Private Lynch" was about the brutality of Saddam's men, about the heroic efforts of the U.S. female soldier, the knight-like warriors who rescued her, and about the grateful help of ordinary Iraqis. The story, which ran on the covers of most respected U.S. newspapers and weeklies, acted as a reminder. The total effect managed to express the chancy and the contingent in terms of the concep-tually tangible, familiarly gendered, and politically sacred. The context in which the story was reminded included past agent images, such as the Americans coming to Europe's rescue in World War II. In the same way, the events in Kosovo in 1999—that is, thousands of refugees, desperate people, oppressive Serbs, and massacres—functioned as reminding agent images. They were seen against politically sacred images. They became revelatory. They inspired and even compelled action. They almost naturally turned into a humanitarian intervention. In the words of Ludwig Wittgenstein (1968, §115): "A picture held us captive. And we could not get outside it, for it lay in our language and language seemed to repeat it to us inexorably."

Notes

Violent Vortexes of Compassion

1. The idea of emotions as entertained here is strongly political and external-ist in that the individual's emotionality is thought to be a by-product and secondary to the emotions contained in the shifting power hierarchies. Here, the argument can be framed in terms of philosophical thought, such as Wittgenstein's ideas of the collective nature of feelings (e.g., Crawford 2000, 116).

Compassion as a Morality Drama at the Profiled EU and U.S. Borders

1. See Arendt 1973, 278.
2. Communication from the Commission to the Council and the European Parliament (52001DC0720).
3. Commission Working Document on the relationship between safeguarding internal security and complying with international protection obligations and instruments (Brussels, 05.12.2001, COM (2001) 743 final).
4. See, for example, Davidson 1989, p. 10; Diehl 1982, p. 97.
5. http://usembassy-australia.state.gov/hyper/2002/0610/epf103.htm
6. The list includes Andorra, Australia, Austria, Belgium, Brunei, Denmark, Finland, France, Germany, Iceland, Ireland, Italy, Japan, Liechtenstein, Luxembourg, Monaco, the Netherlands, New Zealand, Norway, Portugal, San Marino, Singapore, Slovenia, Spain, Sweden, Switzerland, and the United Kingdom.
7. Fact sheet: US-VISIT Program (http://www.dhs.gov/dhspublic/display?content=736).
8. The Office of Foreign Assets (OFAC) maintains an important reference list containing the names of 10,000 known and suspected terrorists, money laun-derers, and narco-traffickers.
9. For example, it details information on diet (such as pure vegetarian, vegetar-ian, lacto, seafood, fiber, and low on fat, calories, cholesterol, sodium, and pro-tein) and also reveals information on ethnic/religious diets (such as Asian vegetarian, Hindu, Muslim, and kosher).
10. Two of the 9/11 terrorists had overstayed their visas.

Compassions at International Airports: The Hub-and-Spoke Pedagogy of the American Empire

1. One of the most central aspects of the airport experience is its gendered nature. For example, the overwhelmingly male sexuality of the airport ranges from airport voyeurism and objectification of stewardesses to airport prostitution and the so-called "mile-high" experience.

2. An airport is generally organized around three layers: the service level, the intermediary arrivals area, and the upper departures area. In many airports, the arrivals area is placed underground. It comprises a large baggage claim area and the narrow gates and corridors of the customs and immigration counters. Piers radiate outward toward the gates, which usually have a hammer-head shape. There are standard types of security and customs areas. These narrow areas contrast with the gates, waiting rooms, check-in halls, and shopping areas.

3. Mallaby (2002, 34), for example, treats imperialism as an age-old solution to the problem posed by both power vacuums and outlawed and failed states.

4. In contemporary American discourse, the negative burden of the word, empire, derives from associations with coercive and forceful occupation of foreign lands (e.g., Ferguson 2003, 56).

5. The dark Kaplanian vision can be connected to a larger conceptual shift in international relations, though toward the medieval or pre-Westphalian imagery (Deibert 1997, 188).

6. For example, Sullivan (2003, 112) reviews the new Philadelphia airport. He points out that the airport has been transformed into "a cosmopolitan hub for the jet set." The airport is "drenched with sunlight . . ., the skylit baggage claim is an elevated . . ., instead of a rectangular arrivals hall, travelers enjoy an iris-shaped room topped with an impressively sloped space frame." All this makes passengers "pinch themselves to make sure they're not dreaming."

7. Recently, there has been a flurry of interest in transmission, mobility, movement, and flow in sociological and cultural studies (e.g., Castells 1996; Martinotti 1999; Urry 2000; Crang 2002).

8. Important for the loci of memory were their clear and conventionally ordered architecture. In this way, the cathedral, with its intricate but strictly conventional architecture, could offer a large capacity locus for memory. The conventionalized complexity of the cathedral is mirrored in the structure of the airport.

Beyond Humanitarian Compassion

1. The status of imagination in postbehavioral international relations has been cumbersome. It may be suggested that through the inherent bias against images, imaginative memory has been reduced to a lesser significance in social sciences or treated as an obstacle to reaching verifiable results. The iconoclasm may be seen in the tendency to think that powerful images distort rational thought and divert attention away from the dialectic processes. At best, images

are regarded as convenient shortcuts, and at worst, they present reality in skewed, deviant, simplified, and reduced forms. Images are often conceptualized in connection with problems such as animosity, xenophobia, and racism. Images of the past, in particular, are considered problematic as Jervis (1976, 217) points out in talking about what he calls "the tyranny of the past." The idea that memory consists of a grossly simplifying collection of myths bears heavily on the ethical worth of "memory images."

2. For neotraditionalism and different versions of it, see, for example, Astrov (2005).

3. One of the first explications of the term by Czech President Vaclav Havel pointed out the identity between the bombing of the Serbs in 1999 and the purely humanitarian aim of protecting the wronged Kosovars.

4. The 1999 intervention in East Timor should also be noted.

5. Nicholar Kristof (June 11, 2002), in his *New York Times* column, gives a good example of this evolution, when he states that "Afghanistan is the latest example of not only a just war, but a humanitarian war. The vaccination efforts and other medical campaigns made possible by the invasion may save a million Afghan lives over the next decade."

6. His memory system was based on Lullism. Lullism was developed by Raymond Lull in the thirteenth century. It put the emphasis on order. The orderly locus did not include strong and striking images. They were considered distractions from both the practical and religious perspectives.

7. The cracking of nature's cipher was supposed to remind one of the more godly hermeneutics.

8. Ramism subsequently became very influential, for example, in American Puritan thought and especially in the first steps of what became Harvard University. The strong influence in the development of more modern religious and secular education is well recorded, as, for example, by White (2005) and McKnight (2003).

9. The images are present, for example, in a highly polished form in the scientific thought in the idea of near mystical notions of "keys" to reality. These striking ciphers or keys may be found in the mathematics and arithmetic equations of modern times (e.g., Pesic 1999). They are also heavily present in the philosophy of education (e.g., White 2005). The later forms of this strand of thought are harder to discern. Its main uses were not in the determinate systems of high religion and scientific rationality. But it had and continues to have a heavy following in the arts. The lasting influence is recorded also in psychoanalysis, in political communication, in marketing, in public relations and, increasingly, in international relations (e.g., van Ham 2002).

10. Thomas Aquinas, in his commentary to Aristotle's *De Memoria et Reminiscencia*, argues influentially that "if we wish to remember easily any intelligible reasons, [we must] bind them, as it were, by certain other *phantasma*." These phantasms of images enable orderly memory, since "things that have subtle and spiritual considerations can less be remembered, whereas things are more memorable that are gross and sensible".

11. The author (III.xxiii) further recommends that a teacher should give to the students a general idea or an example to which they are used to. It is up to

them to apply it further. In this way, the agent images had a sticking power that allowed for easy reapplication.

12. The idea of concentric revolving wheels was already a theme in Raymond Lull's (ca. 1235-1315) writings.

13. The memory technologies of the seventeenth century were much concentrated on the idea of developing universal artificial language. Parallel to this tendency, there developed an important offshoot that led to the further development of calculus and symbolic logic (e.g., Rossi 2000, 178). The common motive for much of these parallel developments was to devise a means of communication which could be easily learned and which would greatly facilitate inter-human understanding.

14. Often, these mental explorations were given an occult nature: The connections and associations in the complexity of earthly reality offered clues and keys to mysteries of a deeper and more cosmological kind.

15. A language game ties words together with simple actions and things: ". . . the term 'language-game' is meant to bring into prominence the fact that the speaking of language is part of an activity, or of a form of life" (Wittgenstein 1968, 34).

16. The source of Apter's thinking is Ricouer's (1967) temporal dynamics: Revolutionary movements redefine the past in order to assert an alternative future (Polletta 1992, 89–90).

17. In an interview in *Independent* (August 5, 1993), the editor of ITN, Mike Jeremy, placed the photos among the "key images" of the war.

18. Plato's story about submergence of Atlantis provides one ancestral illustration of this genre. The ship of state is suddenly caught in a violent storm because of the dark side of human nature.

19. The collection of unusual occurrences accompanying the conversion and expansion of Christianity included such events as healings, exorcisms, celestial signs, and the raising of the dead (McGee 2001, 147, 155).

20. The antislavery tradition remained in people's memories long after its heyday had passed. Humanitarian images of this type were able to mobilize publicity in Britain even in 1870, when activists were able to turn the iconography of injustice into an antislavery crusade in the Pacific Islands (Samson 1998, 117).

Bibliography

Aaltola, Mika. *Rhythm, Exception, and Rule in International Relations: The Case of Mad Cow Disease*. Tampere: University of Tampere, 1999.

———. *Sowing the Seeds of Sacred: Political Religion of the Contemporary World Order and the American Era*. Leiden: Brill, 2008.

Abbot, F.M. "The WTO Medicines Decision: World Pharmaceutical Trade and the Protection of Public Health." *The American Journal of International Law* 99, 2 (2005): 317–58.

Aberbach, David. "Revolutionary Hebrew, Empire and Crisis: Towards a Sociological Gestalt." *The British Journal of Sociology* 48, 1 (1997): 128–48.

Ali, S.H. and R. Keil. "Multiculturalism, Racism and Infectious Disease in the Global City: The Experience of the 2003 SARS Outbreak in Toronto." *Topia* 16 (2006): 23–49.

Anonymous author. *Ad Herennium*. Cambridge: Harvard University Press, 1954.

Apter, David. "The New Mytho/Logics and the Specter of Superfluous Man." *Social Research* 52 (1985): 269–307.

Arendt, Hannah. *The Origins of Totalitarianism*. San Diego: Harcourt Brace Jovanovich, 1973.

Aristotle. "Nicomachean Ethics." In *The Complete Works of Aristotle*, edited by J. Barnes. Princeton: Princeton University Press, 1984.

———. *Politics*. London: Dover Publications, 2000.

Astrov, Alexander. *On World Politics: R. G. Collingwood, Michael Oakeshott and Neotraditionalism in International Relations*. London: Palgrave Macmillan, 2005.

Augé, M. *Non-Places: An Introduction to an Anthropology of Supermodernity*. London: Verso, 1995.

———. *An Anthropology for Contemporaneous Worlds*. Stanford: Stanford University Press, 1999.

Aysha, Emad El-Din. "Huntington's Shift to the Declinist Camp: Conservative Declinism and the 'Historical Function' of the Clash of Civilizations." *International Relations* 17, 4 (2003): 429–52.

Baldwin-Edwards, M. and B. Hebenton. "Introduction." In *Policing across National Boundaries*, edited by M. Anderson and M. den Boer. New York: Pinter, 1994.

Barker, Ernest. *Greek Political Theory: Plato and His Predecessors*. London: Barnes and Noble, 1960.

Barker, H.F. and R.M. Ridley. "What Went Wrong in BSE? From Prion Disease to Public Disaster." *Brain Research Bulletin* 40, 4 (1996): 237–44.

Barthes, Ronald. *Mythologies*. New York: Hill and Wang, 1984.

Beck, Ulrich. *World Risk Society*. Cambridge: Blackwell, 1999.

Beeman, William O. "The Anthropology of Theater and Spectacle." *Annual Review of Anthropology* 22 (1993): 369–93.

Bertier de Sauvigny, Guillaume. *The Bourbon Restoration*. Philadelphia: University of Pennsylvania Press, 1966.

Bhadra, D. and D. Hechtman. "Determinants of Airport Hubbing in the United States: An Empirical Framework." *Public Works Management & Policy* 9, 1 (2004): 26–50.

Bigo, Didier. "The European Internal Security Field: States and Rivalries in a Newly Developing Area of Police Intervention." In *Policing across National Boundaries*, edited by M. Anderson and M. den Boer. New York: Pinter, 1994.

Brantlinger, Patrick. "Victorians and Africans: The Genealogy of the Myth of the Dark Continent." *Critical Inquiry* 12, 1 (1985): 166–203.

Brunt, P.A. "Thucydides and Human Irrationality." *Classical Review* 17, 3 (1967): 278–80.

Burns, B., C. Busby, and K. Sawchuk. *When Pain Strikes*. Minneapolis: University of Minnesota Press, 1999.

Butler, R. and J. Huston. "The Meaning of Size: Output? Scope? Capacity? The Case of Airline Hubs." *Review of Industrial Organization* 14 (1999): 51–64.

Calhoun, Craig. "Identity and Plurality in the Conceptualization of Europe." In *Constructing Europe's Identity: The External Dimension*, edited by Lars-Erik Cederman. London: Lynne Rienner, 2001.

Carruthers, Mary. *The Book of Memory. A Study of Memory in Medieval Culture*. Cambridge: Cambridge University Press, 1990.

———. *The Craft of Thought: Rhetoric, Meditation, and the Making of Images, 400–1200*. London: Cambridge University Press, 2000.

Castells, M. *The Rise of the Network Society*. Oxford: Blackwell, 1996.

Chatterjee, Deen. "Introduction." *The Ethics of Assistance: Morality and the Distant Needy*, edited by Deen Chatterjee. New York: Cambridge University Press, 2004.

Churchill, Winston. "War Prospects." *Vital Speeches of the Day* 6, 9 (1940): 272–74.

Clapham, Christopher. *Africa and the International System. The Politics of State Survival*. Cambridge: Cambridge University Press, 1996.

Clark, Candace. "Sympathy Biography and Sympathy Margin." *American Journal of Sociology* 93 (1987): 290–321.

Cogan, Marc. *The Human Thing*. Chicago: University of Chicago Press, 1980.

Connolly, William E. *Identity\Difference: Democratic Negotiations of Political Paradox*. Minneapolis: University of Minnesota Press, 2002.

Connor, Walter Robert. *Thucydides*. London: Princeton University Press, 1984.

Corcoran, Mary and Michel Peillon. *Uncertain Ireland: A Sociological Chronicle, 2003–2004*. Dublin: Institute of Public Administration, 2006.

Cordesman, A.H. and Abraham R. Wagner. *The Lessons of Modern War: Volume III. The Afghan and Falklands Conflicts*. Boulder: Westview Press, 1990.

Craik, E.M. "Thucydides on the Plague: Physiology of Flux and Fixation." *Classical Quarterly* 51, 1 (2001): 102–8.

Crang, M. "Between Places: Producing Hubs, Flows and Networks." *Environment and Planning* A. 34 (2002): 569–74.

Crawford, Neta. "The Passion of World Politics: Propositions on Emotion and Emotional Relationships." *International Security* 24, 4 (2000): 116–56.

Crawford, T.H. "Imagine the Human Body: Quasi Objects, Quasi Texts, and the Theater of Proof." *PMLA* 11, 1 (1996): 66–76.

Dalby, Simon. "The Environment as Geopolitical Threat: Reading Robert Kaplan's Coming Anarchy." *Ecumene* 3, 4 (1996): 472–96.

Daley, Tad. "Afghanistan and Gorbachev's Global Foreign Policy." *Asian Survey* 29, 5 (1989): 496–513.

Daniels, R., P. Macklem, and K. Roach. *The Security of Freedom: Essays on Canada's Anti-Terrorism Bill*. Toronto: University of Toronto Press, 2001.

Darwin, Charles. *Origin of Species*. London: Murray, 1859.

Dassel, Kurt and Eric Reinhardt. "Domestic Strife and the Initiation of Violence at Home and Abroad." *American Journal of Political Science* 43, 1 (1999): 56–85.

Davidson, Clifford. *Visualizing the Moral Life: Medieval Iconography and the Macro Morality Plays*. New York: AMS Press, 1989.

Davis, Mike. *The Monster at Our Door: The Global Threat of Avian Flu*. New York: New Press, 2005.

Deibert, Ronald J. " 'Exorcismus Theoriae': Pragmatism, Metaphors and the Return of the Medieval in IR Theory." *European Journal of International Relations* 3, 2 (1997): 167–92.

Delaporte, F. *Disease and Civilization: The Cholera in Paris, 1832*. London: The MIT Press, 1986.

Delevie, Brian and Isshaela Ingham. "Unconscionable or Communicable: The Transference of Holocaust Photography in Cyber Space." *Afterimage* (May-June 2004).

Demerath, N.J. and R.H. Williams. *A Bridging of Faiths: Religion and Politics in a New England City*. Princeton, N.J.: Princeton University Press, 1992.

Denich, Bette. "Dismembering Yugoslavia: Nationalist Ideologies and the Symbolic Revival of Genocide." *American Ethnologist* 21, 2 (1994): 367–90.

Deudney, D. and L. Ikenberry. "The International Sources of Soviet Change." *International Security* 16, 3 (1991): 76–7.

Dewey, John. *Experience and Nature*. Dover: New York, 1958.

Dewey, John. *Art as Experience*. New York: Perigee, 1980.

Diamond, Jared. *Collapse: How Societies Choose to Fail or Succeed*. New York: Viking, 2004.

Diehl, Houston. "Inversion, Parody, and Irony: The Visual Rhetoric of Renaissance English Tragedy." *Studies in English Literature, 1500–1900* 22, 2 (1982): 197–209.

Dodge, Martin and Rob Kitchin. "Flying through Code/Space: The Real Virtuality of Air Travel." *Environment and Planning* 36 (2004): 195–211.

Durkheim, Emile. *The Elementary Forms of the Religious Life*. New York: Free Press, 1965.

Edmunds, Lowell. "Thucydides' Ethics as Reflected in the Description of Stasis." *Harvard Studies in Classical Philology* 79 (1975): 73–92.

Edwards, Brian. *Modern Terminal: New Approaches to Airport Architecture.* New York: E & FN Spon, 1998.

Edwards, John. "Asylum Seekers and Human Rights." *Res Publica* 7 (2001): 159–82.

Eliade, Mircea. *The Sacred and the Profane: The Nature of Religion.* Trans. Willard R. Trask. London: Harcourt, Brace & World, 1959.

———. *Cosmos and History.* London: Bollingen, 1971.

Ellis, Caroly. "Shattered Lives: Making Sense of September 11th and Its Aftermath." *Journal of Contemporary Ethnography* 31, 4 (2002): 375–410.

Enders, Walter and Todd Sandler. "Transnational Terrorism in the Post-Cold War Era." *International Studies Quarterly* 43 (1999): 145–67.

Entralgo, Lain. *The Therapy of the Word in Classical Antiquity.* New Haven: Yale University Press, 1970.

Erdman, David V. "Blake's Vision of Slavery". *Journal of the Warburg and Courtauld Institutes* 15, 3–4 (1952): 242–52.

Ericson, Richard V. "How Journalists Visualize Fact." *The Annals of the American Academy of Political and Social Science* 560, 1 (1998): 83–95.

Ferguson, J. *The Anti-Politics Machine: "Development," Depoliticization, and Bureaucratic Power in Lesotho.* Cambridge: Cambridge University Press, 1990.

Ferguson, Niall. "Hegemony or Empire." *Foreign Affairs* 82, 5 (2003): 56–60.

Fiering, Norman S. "Irresistible Compassion: An Aspect of Eighteenth-Century Sympathy and Humanitarianism." *Journal of the History of Ideas* 37, 2 (1976): 195–218.

Fine, Gary Alan and Philip Manning. "Erving Goffman." In *The Blackwell Companion to Major Contemporary Social Theorists, Part II*, edited by George Ritzer. London: Blackwell, 2003.

Finucane, Melissa L. "Mad Cows, Mad Corn and Mad Communities: The Role of Socio-Cultural Factors in the Perceived Risk of Genetically-Modified Food." *Proceedings of the Nutrition Society* 61, 1 (2002): 31–7.

Freedman, Amy. "The SARS Crisis and Challenges to Regimes Legitimacy in China." *Conference papers–NewEngland Political Science Association*, 2004.

Gaines, Jane M. "Everyday Strangeness: Robert Ripley's International Oddities as Documentary Attractions." *New Literary History* 33, 4 (2002): 781–801.

Garcia-Zamor, Jean-Claude. "Conundrums of Urban Planning in a Global Context: The Case of the Frankfurt Airport." *Public Organization Review: A Global Journal* 1 (2001): 415–35.

Gelpi, Christopher. "Democratic Diversion: Governmental Structure and the Externalization of Domestic Conflict." *Journal of Conflict Resolution* 41, 2 (1997): 255–82.

Glover, Jonathan. *Humanity: A Moral History of the Twentieth Century.* New Haven: Yale University Press, 2000.

Giesecke, J. "Prevention, Not Panic. Epidemics and Trade Sanctions." *The Lancet* 356, 9229 (2000): 588.

Ginzburg, Carlo. "Killing a Chinese Mandarin: The Moral Implications of Distance." *Critical Inquiry* 21, 1 (1994): 46–60.

Goffart, Walter. "Zosimus, The First Historian of Rome's Fall." *The American Historical Review* 76, 2 (1971): 412–41.

Goffman, Erving. *Frame Analysis*. New York: Harper, 1974.

———. *Goffman Reader*. London: Blackwell, 1997.

Goldblatt, Patricia. "How John Dewey's Theories Underpin Art and Art Education." *Education and Culture* 22, 1 (2006): 17–34.

Goldmann, Lucien. *The Hidden God: A Study of Tragic Vision in the Pensees of Pascal and the Tragedies of Racine*. London: Routledge and Kegan Paul, 1964.

Goode, E. and N. Ben-Yehuda. *Moral Panics: The Social Construction of Deviance*. Cambridge: Blackwell, 1994.

Goodman, Ryan. "Humanitarian Intervention and Pretexts for War." *The American Journal of International Law* 100, 1(2006): 107–41.

Gonos, George. "'Situation' versus 'Frame': The 'Interactionist' and 'Structuralist' Analyses of Everyday Life." *American Sociological Review* 42, 6 (1997): 854–67.

Gottdiener, Mark. *Life in the Air: Surviving the New Culture of Air Travel*. Boulder: Rowman & Littlefield, 2001.

Govean, Rodger M. and Gerald T. West. "Riot Contagion in Latin America, 1949–1963." *Journal of Conflict Resolution* 25, 2 (1981): 349–68.

Graham, Thomas E. *Russia's Decline and Uncertain Recovery*. Washington: Carnegie Endowment for International Peace, 2002.

Gruman, Gerald. " 'Balance' and 'Excess' as Gibbon's Explanation of the Decline and Fall." *History and Theory* 1, 1 (1960): 75–85.

Hahn, Cynthia. "Seeing and Believing: The Construction of Sanctity in Early-Medieval Saints' Shrines." *Speculum* 72, 4 (1997): 1079–106.

Hamilton, L.C. and J.D. Hamilton. "Dynamics of Terrorism." *International Studies Quarterly* 27, 1 (1983): 39–54.

Herdt, Gilbert. *Gay Culture in America*. Boston: Beacon Press, 1992.

Hildebrandt, G., J. Luy, and O. Simon. "Kannibalismus und Rinderwahn: Ein Argument Gegen Jegliche Tiermehlfuetterung?" *Tieraerztliche Umschau* 57, 2 (2002): 77–89.

Hill, Stuart and Donald Rothchild. "The Contagion of Political Conflict in Africa and the World." *Journal of Conflict Resolution* 30, 4 (1986): 716–35.

Hobsbawm, Eric. *Bandits*. New York: Dell, 1969.

Hoffman, B. "Rethinking Terrorism and Counterterrorism since 9/11." *Studies in Conflict & Terrorism* 25 (2002): 303–16.

Hollander, Paul. *Political Will and Personal Belief: The Decline and Fall of Soviet Communism*. New Haven: Yale University Press, 1999.

Hoy, S. and W. Nuget. "Public Health or Protectionism? The German-American Pork War." *Bulletin of the History of Medicine* 62 (1989): 45–52.

Huntington, Samuel P. "Political Development and Political Decay." *World Politics* 17, 3 (1965): 386–430.

———. "The Clash of Civilizations." *Foreign Affairs* 72, 3 (1993): 22–8.

———. "The Erosion of American National Interests." *Foreign Affairs* 76, 5 (1997): 28–49.

———. *The Clash of Civilizations and the Remaking of World Order*. New York: Simon & Schuster, 1998.

———. "The Hispanic Challenge." *Foreign Policy* (March/April 2004): 30–45.

James, William. *Varieties of Religious Experience*. London: Penguin Classics, 1985.

Jasanoff, S. "Civilization and Madness: The Great BSE Scare of 1996." *Public Understanding of Science* 6, 3 (1997): 221–32.

Jasper, James M. "The Emotions of Protest: Affective and Reactive Emotions In and Around Social Movements." *Sociological Forum* 13, 3 (1998): 397–424.

Jennings, Roy and Robert Read. *From Influenza: Human and Avian in Practice*. London: Royal Society of Medicine, 2006.

Jervis, Robert. *Perception and Misperception in International Politics*. Princeton: Princeton University Press, 1976.

Joppke, Christian. "Why Liberal States Accept Unwanted Immigration." *World Politics* 50, 2 (1998): 266–93.

Jung, Carl G. *On the Psychology of the Trickster-Figure*. Four Archetypes. Princeton: Princeton University Press, 1973.

Kalimtzis, Kostas. *Aristotle on Political Enmity and Disease: An Inquiry into Stasis*. Albany: State University of New York Press, 2000.

Kallet, Lisa. "The Diseased Body Politic, Athenian Public Finance, and the Massacre at Mykalessos (Thucydides 7.27–29)." *American Journal of Philology* 120 (1999): 223–44.

Kaplan, Robert D. "The Coming Anarchy." *The Atlantic Monthly* 273 (1994): 44–75.

Karlen, A. *Napoleon's Glands and Other Essays in Biohistory*. Boston: Little, Brown, 1984.

Katzenstein, Peter. "Alternative Perspectives on National Security." In *The Culture of National Security: Norms and Identity in World Politics*, edited by Peter J. Katzenstein. New York: Columbia University Press, 1996.

Kaziak, Barbara. "Homeric Thumos: The Early History of Gender, Emotion, and Politics." *The Journal of Politics* 61, 4 (1999): 1068–91.

Keele, B.F., F. Van Heuverswyn, and Y. Li. "Chimpanzee Reservoirs of Pandemic and Non-Pandemic HIV-1." *Science* 313 (2006): 523–26.

Kelm, Mary-Ellen. *Colonizing Bodies: Aboriginal Health and Healing in British Columbia, 1900–50*. Vancouver: University of British Columbia Press, 1998.

Kemper, T.D. "How Many Emotions Are There? Wedding the Social and the Autonomic Components." *The American Journal of Sociology* 93, 2 (1987): 263–89.

———. "Social Constructionist and Positivist Approaches to the Sociology of Emotions." *The American Journal of Sociology* 87 (1981): 337–62.

———. "Predicting Emotions from Social Relations." *Social Psychology Quarterly* 54 (1991): 330–42.

Kennedy, P. *The Rise and Fall of the Great Powers*. New York: Random House, 1987.

Kleinert, S. "The Mad Cow Crisis – the Mad, the Bad, and the Ugly." *Lancet* 352, 28 (1998): 584.

Kocur, Zoya and Simon Leung. *Theory in Contemporary Art since 1985*. Blackwell: London, 2004.

Koslowski, Rey and Friedrich Kratochwil. "Understanding Change in International Politics: The Soviet Empire's Demise and the International System." *International Organization* 48, 2 (1994): 215–47.

Kreutzmann, Hermann. "From the Modernization Theory Towards the 'Clash of Civilizations': Directions and Paradigm Shifts in Samuel Huntington's Analysis and Prognosis of Global Development." *GeoJournal* 46 (1999): 255–65.

Kupchan, Charles A. *The End of the American Era: U.S. Foreign Policy and the Geopolitics of the Twenty-first Century.* New York: Alfred A. Knopf, 2002.

Landow, George P. *Images of Crisis: Literary Iconology, 1750 to the Present.* London: Routledge & Kegan Paul Books, 1982.

Laqueur, Walter. "Gorbachev and Epimetheus: The Origins of the Russian Crisis." *Journal of Contemporary History* 28, 3 (1993): 387–419.

Larrey, J.D. *Mémoire sur le Cholera-Morbus. Paris, 1831.* Quoted in *Disease and Civilization: The Cholera in Paris,* F. Delaporte, 27–33. London: The MIT Press, 1986.

Latour, Bruno. *The Pasteurization of France.* Cambridge: Harvard University Press, 1988.

Lebow, Richard. *Between Peace and War.* Baltimore: Johns Hopkins University Press, 1981.

L'Etang, H. *Fit to Lead?* London: Heinemann, 1970.

Levy, Jack S. "Domestic Politics and War." *Journal of Interdisciplinary History* 38, 4 (1988): 653–73.

———. "Diversionary Theory of War: A Critique." In *Handbook of War Studies,* edited by M. Midlarsky. London: Unwin-Hyman, 1989.

Lewis, H. *Shame and Guilt in Neurosis.* New York: International Universities Press, 1971.

Li, Richard P.Y. and William R. Thompson. "The 'Coup Contagion' Hypothesis." *The Journal of Conflict Resolution* 18, 1 (1975): 63–88.

Lieven, Dominic. "Western Scholarship on the Rise and Fall of the Soviet Regime: The View from 1993." *Journal of Contemporary History* 29, 2 (1994): 195–227.

———. "Dilemmas of Empire 1850–1918. Power, Territory, Identity." *Journal of Contemporary History* 34, 2 (1999): 163–200.

Lin, S.G. "Geopolitics of Communicable Diseases: Plague in Surat, 1994." *Economic and Political Weekly* (November 18, 1995): 35.

Lindenbaum, Shirley. "Kuru, Prions, and Human Affairs: Thinking about Epidemics." *Annual Review of Anthropology* 30 (2001): 363–85.

Lintott, Andrew. "What Was the 'Imperium Romanum'?" *Greece & Rome* 28, 1 (1981): 53–67.

Lodge, Juliet. "Sustaining Freedom, Security and Justice – From Terrorism to Immigration." *Liverpool Law Review* 24 (2002): 41–71.

Lutz, Catherine A. and Lila Abu-Lughod, eds. *Language and the Politics of Emotion.* London: Cambridge University Press, 1990.

Macfarlane, S.N., C.J. Thielking, and T.G. Weiss. "The Responsibility to Protect: Is Anyone Interested in Humanitarian Intervention?" *Third World Quarterly* 25, 5 (2004): 977–92.

Mack, Alistair. "The Humanitarian Operations Centre, Kuwait: Operation Iraqi Freedom." *International Peacekeeping* 11, 4 (2004): 683–96.

Mahroum, Sami. "Europe and the Immigration of Highly Skilled Labour." *International Migration* 39, 5 (2001): 27–44.

Mahy, Brian W.J. and C.C. Brown. "Emerging Zoonoses: Crossing the Species Barrier." *Revue Scientifique et Technique de l'Office International des Epizooties* 19, 1 (April 2000): 33–40.

Malkki, Liisa. "Speechless Emissaries: Refugees, Humanitarianism, and Dehistoricization." *Cultural Anthropology* 11, 3 (1996): 377–404.

Mallaby, Sebastian. "The Reluctant Imperialist: Terrorism, Failed States, and the Case for American Empire." *Foreign Affairs* 81, 2 (2002): 34–41.

Manicas, Peter. "War, Stasis, and Greek Thought." *Comparative Studies in Society and History* 24, 4 (1982): 673–88.

Mendelson, Sarah. "Internal Battles and External Wars: Politics, Learning and the Soviet Withdrawal from Afganistan." *World Politics* 45 (1993): 327–60.

Marshall-Cornwall, J. *Napoleon as Military Commander.* Princeton: Van Nostrand, 1967.

Martinotti, G. "A City for Whom? Transient and Public Life in the Second-Generation Metropolis." In *The Urban Moment: Cosmopolitan Essays on the Late-20th-Century City*, edited by R. Beauregard and S. Body-Gendrot. London: Sage, 1999.

Mayer, Arno J. "Internal Causes and Purposes of War in Europe 1970–1956: A Research Assignment." *The Journal of Modern History* 41, 3 (1969): 291–303.

McGee, Gary B. "Miracles and Mission Revisited." *International Bulletin of Missionary Research* 25, 4 (2001): 146–56.

McGovern, Charles. "The Politics of Consumption: Material Culture and Citizenship in Europe and America." *Journal of Interdisciplinary History* 34, 1 (2003): 45–65.

McKnight, Douglas. *Schooling, the Puritan Imperative, and the Molding of an American National Identity: Education's Errand into the Wilderness.* Mahwah: Lawrence Erlbaum Associates, 2003.

McNeill, W.H. *Plagues and People.* Oxford: Basil Blackwell, 1977.

Midlarsky, Manus I., Martha Crenshaw, and Fumihiko Yoshida. "Why Violence Spreads." *International Studies Quarterly* 24, 2 (1980): 262–98.

Minh Ha, Trinh. "All Owning Spectatorship." In *Theory in Contemporary Art since 1985*, edited by Zoya Kocur and Simon Leung. London: Wiley-Blackwell, 2004.

Modelski, G. "Long Cycles of World Leadership: An Annotated Bibliography." *International Studies Notes* 10 (1983): 1–5.

Monoson, S.S. and Michael Loriaux. "The Illusion of Power and the Distribution of Moral Norms: Thucydides' Critique of Periclean Policy." *American Political Science Review* 92, 2 (1998): 285–97.

Most, Ben and Harvey Starr. "Diffusion, Re-inforcement, Geopolitics, and the Spread of War." *American Journal of Political Science* 74, 4 (1980): 932–46.

Muus, Philip. "International Migration and the European Union, Trends and Consequences." *European Journal on Criminal Policy and Research* 9 (2001): 31–49.

Naylor, David. *National Advisory Committee Report on SARS and Public Health.* Ottawa: Health Canada, 2003.

Nelkin, D. and S.L. Gilman. "Placing Blame for Devastating Disease." In *In the Time of Plague: The History and Social Consequences of Lethal Epidemic Disease*, edited by A. Mack. New York: New York University Press, 1991.

Nicholson, Beryl. "The Wrong End of the Telescope: Economic Migrants, Immigration Policy, and How It Looks from Albania". *Political Quarterly* 73, 4: 436–45.

Nicholson, K., R. Webster, and A. Hay. *Textbook of Influenza.* Oxford: Blackwell, 2007.

Padel, Ruth. *In and Out of the Mind: Greek Images of the Tragic Self.* Princeton: Princeton University Press, 1992.

Padmawati, Siwi and Mark Nichter. "Community Response to Avian Flu in Central Java, Indonesia." *Anthropology & Medicine* 15, 1 (2008): 31–51.

Palumbo-Liu, David. "Multiculturalism Now: Civilization, National Identity, and Difference Before and After September 11th." *Boundary* 2 29, 2 (2002): 109–27.

Park, B. *The Impact of Illness on World Leaders.* Philadelphia: University of Pennsylvania Press, 1986.

Patterson, D.K. *Pandemic Influenza, 1700–1900: A Study in Historical Epidemiology.* London: Rowman & Littlefield Publishers, Inc., 1986.

Perelmuter, Rosa. "The Rogue as Trickster in 'Guzmán de Alfarache'." *Hispania* 59, 4 (1979): 820–26.

Pesic, Peter. *Labyrinth: A Search for the Hidden Meaning of Science.* London: The MIT Press, 1999.

Phillips, et al. "Report of the BSE Inquiry." London: House of Commons, 2000.

Piiparinen, Touko. "The Lessons of Darfur for the Future of Humanitarian Intervention." *Global Governance* 13, 3 (2007): 365–90.

Polletta, Francesca. "Politicizing Childhood: The 1980 Zurich Burns Movement." *Social Text* 33 (1992): 82–102.

Reicher, S., C. Cassidy, I. Wolpert, N. Hopkins, and M. Levine. "Saving Bulgaria's Jews: An Analysis of Social Identity and the Mobilization of Social Solidarity." *European Journal of Social Psychology* 36 (2006): 49–72.

Retzinger, Suzanne M. *Violent Emotions: Shame and Rage in Marital Quarrels.* Newbury Park: Sage, 1991.

Ricoeur, Paul. *The Symbolism of Evil.* Boston: Beacon Press, 1967.

Roberts, Adam. "Transformative Military Occupation: Applying the Laws of War and Human Rights." *The American Journal of International Law* 100, 3 (2006): 580–622.

Robins, R.S. "Disease, Political Events, and Populations." In *Biocultural Aspects of Disease,* edited by H. Rothschild and C. Chapman. London: Academic Press, 1981.

Rorty, Amélie Oksenberg. "Akrasia and Conflict." *Inquiry* 23.2 (1980): 193–212.

———. "The Social and Political Sources of Akrasia." *Ethics* 107 (1997): 644–57.

Rorty, Richard. *Contingency, Irony, and Solidarity.* Cambridge: Cambridge University Press, 1989.

Rosenberg, C. *Explaining Epidemics and Other Studies in the History of Medicine.* Cambridge: Cambridge University Press, 1992.

Rossi, Paolo. *Logic and the Art of Memory.* Chicago: University of Chicago Press, 2000.

Rotberg, Robert. "The New Nature of Nation-State Failure." *The Washington Quarterly* 25, 3 (2002): 85–96.

Samson, Jane. *Imperial Benevolence: Making British Authority in the Pacific Islands.* Honolulu: UHP, 1998.

Scarry, Elaine. *The Body in Pain: The Making and Unmaking of the World.* London: Oxford University Press, 1985.

Scheff, Thomas J. *Bloody Revenge.* Bounder: Westview, 1993.

Scherpe, Klaus. "Reading the Aesthetics of Resistance: Ten Working Theses." *New German Critique* 30 (1983): 97–105.

Shaoul, J. "Mad Cow Disease: The Meat Industry is Out of Control." *Ecologist* 27, 5 (1997): 182–87.

Sharrad, Paul. "The Art of Memory and the Liberation of History: Wilson Harri's Witnessing of Time." *Calloloo* 18, 1 (1995): 94–108.

Shimkus, J. "Infection Control. Mad Cows and Weird Science." *Hosp-Health-Netw.* 72, 11(1998): 62.

Siddiqi, Javed. *World Health and World Politics: The World Health Organization and the UN System*. Columbia: University of South Carolina Press, 1995.

Singer, Alan. *Aesthetic Reason: Artworks and the Deliberative Ethos*. Philadelphia: Pennsylvania State University Press, 2003.

Slack, Paul. "Responses to Plague in Early Modern Europe: The Implications of Public Health." In *In Time of Plague: The History and Social Consequences of Lethal Epidemic Disease*, edited by A. Mack. New York: New York University Press, 1991.

Slim, Hugo. "Violence and Humanitarianism." *Security Dialogue* 32, 3 (2001): 325–39.

Smith, Alastair. "International Crises and Domestic Politics." *The American Political Science Review* 92, 3 (1998): 623–38.

Smith, D.M. "How Far Should We Care? On the Spatial Scope of Beneficence." *Progress in Human Geography* 22: 15–38.

Snyder, L. "The American-German Pork Dispute, 1879–1891." *Journal of Modern History* 17 (1961): 16–28.

Sontag, Susan. *Illness as Metaphor and AIDS and Its Metaphors*. New York: Picador, 1990.

Spilerman, S. "The Causes of Racial Disturbances: A Comparison of Alternative Explanations." *American Sociological Review* 35 (1970): 627–29.

Spitzer, Leo. "Ragamuffin, Ragman, Rigmarole and Rogue." *Modern Language Notes* 62, 2 (1947): 85–93.

Stahl, Hans-Peter. *Die Stellung des Menschen im Geschichtichen Prozess*. Munich: Beck, 1966.

Starn, Randolph. "Meaning-Levels in the Theme of Historical Decline." *History and Theory* 14, 1 (1975): 1–31.

Steinglass, Matt. "Hell on Wings." *NYT Book Review Desk* (November 27, 2005).

Sullivan, C.C. "Making Concessions." *Architecture* 92, 12 (2003): 111–16.

Summers-Effler, Erika. "The Micro Potential for Social Change: Emotion, Consciousness, and Social Movement Formation." *Sociological Theory* 20, 1 (2002): 41–60.

Sznaider, Natan. "Consumerism as a Civilizing Process: Israel and Judaism in the Second Age of Modernity." *International Journal of Politics, Culture and Society* 14, 2 (2000): 297–313.

Taylor, Barbara. *Mary Wollstonecraft and the Feminist Imagination*. Cambridge: Cambridge University Press, 2003.

Thompson, W.R. and G. Zuk. "World Power and the Strategic Trap of Territorial Commitments." *International Studies Quarterly* 30, 3 (1986): 249–67.

Thürer, Daniel. "The 'Failed State' and International Law." *International Review of the Red Cross* 836 (1999): 731–61.

Todd, Emmanuel. *After the Empire: The Breakdown of the American Order*. New York: Columbia University Press, 2003.

Troy, K. "The Plague that Wasn't." *Newsweek*, December 9, 1996.

Turner, V. *Schism and Continuity in an African Society*. Manchester: Manchester University Press, 1957.

Tuan, Yi-Fu. *Landscapes of Fear*. London: Pantheon Books, 1979.

Ungar, Sheldon. "Hot Crises and Media Reassurance: A Comparison of Emerging Diseases and Ebola in Zaire." *British Journal of Sociology* 49, 1 (1998): 36–56.

Urry, John. *Sociology Beyond Societies: Mobilities for the Twenty-First Century*. London: Routledge, 2000.

Vandermeerch, Patrick. "Psychotherapeutic and Religious Rituals: The Issue of Secularization." In *Current Studies on Rituals: Perspectives for the Psychology of Religion*, edited by H. Heimbrock and H. Boudewijnse. Atlanta: Rodopi, 1990.

van der Ploeg, Irma. "The Illegal Body: 'Eurodac' and the Politics of Biometric Identification." *Ethics and Information Technology* 1 (1999): 295–302.

van Ham, Peter. "Branding Territory: Inside the Wonderful Worlds of PR and IR Theory." *Millennium: Journal of International Studies* 31, 2 (2005): 107–131.

Voegelin, Eric. *History of Political Ideas: Volume I, Hellenism, Rome, and Early Christianity*. Columbia: University of Missouri Press, 1997.

Weiner, Myron. *The Global Migration Crisis: Challenge to States and to Human Rights*. New York: HarperCollins, 1995.

Wendt, Alexander. "Anarchy is What States Make of It." *International Organization* 46, 2 (1992): 391–426.

Willer, David, Michael Lovaglia, and Barry Markovsky. "Power and Influence: A Theoretical Bridge." *Social Forces* 76, 2 (1997): 571–603.

White, J. "Puritan intelligence." *Oxford Review of Education* 31, 3 (2005): 423–42.

White, Mark J. *The Cuban Missile Crisis*. New York: New York University Press, 1996.

Williams, R.H. and N.J. Demerath. "Religion and Political Process in an American City." *American Sociological Review* 56 (1991): 417–31.

Wittgenstein, Ludwig. *Philosophical Investigations*. Oxford: Basil Blackwell, 1968.

———. *On Certainty*. Oxford: Basil Blackwell, 1972.

Wohl, Dahl. *Love Among the Ruins: The Erotics of Democracy in Classical Athens*. Princeton: Princeton University Press, 2003.

Wohlforth, William. "The Strange Death of the USSR." *Georgetown Journal* 1, 1 (2000): 45–9.

Yam P. "Mad Cow's Human Toll." *Scientific American* 284, 5 (2001):12–3.

Yates, Frances. *The Art of Memory*. London: The University of Chicago Press, 1966.

Young-Bruehl, Elisabeth. "What Thucydides Saw." *History and Theory* 25, 1 (1986): 1–16.

Zartman, I.W. "Introduction: Posing the Problem of State Collapse." In *Collapsed States: The Disintegration and Restoration of Legitimate Authority*, edited by I.W. Zartman. Boulder: Lynn Rienner Publishers, 1995.

Zhang, Letian and Tianshu Pan. "Surviving the Crisis: Adaptive Wisdom, Coping Mechanisms and Local Responses to Avian Influenza Threats in Haining, China." *Anthropology & Medicine* 15, 1 (2008): 19–30.

Index